リーダーのための

ビジネス英会話フレーズブック

小林真美

Kobayashi Mami

はじめに

　ここ数年、外国人と働く環境で、リーダー的な役割を担う日本人が少しずつ増えてきていると感じます。業務提携や組織の指揮系統の変更で、待ったなしで英語をなんとかしなければ仕事にならないと、悲鳴を上げる管理職の方のご相談にも乗ってきました。

　英語で仕事をする時のコミュニケーションは、日本人同士が日本語で語っていることを、そのまま英語にするだけではうまく行きません。話の持って行き方から始め、伝え方や、適切な言葉の選び方、切り出すタイミングなど、異文化コミュニケーションだからこそ、配慮しなければならないことがたくさんあります。

　本書は、グローバルな外資系企業や、外国人が多い職場で長くリーダー職を務めてきた私自身の経験をもとに、実務で使ってきたフレーズを状況別にまとめています。
　ご紹介するフレーズの中には、いざという時に口から出てきて窮地を救ってくれたフレーズから、実際はうまく言えず、本当はこんなフレーズが言えれば良かったのにと、苦い思い出のある表現もたくさん含めました。
　外国人と働く上では、わかってもらいたいことを言葉で表現する、それをタイミングを逃さず、自信をもって伝えることがとても大切です。

　リーダーが伝えるべきことには、日本人同士であれば敢えて口に出さない感謝やお礼の言葉や、日本語にすると歯がゆいような賞賛の言葉も含まれます。予期せぬピンチの時には、チームの士気を上げるような励ましの言葉も必要でしょう。また、部下やチームメンバーに改善点を伝えるなど、ちょっと難しい状況でも曖昧にせず、適切な表現で相手がわかるまで伝えることも必要になります。

　私自身、自分の英語力が大きく伸びたのはいつだったかを振り返ると、アメリカの大学院に留学した頃と、仕事の責任が増えた30代後半を思い出します。自分がチャンスを逃さずにきちんと発言しないと、会社が誤った決断をしたり、チームメンバーや部下に迷惑がかかって

しまう、管理職になってから真剣度が増したのです。外国人の同僚や部下とは、日頃のコミュニケーションを密にすることで、チームがより良く機能することを学んだのもこの頃です。

　若干語弊がありますが、ノンネイティブではない私たちが大事なことを伝えたい時は、大げさに言うくらいがちょうど良い場面がよくあります。このまま話が進んでしまったら問題だというプロジェクトや、過大な仕事量をなんとか調整したい、人事評価などにつながる誤解を解きたいなど。

　日常のビジネスの現場では、いろいろな難題がつきものですよね。そういった場面で、焦らず冷静に、失礼にならない適切な表現ながら的確に、相手の理解を求める主張ができる表現力がリーダーには必要です。

　一方、本書は単純に欧米流のリーダーを目指したものではありません。外国人を雇用している日系企業はもとより、外資系といっても、日本にある拠点では日本人の同僚や部下も多く、彼ら、彼女らと信頼関係を築くには、共通する文化的・社会的背景の理解にもとづくコミュニケーションが期待されます。日本人を含めた、多様なチームをまとめる、バランス感覚に優れたリーダー像を想定して、執筆しました。

　世界的に、現在はチーム全体でよりパフォーマンスを上げることが求められる時代になっていると感じます。私が20数年前にビジネススクールを出た頃の欧米企業は、今よりもはるかに個人の業績が重視されていました。

　現在は、自分自身のパフォーマンスを上げるのは当然ながら、部下やチームメンバーをしっかりまとめるスキルがリーダーに求められ、率いるチーム全体の実績が評価される時代ではないでしょうか。

　協調性をもつ優れた日本的なリーダー像に加え、いざという時はチームのため、自分のために "バシッ" と英語で意見が言える、そんなリーダーを目指す方に、本書が少しでもお役に立てれば幸いです。

小林真美

音声ダウンロードについて

　本書の Chapter 1 から Chapter 6 までの英語フレーズをネイティブ（男女）がナチュラルスピードで読んでいます。

下記 URL より音声をダウンロードすることができます。
https://www.asuka-g.co.jp

＜ナレーター＞
Josh Keller,　Karen Haedrich

	〔トラック番号〕	〔該当ページ〕
Chapter 1	Track　1 ～ 23	pp14 ～ 91
Chapter 2	Track　24 ～ 50	pp94 ～ 165
Chapter 3	Track　51 ～ 70	pp168 ～ 235
Chapter 4	Track　71 ～ 80	pp238 ～ 305
Chapter 5	Track　81 ～ 119	pp308 ～ 378
Chapter 6	Track　120 ～ 133	pp382 ～ 439

※付録（pp441 ～ 477）の例文は収録されていません。

Contents

はじめに

■ Chapter 1　仕事を円滑に進めるための最強フレーズ

1　社内の日常コミュニケーション

1　部下やチームメンバーとの日常会話　　　　　　　　　　14
2　部下や同僚に何かをうまく依頼する　　　　　　　　　　21
3　アシスタントや部下に仕事の指示を出す　　　　　　　　23
4　作業を依頼する　　　　　　　　　　　　　　　　　　　26
5　部下に仕事の進捗や調子を聞く　　　　　　　　　　　　28
6　仕事がうまく進んでいない部下をフォローする　　　　　29
7　仕事がうまく進んでいない部下をサポートする　　　　　31
8　部下に感謝や賞賛の気持ちを伝える　　　　　　　　　　33

2　会議・チームミーティング・営業会議

1　会議を開始する、進行を仕切る　　　　　　　　　　　　36
2　活発な意見を促し、会議を仕切る　　　　　　　　　　　38
3　会議をまとめる　　　　　　　　　　　　　　　　　　　50
4　経営会議で営業や財務報告をする　　　　　　　　　　　52

3　オンライン会議（ウェブ会議、電話会議）

1　会議を招集する　　　　　　　　　　　　　　　　　　　58
2　会議を開始時の挨拶や自己紹介　　　　　　　　　　　　58
3　会話をコントロールする　　　　　　　　　　　　　　　62
4　オンライン会議特有の問題（技術的問題など）や状況に対処する　64
5　会議をまとめて指示を出す　　　　　　　　　　　　　　68

4　雑談、スモールトーク

1　同僚との何気ない雑談　　　　　　　　　　　　　　　　70
2　ビジネス交流会などでの初対面の人との雑談　　　　　　74

3　会合や商談の前や休憩中での雑談　　　　　　　　78

4　気の利いた相づちや沈黙を埋めるフレーズ　　　87

5　会話が聞き取れなかった時　　　　　　　　　　89

6　スマートに雑談を終了する　　　　　　　　　　90

Column ❶　オンライン英語会議の攻略法　　　　　　　　92

■ Chapter 2　人を育てるための最強フレーズ

1　優秀な人材の採用（面接）

1　相手を知る雑談（自己紹介）　　　　　　　　　94

2　志望動機を聞き出し、深掘りする　　　　　　　97

3　長所や短所を聞き出し、深掘りする　　　　　　98

4　これまで達成したこと・人生に影響を与えた経験について　99

5　今後の夢やキャリア展望を聞く　　　　　　　102

6　転職の理由を聞き出す　　　　　　　　　　　103

7　価値観や大切にしていることを聞く　　　　　104

8　質問を促し、真摯に答える　　　　　　　　　107

2　部下を育てるためのフレーズ

1　部下の不安を取り除く日頃の声かけ　　　　　112

2　部下のモチベーションを上げる　　　　　　　113

3　部下の仕事の進捗を確認する　　　　　　　　116

4　困っている部下を助ける　　　　　　　　　　117

5　部下のキャリアアップを助ける　　　　　　　119

3　日頃のフィードバックに使えるフレーズ

1　良かったことをこまめに伝える　　　　　　　121

2　改善点をポジティブに伝える　　　　　　　　123

3　現状の問題点について　　　　　　　　　　　126

4　改善が見られない部下に指導をする　　　　　128

4　人事考課のための最強フレーズ

1　年初に目標設定を促す	132
2　スキルアップを目指す	134
3　達成度合いを客観的に伝える	135
4　良かった点・達成できなかった点を効果的に伝える	139
5　部下からの質問・反論に対する適切な回答をする	146
6　部下との誤解を解消してフォローする	148
7　部下のモチベーションを上げる	152
8　改善点をポジティブに伝える	155
9　改善が見られない部下に一歩踏み込んだ指導をする	157
10　キャリア・デベロップメントを話し合う	163

Column ❷　瞬発力を鍛えることを意識しよう	166

■　Chapter 3　チームを率いるための最強フレーズ

1　チームを作る

1　チームメンバーに自分の信念を語る	168

2　チームを一段ワンランクアップさせる

1　チームワークを強固にする	173
2　チームメンバーの成長をさらに促す	176
3　交渉力を高めるための指導的なフレーズ	180
4　社内交渉を円滑に進めるための準備を話し合う	181

3　部下を指導する

1　会社の閑散期に部下のモチベーションを維持する	185
2　厳しい状況、緊急事態の時	187
3　コーチングを使って、部下を育てる	194
4　自信のない部下を励まして力を発揮させる	202
5　自信過剰な部下をコントロールする	204
6　困難な状況にいる部下を励ます	205

4 社内とチームの関係を調整する

1	社内交渉を円滑に進める	207

5 チームの仕事環境

1	自分のチームに必要なリソースを勝ち取るためのフレーズ	212
2	チームを過剰な仕事量から守る	215

6 チームの結果に責任をもつ

1	チームの失敗をかばう	222
2	チームの功績をたたえる	224
3	ふり返る（評価、反省）	225

7 チーム、部下を守る

1	会社の上層部とのちょっと難しい局面でのやり取り	227
2	自分の部下・チームをリストラから守る	232
3	経費削減、人員削減について	234

Column ❸ 単語を覚える時は連想ゲームの発想で　　236

■ Chapter 4　キャリアアップのための最強フレーズ

1 グローバル企業にチャレンジ（面接）

1	自分が達成してきたことを効果的に伝える	238
2	長所をどのように生かしたか具体的な事例を伝える	244
3	短所をうまく伝え、長所ともとれるように伝える	253
4	自分のキャリアの機会がどのようなものか前向きに聞く（夢を語る）	257
5	会社の環境やカルチャーが自分に合うか、適切な言葉で聞き出す	260
6	転職の理由をポジティブに表現する	269
7	過剰にアグレッシブにならない程度に自分を売り込む	274

2　社内での昇進にチャレンジ

1　自分が社内で達成してきたことを客観的に伝える	280
2　自分が昇進後のポジションにいかにふさわしいかをアピールする	287
3　今回の昇進がダメでも次につながるように好印象を残す	296

Column ❹　ビジネスシーンの英会話は大げさなくらいがちょうどいい	306

■　Chapter 5　ビジネスを急成長させるための最強フレーズ

1　効果的な自己紹介

1　初対面の挨拶、社名やポジションを伝える	308
2　自分の経験やスキルをアピールする	311
3　印象づける自社紹介のフレーズ	313
4　スマートに連絡先を交換して会話を終える	314

2　商談・交渉

1　商談をスムーズに始める	316
2　自社の商品やサービスを紹介・提案する	319
3　具体的なリクエスト、提案や質問をする	320
4　質問に対して即答できない時	323
5　相手の考えや懸念点を確認する時	325
6　反論・説得・反対意見を言う時	326
7　誤解を解く時	328
8　妥協案を話し合う時	329
9　時間を稼ぐ時	330
10　解決策を話し合う時	331
11　合意に達しないため、交渉をいったん打ち切る時	332
12　後ほど返事を聞く場合	335
13　合意した時	335
14　価格について交渉する時	338
15　発注する時	340

3 海外企業とのＭ＆Ａ・事業再編・ジョイントベンチャー

1 市場リサーチを行う　　342
2 交渉相手のビジネスを分析する　　345
3 交渉相手と条件をつめる　　347
4 感想・考えを述べる　　351
5 弁護士などの専門家を交渉に使う　　355

4 接待と会食

1 クライエントを接待に誘う　　356
2 相手の好みを確認する　　357
3 会食を楽しい会話で盛り上げる　　359
4 会食中の気配りフレーズ　　361
5 スマートに支払いを済ませる　　363
6 その他の接待・さわやかなお見送りのフレーズ　　363
7 誘う　　364
8 接待を受けた後のお礼　　365
9 バーなどでのカジュアルな会話　　366
10 日本食・日本酒の説明をする　　366

5 海外出張

1 訪問先とアポをとる　　370
2 旅行手配と旅行中の会話　　374
3 たずねる、依頼する　　375
4 海外出張中のトラブル対応　　377
5 体調が良くない時　　378

Column ❺ パワー単語を活用して、リーダーのフレーズを格上げしよう　　379

■ Chapter 6　グローバルリーダーの最強フレーズ

1　効果的なオープニング

1　プレゼンに適切な挨拶と自己紹介　382
2　プレゼンの目的を効果的に伝える　389
3　相手に語りかけて関心を引く　395

2　インパクトのあるプレゼンテーション

1　メインパートをわかりやすく伝える　398
2　グラフやデータを使って効果的に説明する　405
3　相手の理解の確認をする　413
4　大事なメッセージを強調する方法　414
5　接続詞・接続句を駆使してスムーズに話を展開　418

3　質問への対応

1　プレゼンの流れに沿った質問の受け方　425
2　質問へ移行する　427
3　予期せぬ質問への対応　431
4　本題と無関係な質問を受けた場合の対応　435

4　クロージング

1　効果的にまとめる　436
2　参加者へのお礼　438

Column ❻　ブツブツひとりごとの自主練でアウトプットの習慣を　440

＜付録＞　プロフェッショナルが書く最強文章術　441

おわりに

カバーデザイン　大場君人

Chapter 1

仕事を円滑に進めるための
最強フレーズ

　欧米社会では個人の成果が重視される一方、ビジネスの場での円滑なコミュニケーション力は、チーム全体のパフォーマンスを向上させるためにも、リーダーにとって非常に大切な資質と考えられています。時間を大切にする意識も強く、会議の時間管理や、タイムリーな情報共有なども非常に大切です。

1. 部下やチームメンバーとの日常会話　　　Track 1

Good morning. How are you today?

おはよう。今日は元気？

How was your weekend?

週末はどうだった？

Did you have a good weekend?

良い週末を過ごした？

What is your schedule today?

今日の予定はどうなっている？

We have a meeting from 10 am.

午前10時から会議があるからね。

Please be sure to come on time.

遅れないようにね。

I am going to miss the meeting this morning because of an urgent matter.

緊急な案件があって、今朝のミーティングには出られそうもないな。

I would like you to take care of the meeting on my behalf.

私の代わりにミーティングを取り仕切ってくれないか。

Let me know how it goes.

後でどうなったか教えてね。

What happened?

何かあったの？

Is there anything wrong with your project?

プロジェクトに何か問題でもあるの？

Would you like to grab a coffee to catch up this afternoon?

午後にコーヒーでも飲みながら近況報告してくれないか？

Are you free for lunch sometime this week?

今週、ランチでフリーな日ある？

I would like to talk about our next project over lunch, if possible.

できればランチしながら次のプロジェクトについて話したいな。

Could you fill me in what you discussed with the customer yesterday?

昨日の顧客との商談はどんな話だったか、教えてくれる？

Would it be difficult to make it happen this week?

今週は難しそうかな？

How about next week?

来週はどう？

I'm heading off to lunch.

ランチに行って来る。

I'll be back in an hour.

1時間で戻るよ。

I am going to have a lunch meeting with our client, then I won't be back until around 3 pm.

クライエントとのランチミーティングがあるので午後3時頃まで戻らないよ。

Could you remind me where the meeting will take place?

ミーティングはどこで開催されるか教えてくれる？

Could you confirm what time the meeting will start?

ミーティングは何時に始まるか確認してくれる？

I would like to have someone fix my PC quickly.

早急に私のパソコンを直してほしいんだ。

Do you have the file on the monthly report?

月次レポートのファイルを持っている？

Do you have any idea what's wrong with this screen?

この画面、何が問題かわかる？

I'm sorry to bother you.

忙しいところごめんね。

Do you have a minute?

今ちょっといい？

Just a quick question.

ちょっと質問があるんだけど。

I have to share some bad news with you.

悪い知らせを君に伝えないといけない。

Are you available around 10 o'clock this morning?

今朝10時頃、時間をとってくれる？

I understand you are tied up at this moment.

今はちょっと忙しいようだね。

Please come to see me when you are done.

終わったら私のところに来て。

I would like to bring something to your attention.

ちょっと話したいことがあるんだ。

I understand that we are receiving complaints from our clients.

クライエントから苦情が来ているそうだね。

You should inform the manager about this issue immediately.

この問題はすぐにマネージャーに報告すべきだね。

Don't get me wrong.

誤解しないでね。

I just want to have a better understanding of the situation.

状況をよく理解したいだけなんだ。

You seem to be exhausted.

疲れ果てているようだよ。

Why don't you take a day off?

一日休みをとったら？

You really should take the rest of the day off.

今日は早く帰ったほうがいいよ。

I'm leaving now.

そろそろ帰るよ。

Have a good evening.

お疲れさま。

See you tomorrow.

また明日。

Let's go home now and finish this tomorrow.

今日はここまでにして、明日これを終わらせよう。

I've got to go now as I have a client dinner tonight.

今夜はクライアントの接待があるから、もう行くね。

I always appreciate your hard work.

今日もご苦労さま。

Enjoy the rest of your day.

残りの一日を楽しんでね。

I will be late tomorrow as I have a doctor's appointment.

明日は病院の予約があるから、出社は遅れるよ。

I'll take the morning off tomorrow.

明日は午前半休の予定だよ。

I am going to take tomorrow off.

明日は休暇をとるよ。

I'm counting on your help.

頼むね。

Shall we go for a drink tonight?

今夜飲みに行かない？

It's on me.

おごるよ。

Do you mind if Tom comes along?

トムも誘っていい？

Would you ask other members to join us?

他のメンバーも誘ってみて。

Thanks for inviting me to the gathering.

懇親会に誘ってくれてありがとう。

I'll just leave you guys to enjoy the night without me.

今回は私抜きで、皆で楽しんで。

This is my small contribution to the party.

これ、少しだけの会計の足しにして。

Too bad I won't be able to make it, as I have a conference call tonight.

残念だけど今夜は電話会議があって、参加できないんだ。

What do you say if we grab dinner on Monday instead?

かわりに月曜に夕食どう？

I would like to treat the team as we all have been working so hard for the last few months.

ここ数ヶ月、皆とても頑張ってくれたので、ごちそうしたいな。

What are you in the mood for? Japanese? Steaks? Pasta?

何を食べたい？　和食？　ステーキ？　パスタ？

It's been a crazy week. Thank you for all your hard work.

今週は忙しかったけど、皆ご苦労さま。

Are you ready for the weekend?

週末は楽しみだよね。

Do you have any plans for the weekend?

週末は何か予定はあるの？

What are you up to this weekend?

今週末は何をする予定？

Next week will be another busy week for us.

来週も忙しい週だからね。

Hope you will have some rest during the weekend.

週末はゆっくり休んでね。

Have a nice weekend.

良い週末を。

Don't check your work emails during the weekend.

週末は仕事のメールは見ないようにね。

2. 部下や同僚に何かをうまく依頼する　　　Track 2

It would be great if you could help me.

手伝ってもらえたら、助かるな。

Would you give me a hand?

ちょっと手を貸してくれる？

I was wondering if you could help me file these documents.

これらの書類をファイルするのを手伝ってくれないかな。

Don't hesitate to ask for my help.

私の助けが必要だったら遠慮しないでね。

Actually, I was about to ask for help.

実は、あなたに手伝いを頼もうとしていたところだよ。

It needs to be proofread.

校正する必要があるんだ。

Can you help?

助けてくれる？

My comments are written in red text.

私のコメントは赤字で書かれています。

Do you mind checking this document?

この書類をチェックしてもらえる？

Could you double-check these numbers to make sure they are final?

これらの数字が最新になっているか、ダブルチェックしてもらえる？

Please check this document first thing tomorrow.

明日一番にこの書類のチェックをしてください。

Would you like me to take over?

引き継ごうか？

I would be happy to do the rest.

残りは私に任せてもらうね。

I need you to use the same format for all the sales reports.

すべての販売レポートに同じ形式を使用する必要があるからね。

Thank you for the well-analyzed report.

よく分析されたレポートをありがとう。

I am going to use your report to conduct a market analysis.

あなたのレポートを使用して市場分析を行います。

I suggest you go through last year's reports.

昨年のレポートを見てみるといいよ。

It might be helpful for you to attend this seminar.

このセミナーに参加すると君の役に立つかもね。

I expect the report to be comprehensive.

このレポートは包括的なものにしてください。

Please make sure there is nothing you overlooked.

見落としがないようにね。

3. アシスタントや部下に仕事の指示を出す　Track 3

Could you make 10 copies of these documents?

この書類を 10 部、コピーをお願いできる？

Could you make enlargements?

拡大してくれる？

Could you make 10 double-sided copies?

10 枚の両面コピーを作成してくれる？

Please hold all calls today.

今日は電話を取り次がないで。

Could you staple these documents and make 5 sets?

これらのドキュメントをホッチキスでとめて、5 部の資料を作ってくれる？

Could you file this contract and store it in the cabinet?

この契約書をファイルして、キャビネットに保管してくれる？

Please lock the cabinets before you leave.

退社する前にキャビネットをロックしてください。

Please recycle all the non-confidential papers.

非機密文書はすべてリサイクルしてください。

This is a sensitive document.

これは機密文書です。

Please handle this appropriately.

適切にこれを扱ってください。

Please send it by FedEx.

これを国際宅配便で送ってね。

I would like you to send this by courier.

これを宅配便で送っておいて。

I need you to handle this immediately.

至急これをお願いね。

I need your quick help.

ちょっと君の助けが必要なんだ。

Please remind me later.

後で思い出させてね。

Could you find the number to call quickly?

どこに電話すればいいか、急いで確認してくれる？

Please note that I will be out of the office this afternoon.

今日の午後は外出します。

Would you settle the travel expenses by the end of the month?

今月末までに旅費精算書を申請しておいてもらえる？

Please claim only the legitimate travel expenses.

正当な旅費のみを請求してください。

Please find the additional information in the attachment.

添付で追加情報を確認くださいね。

Could you arrange the cash advance for my business trip?

出張費の前払いをアレンジしてくれる？

Could you find a good place to entertain our clients?

どこかクライアントの接待に良い場所を探してもらえる？

Could you finish your sales report by the end of this week?

今週末までに売上報告を完了することはできそう？

I would like to have the report before the management meeting.

経営会議の前にレポートを見たいんだ。

Do you think it would be possible?

間に合いそう？

I got to ask you something confidentially.

機密事項で頼みたいことがあるんだけど。

I would like you to do some overtime work this week to finish your reports.

今週はレポートを完成するために残業してもらう必要がありそうだよ。

I am forwarding some materials that could be helpful for you.

役立ちそうな資料を転送するね。

Would you be able to work overtime for one hour or so today?

今日1時間くらい残業を頼める？

Call me anytime when you have a question.

質問があったら、いつでも電話してね。

4. 作業を依頼する　　　　　　　　　　　　　Track 4

Can you input this in the excel sheet?

これを Excel シートに入力しておいてくれる？

Please scan this document and share it with the team.

このドキュメントをスキャンして、チームとシェアしておいて。

I need you to process this order by the end of today.

この注文、今日中に処理お願いね。

Have we heard from Company A today?

今日、A 社から連絡はあった？

Please send the quotation of this matter to the client.

この案件の見積書を先方に送っておいて。

Go ahead and place the order of 5,000 pieces.

5000 個で発注しておいて。

Can we make it on time for March 1st delivery date?

3 月 1 日の納期で問題ないよね？

Please make sure that they will fill our order by the end of this month.

今月末までに先方が納品できるか、確認しておいて。

The unit price has been going up, so we need to negotiate with them.

単価が上がっているから、先方と交渉しないといけない。

Can you email me the template of the contract?

契約書のひな型をメールで送ってもらえる？

Can you check the stock in the warehouse?

倉庫の在庫の確認をしてもらえる？

Please send an invoice to Company B.

B 社に請求書を送っておいて。

The date of the delivery note should be 〜 .

納品書の日付は〜でお願い。

Can I get a list of potential customers sometime this week?

顧客見込みリストを今週中にもらえる？

5. 部下に仕事の進捗や調子を聞く

Here is your new assignment.

これが新しい仕事です。

Please have a look and let me know if you have any questions.

確認して、何か質問があれば知らせてね。

Could you give me an update on what you are working on?

今やっている仕事の進捗を教えてくれる？

What's your priority today?

今日の最優先の事は何かな？

What is the status of the sales report?

セールスレポートの進捗はどう？

Are you getting the help you need to finish this assignment?

この仕事を終わらせるのに必要なサポートはもらえてる？

Is there anything you need from me?

私が何か手伝えることはある？

I would like you to give me an update first thing in the morning tomorrow.

明日の朝一番に報告してください。

Would you come and see me right away?

私のところにすぐに来てくれる？

Could you email your sales report to me by 3 pm today?

販売報告書を今日午後3時までにメールしてもらえる？

It would be okay if you finished it by 10:00 tomorrow.

明日10時までに終わらせてくれれば大丈夫。

6. 仕事がうまく進んでいない部下をフォローする　Track 6

Let's sit down and talk about your current work.

ちょっと時間をとって、君の抱えている仕事について話そう。

You seem to struggle to meet the deadline.

締切に間に合わせるのに苦戦しているようだね。

How comfortable is your workload?

仕事量は大丈夫？

As you know, we need you to keep up with the schedule.

わかっていると思うけど、スケジュール通りに進める必要があるよ。

Do you have any idea why your report wasn't delivered on time?

レポートが間に合わなかった理由はわかっているのかな？

As you know, the management uses your reports to review the sales performance.

経営陣が君のレポートを使って、売上状況を確認しているのは知っているよね。

If you are late on the reports, it slows down their critical discussion.

レポートが遅れると、彼らの大事な議論も遅れてしまうんだよ。

How can I support you in meeting the deadline?

締切に間に合うように、私はどんなサポートができるかな？

Are there any skills you would like to develop to perform the job?

仕事を遂行するために身につけたいスキルがあるかな？

Could you make sure to report any problem immediately?

どんな問題でもすぐに報告するようにしてくれる？

It is critical that everyone completes the task on time.

全員が予定通りに仕事を終わらせることが重要だよね。

You also need to understand the importance of paying attention to details.

細かい点に気を配ることが重要だとも理解してほしいな。

I have reviewed your workload and prioritized the tasks for this week.

君の仕事量を確認して、今週の仕事の優先順位をつけたよ。

If you need further information, please come to see me.

さらに必要な情報があれば、私に知らせてね。

I can set up 15 minute meetings every morning to talk about your progress.

毎朝 15 分、君の仕事の進捗を確認するミーティングを持つこともできるよ。

I am sure you will do better next time.

次はもっとうまくできるはずだよ。

Is your workload too stressful?

仕事量がストレスになってる？

I am here to help you.

助けるよ。

I am happy to set up a time to clarify your roles and responsibilities, if it helps.

君に期待されている役割と職務を確認する機会を持つこともできるからね。

7. 仕事がうまく進んでいない部下をサポートする　Track 7

I assume you know how much you are behind from your target of the month.

今月の目標とどれくらい差があるかわかっているよね。

How much of your work is still working in progress?

仕掛かりの仕事はどれくらいあるの？

Do you have any idea what should be done immediately?

今、直近でやると効果的なことは何だと思う？

What can you do to improve the accuracy of taking orders (work)?

受注（仕事）の精度を上げるにはどうすればいいかな？

Are you on target as planned?

当初の予定通りに進められているのかな？

Are you approaching clients?

顧客へのアプローチはできているのかな？

Why don't you propose a new promotional idea?

新しい販促案を出してみてよ。

Should I come with you to visit them?

先方訪問に同行しようか？

I suggest you review all of your current tasks.

今の仕事の棚卸しをするといいよ。

You can delegate this part to your assistant.

この部分はアシスタントに依頼すればいいよ。

I would like to have a look when you complete the first half of the assignment.

課題の半分ができたところで、私に見せてよ。

---

8. 部下に感謝や賞賛の気持ちを伝える　　Track 8

Well done!

よくやりましたね！

You've done a great job!

すごい仕事をしましたね！

What do you think about your new colleague?

新しい同僚はどう？

Thank you for your extra help to bring her up to speed.

彼女が仕事を覚えるのを助けてくれてありがとう。

I am impressed by your leadership to manage this project.

このプロジェクトで発揮した、あなたのリーダーシップに感心したよ。

I don't know what we would have done without you.

あなたがいなければ、私たちはどうなっていたかわからないよ。

You are really creative.

君は本当にクリエイティブだね。

You are incredible.

君は本当にすばらしい。

I am always counting on you.

いつも頼りにしているよ。

I have been very impressed with your work so far.

あなたのこれまでの仕事は本当にすばらしい。

I know it was tough to meet the deadline, but you did it!

締切が厳しかったはずですが、やりましたね！

I am proud of you.

あなたを誇りに思います。

Keep up the good work.

いい仕事を続けてください。

That was awesome.

すばらしいです。

Thank you for being so flexible.

フレキシブルに対応してくれてありがとう。

It's amazing how thorough your work is.

完璧な仕事で驚きです。

Let's get through this together.

次も一緒に頑張りましょう。

This has been a great joint effort by everyone.

全員でのすばらしい共同作業でした。

I want to know how you did it.

どうやったのか教えてほしいです。

You are always so quick to show leadership.

いつもすぐにリーダーシップを発揮してくれて助かるよ。

You've really made a difference here.

大きな変化をもたらしてくれました。

I'm glad you joined the team.

あなたがチームに参加してくれてうれしいです。

Thank you for being an invaluable member of our team.

チームのかけがいのないメンバーでいてくれてありがとう。

I am proud of my entire team.

チームのみんなを誇りに思うよ。

Let's work together and do our best again next time.

次回も最善を尽くして一緒に頑張りましょう。

2 会議・チームミーティング・営業会議

1. 会議を開始する、進行を仕切る　　　　　Track 9

Good morning, everyone.

皆さん、おはよう。

I hope you are doing well this morning.

今朝も皆さん調子が良いといいのですが。

Thank you for coming today.

今日集まってくれてありがとう。

Let's get down to business.

それでは始めようか。

Let's get the ball rolling.

そろそろ始めましょう。

Ok, let's get started.

では、始めよう。

If everyone is here, I think we'll get started.

皆さん揃っているようであれば、始めましょう。

First, let's go over the minutes from our last meeting.

まずは、前回のミーティングの議事録を確認しましょう。

There are three items on the agenda today.

今日は3つの議題があります。

Today, I need to bring you up to speed on how the business is doing.

今日は、ビジネスの状況についての最新情報を提供します。

We're here today to discuss the upcoming workshop.

本日は間近に控えているワークショップについて話す予定だよ。

The purpose of this meeting is to decide the location of our annual sales meeting.

この会議の目的は、当社の年次営業会議の開催場所を決定することです。

I think the meeting will last for one hour or so.

会議は約1時間と思います。

The meeting is scheduled to finish by 5 pm.

会議は午後5時までには終わる予定です。

Please let me know if you have any items to add to the agenda today.

本日の議論に加えたいことがあれば、ご連絡ください。

I'm afraid Mr. Kato can't be with us today. He's in Osaka, meeting with clients.

加藤さんは大阪で顧客訪問のため、本日は欠席です。

I appreciate your help to finish the meeting on time.

会議が時間通りに終わるように協力頼むね。

We will hear a short report on each point first, followed by a discussion around the table.

最初にそれぞれのポイントについての短い報告を聞き、その後、全員で議論しよう。

We'll have to keep each item to 15 minutes.

各トピックについては 15 分で話しましょう。

Each agenda is allocated 15 minutes.

各議題につき 15 分ずつ議論する予定でいます。

The first item on the agenda is the progress of project A.

最初の議題はプロジェクト A の進捗についてだね。

Let's start with the new hiring plan.

新規採用のプランから始めましょう。

Ms. Suzuki, can you tell us how the ABC project is progressing?

鈴木さん、ABC プロジェクトの進行状況を報告してもらえますか？

Can you give me an update on your research?

あなたの調査についてアップデートをお願いできる？

2. 活発な意見を促し、会議を仕切る　　　Track 10

Ken, can we get your input?

ケン、意見をもらえる？

How do you feel about this proposal?

この提案についてはどう思う？

Ms. Suzuki, what are your thoughts on that?

鈴木さん、それについてはどう思いますか？

Tom, what do you think about this?

トム、この件についてどう思いますか？

Perhaps you could tell us what you think about that?

その件についてどのように考えているか、教えてもらえる？

Ms. Tanaka, would you like to comment on that idea?

田中さん、そのアイデアについてコメントしてくれますか？

Ken, could you give me a sense of what's going on in your responsible area?

ケン、君の担当分野の状況がどんな感じか教えてくれるかな？

Would you like to add anything?

何か付け足すことはありますか？

Now, I would like to hand things over to Ken to explain our plans in detail.

では、我々のプランの詳細を説明するのに、ケンに引き継ぎたいと思います。

Can I say something?

ひとこと発言してもいいかな？

May I interrupt you for a moment?

ちょっと割り込んでもいいかな？

That's a good point.

それは良いポイントです。

You made a good point.

もっともだね。

That's exactly the way I feel.

私もまさに同感です。

It doesn't make any difference to me.

どちらでも私にはあまり違いがないと思う。

I have no opinion on the matter.

この件に関して、意見はありません。

I don't have any strong views on this matter.

この件に関しては、強い意見はありません。

In my opinion, their request sounds reasonable.

私の意見では、彼らの要求はもっともだと思いますよ。

I suggest we break up into groups and have a brainstorming session.

グループに分かれてブレーンストーミングセッションをしよう。

Why don't you share your draft with us?

君のドラフトをシェアしてみてくれない？

How about assigning the tasks to all?

全員に仕事を割り当てるのはどう？

May I suggest a ten-minute break?

10 分間の休憩を入れようか？

From my perspective, it's a little different.

私の見方では、少し異なります。

Let me explain.

説明させてください。

Could you say that again?

もう一度、言ってもらえますか？

I'm afraid I don't understand how you will implement your suggestion.

悪いけど、あなたの提案をどう導入するのか理解できない。

Could you explain that again for me?

もう一度、説明してもらえますか？

I don't quite follow you.

ちょっとあなたの言うことについていけてないようだ。

What exactly do you mean?

正確にはどういう意味？

Excuse me. Let me finish first.

すみません。私の話をまず全部聞いて。

Just one more minute and I'll be done.

あと 1 分で私の話は終わるから。

I would like to hear your opinion after I have completed mine.

私の話をした後に、みんなの意見を聞くよ。

Let me put it another way.

別の言い方をするね。

I am not saying that this is completely irrelevant.

私はそれが完全に無関係であると言っているのではないよ。

We must focus on the main issue.

我々は主要な問題にフォーカスしないといけません。

Here is the bottom line.

ここが一番重要なところです。

To the best of my knowledge, this is the most attractive offer.

私の知る限りでは、これが最も魅力的な提案です。

I would like to make myself clear about this.

この点については正確に話します。

I need to emphasize this point.

この点は強調したいと思います。

I think we should get more clarity on this issue.

この問題については、もっとはっきりさせないといけないな。

Could you simplify the matter?

問題を簡単に説明してもらえる？

We should avoid complicating matters unnecessarily.

不必要に物事を複雑にするのは避けたほうがいい。

What is the upside of your proposal?

あなたの提案の良いところは何ですか？

This is not a manufacturing issue or a marketing issue.

これは製造上の問題でもマーケティングの問題でもないんだ。

I need to remind you that we all have to own the results.

全員が結果に責任があるということを思い出してくれよ。

We have to work together to turn around the business.

ビジネスを好転させるためには、協力しなければいけないよ。

All we have to do now is to develop a realistic strategy.

今やらなければいけないことは、現実的な戦略を立てることだよ。

I suggest we stick to the original strategy.

元々の戦略を貫くのをすすめるよ。

Let me see if I've understood you correctly.

あなた（の提案）を正しく理解できているか確認させてほしいな。

Are you proposing to postpone the advertisement?

広告の延期を提案しているのかな？

I'm afraid I don't understand what you are getting at.

君が何を言いたいのか、理解できてないようだよ。

Could you explain to me how that is going to work?

それがどのようにうまく行くのか、説明してくれる？

I don't see what you mean.

言っている意味がわからないなあ。

Could we have some more details, please?

もう少し詳細を教えてくれる？

Have I made everything clear?

私の言ったことは全て明確になったかな？

I would be happy to clarify anything that's not clear.

もし明確でないところがあれば、喜んで説明するよ。

Let's go through how we're going to decide the next step again.

次のステップをどう決めるのか、再度確認しよう。

I want to make sure everyone is on the same page.

全員が状況を理解しているかを確認したい。

Is there something else you would like to share with us?

何か他にシェアしたい点はある？

What does everyone else think?

他のみんなはどう思うかな？

I would like you all to focus on the discussion.

全員、議論に集中してください。

It seems to me that we are far behind the schedule of this project.

このプロジェクト、予定よりかなり遅れているね。

In my experience, it will be difficult to catch up with the schedule.

経験上、予定に追いつくには難しいのではないかな。

I strongly believe that we need to change our plan now.

今、予定を変更すべきです。

There's no question that we are losing our share.

我々のシェアが落ちているのは、明らかだ。

I agree with your comments.

その通りだね。

I completely agree with his proposal.

彼の提案にまったく賛成です。

I'm in agreement.

賛成です。

Exactly.

その通りです。

Absolutely.

まったくそうです。

That's so true.

まさにその通りです。

That's for sure.

確かにそうですね。

I'm all for that idea.

その考えに大賛成です。

I couldn't agree with you more.

まさしくその通りです。

That's exactly what I think.

まさしく私が考えていた通りです。

I agree with them in principle.

基本的には彼らの意見に賛成です。

That's exactly how I feel.

まさしく私が感じていた通りです。

Well, it depends.

そうだな、それは状況次第だよ。

I agree with you up to a point.

ここまでは賛成。

Well, I don't think so.

う〜ん、そうは思わないな。

I'm afraid I don't agree.

悪いけど賛成できないな。

I'm sorry but I can't agree with you on that.

残念ながら、その点については合意できかねるよ。

I'm not so sure about that.

それはどうだろうか。

That's not how I see it.

私の見方と異なるよ。

Not necessarily.

必ずしもそうではないよ。

I see what you're saying, but I have a different opinion.

あなたが言っていることはわかるけど、私の意見は異なります。

I understand where you're coming from, but I can't agree with you.

なぜ君がそう考えるのかは理解できるけれど、合意できないな。

Well, I'd have to think about that.

そうだな、その点については考えてみなければならないな。

Unfortunately, I see it differently.

あいにく、私は違う見解です。

That's not really how I see it.

私の見方は異なります。

I am not comfortable with the plan.

その計画には賛成しかねます。

I'm sorry, but I completely disagree.

申し訳ないが、完全に反対意見です。

Well, I don't know. It depends on the situation.

えっと、それはどうかな。状況次第ではないかと思うよ。

I would rather suggest a different approach.

むしろ別のアプローチを提案します。

Sorry, that's not quite right.

すみません、それはちょっと正しくありません。

I'm afraid you don't understand what I'm saying.

残念ながら、私の話を理解してもらえていないようだ。

That's not what I meant.

それは私が意図したことではないよ。

I think you might have misunderstood me.

私の発言を誤解されているようだね。

Please allow me to clarify it once more.

もう一度、説明させてもらうよ。

We are here today to discuss our marketing plan.

今日はマーケティングプランを議論するために集まっているよ。

Would it be OK to talk about different issues later?

別の問題については後にしてもらえる？

That's not really why we're here today.

その件を話すために今日ここに集まっている訳ではないよね。

I think we're getting a bit off topic.

話がちょっとそれてきていると思うよ。

We'll have to leave that to another time.

その件は別の機会に話しましょう。

Please be brief.

簡単にお願いね。

Why don't we return to the main focus of today's meeting?

本日の議題に戻ろうか？

Now, let's move onto the next item.

では、次の議題に移ろう。

Next, I'd like to discuss the second agenda.

次に、2番目の議題について話そう。

I think we've spent enough time on this topic.

この話題については、十分議論したね。

We don't seem to be getting anywhere with this today.

今日のところは、どうにもまとまらないようだな。

Let's discuss it further at the next meeting.

次の会議で再度話そう。

Let's try to find a middle ground.

妥協点を見つけよう。

Why don't we try to reach a compromise?

妥協しませんか？

For now, we have to agree to disagree.

現時点では、合意しないということに同意しましょう。

Why don't we leave it to our boss?

この件はボスに任せてはどうですか？

Let's transit to our next item of agenda.

アジェンダにある次の項目に移りましょう。

I suggest we all sleep on it and get together tomorrow.

いったん保留にして、明日また集まることを提案します。

3. 会議をまとめる　　　　　　　　　Track 11

Is there anything else we need to discuss?

他に何か議論しなくてはいけないことはあるかな？

Has anyone else gotten anything to contribute?

誰か他に意見ありますか？

Are there any more comments?

何か他にコメントありますか？

Unfortunately, we're running short of time.

あいにく、時間がなくなってきました。

We'll have to leave that till another time.

その件は次の機会に話をしよう。

It looks like we've covered all topics on the agenda.

アジェンダにある全ての話題をカバーしたようだね。

Before we close, let me just summarize the main points.

終了する前に、主要ポイントをまとめます。

Let me quickly go over today's main points.

簡単に今日の主要ポイントを確認します。

Let's wrap up.

まとめましょう。

In this meeting we have discussed three things.

今回のミーティングでは、3つのことを話しました。

Let's meet again in a few weeks.

数週間のうちに再度集まりましょう。

How about Wednesday in two weeks?

2週間後の水曜はどうですか？

Our next meeting will be on June 5th.

次のミーティングは6月5日です。

Let's get together three weeks from today.

3週間後にまた集まりましょう。

I'd like to thank everyone for coming today.

今日は参加してくれてありがとう。

Thank you very much for making the time in your schedule for today's meeting.

今日のミーティングのためにスケジュールの時間を割いてくれてありがとう。

I appreciate everyone's contribution today.

本日の皆さんの貢献に感謝します。

The meeting was very productive.

とても有効なミーティングでしたよ。

That will be all for today.

これで今日は終了です。

4. 経営会議で営業や財務報告をする　　　Track 12

I would like to give you some highlights of our sales performance last month.

先月の当社の売上実績の注目点をご紹介します。

Sales of our new products are strong.

新製品の売り上げは好調です。

Sales are in good shape.

売上は好調です。

Compared to last month, sales went up 12% this month.

前月に比べて、今月は売上が12%伸びました。

We hit a record 42% share in September. Up 11% versus a year ago.

9月のシェアは42%となり、前年同月と比べて11%上昇しました。

This month, sales were significantly better than we had expected.

今月、売上は予想を大きく上回りました。

The total revenue exceeded our target by 10%.

総売上は目標を10%超えました。

Unfortunately, this was the worst month I've ever experienced.

残念ながら、今月はこれまでになく厳しい月でした。

We missed the profit target for the first time in this fiscal year.

今年度初めて利益目標に到達しませんでした。

Sales were far more sluggish than last month due to the competition.

競争のため、先月に比べて売上はかなり落ちました。

The new model was by far our top selling product.

新しいモデルは、当社で最も売れる商品になりました。

This marked the best performance of this division since 2019.

この結果、2019 年以降、当部門の売上は最高となりました。

We had disappointing sales last month due to the bad weather.

悪天候のため、先月の売上は残念な数字でした。

We have seen a declining trend in our sales of core products.

主力製品の売上が低下傾向にあります。

One of the challenges we are facing is the hike of the price of oil.

私たちが直面している課題の 1 つは、原油価格の上昇です。

The reasons for our sales decline are still under investigation.

売上減少の理由はまだ調査中です。

We will share our findings and corrective actions at the next meeting.

次の会議で、調査結果と今後の対策を共有します。

The following are highlights, trends, and issues from our financial results of the year.

以下は、当年度の業績からの注目点、傾向、および懸念点です。

Revenue is $200,000 this year. Down by 2% compared to last year.

今期の収益は 200,000 ドルで、前期に比べて 2%ダウンしました。

Online sales now make up 30% of total sales.

オンラインの売上は全売上の 30%を占めます。

This number is expected to rise to 40% in the following year.

この数字は翌年には 40% に達する見込みです。

The source of growth for the period is the new product.

期間の売上の伸びを牽引したのは新製品です。

We continue to see that the new advertising is driving the increase in sales.

新しい広告が売上の増加を牽引していくと考えています。

One of the issues is high account receivables.

懸念点の一つは売上債権が増えていることです。

We have implemented the new policies and procedures to counter this issue.

この問題に対処するための新しいポリシーと手順を実施しました。

We expect that the price competition is getting tougher with the entry of foreign competitors.

私たちは海外の競合の参入によって価格競争が激化すると考えています。

We have implemented several initiatives to achieve the 5% cost reduction in administrative expenses.

管理費 5% 削減を実現するために、いくつかの取り組みを実施しました。

We have planned to improve the gross margin by 0.1% by changing sourcing strategies.

調達戦略を変更することで、売上総利益率を 0.1% 改善することを計画しています。

We have hired outside consultants to develop a lean organizational structure.

無駄のない組織構造を構築するために外部のコンサルタントを雇いました。

Today, I would like to talk about how to turn around the disappointing sales of Product XYZ.

今日、私は製品 XYZ の期待はずれの売上を好転させる方法についてお話しします。

In my opinion, the first thing we need to do is to increase brand awareness.

私の考えでは、ブランドの認知度を高めることを最初に行うべきです。

I propose to advertise more in magazines and online this year.

今年は雑誌やオンラインでもっと宣伝することを提案します。

The last market research suggests our products have the greatest potential with the younger generation.

前回の市場調査によると、当社の製品は若い世代に最大の可能性があります。

I would like to propose to increase our budget to launch our revolutionary product.

当社の画期的な製品の発売にあたり、予算の増額を提案したいと思います。

With this innovative product, we are confident to beat competition.

この革新的な製品で、競合に打ち勝つ自信があります。

I must say that we have underestimated the competition.

競合を過小評価していたと言わざるを得ません。

We should get more facts about the market before we do something different.

別の手を打つ前に市場について、もっと多くの事実を理解すべきと考えます。

We need to fix this issue as quickly as possible.

この問題は早急に解決しなければなりません。

I strongly suggest taking corrective action to recover our sales.

売上を回復させるために是正措置を講じるべきです。

We will come back to present further concrete corrective action next month.

来月、さらに具体的な是正プランを提示させていただきます。

I appreciate your encouragement and support for our sales team.

営業チームへの励ましとサポートに感謝します。

3 オンライン会議（ウェブ会議、電話会議）

1. 会議を招集する　　　　　　　　　　　Track 13

Please join our conference call which is indicated down below.

下記の電話会議に参加お願いいたします。

The main purpose of the conference call is to discuss our next year budget.

今回の電話会議の主な目的は、来年度の予算について話すことです。

If there's anything you think should be added, please let me know.

何か追加すべきものがあれば、私に教えてください。

Feel free to make any comments on the agenda.

アジェンダについて、自由にコメントしてください。

Before the conference call next week, I would appreciate it if you could think about your proposal.

来週の電話会議まで、各自の提案について考えておいてください。

2. 会議を開始する時の挨拶や自己紹介　　　Track 14

Are we all on?

全員準備できたかな？

Can everybody hear me?

皆さん、聞こえますか？

Do we have John on the call?

ジョンは参加してる？

Are we waiting for anyone else?

まだ参加できてない人はいるかな？

Now that we're all connected, let's begin.

全員つながったね、では開始しましょう。

Good afternoon, everyone. I think we are ready to begin.

皆さん、こんにちは。準備はできていますね。

Can I ask that we all state our names, please?

全員、名前を言ってもらえますか？

Can I ask that we all briefly introduce ourselves, please?

皆さん、簡単に自己紹介してくださいますか？

It's Lisa in Tokyo, the facilitator of today's conference call.

今日の電話会議を取りまとめる、東京のリサです。

Unfortunately, members from the Osaka office are not with us today.

あいにく、大阪オフィスからは今日は誰も参加してないようです。

Something came up today, so they need to skip the conference call.

今日は緊急案件があって、電話会議には参加できないと聞いています。

I have received an apology from Mr. Suzuki for being absent.

鈴木さんから欠席のおわびの連絡をもらっています。

He has an emergency he has to deal with this morning.

今朝、急用が発生したそうです。

However, we need to carry on without them.

あいにくですが、彼らなしで進めましょう。

Today we have two Johns. Please make sure to add surnames when speaking.

今日は参加者に2人のジョンがいます。話す時は（どちらのジョンかわかるように）苗字をお願いしますね。

Please join me in welcoming Mr. Suzuki, who is new to our group.

グループの新メンバーの鈴木さんを歓迎しましょう。

He would like to say a few words of introduction.

彼に簡単に自己紹介してもらいます。

Now let's move on to the main topic.

ではさっそく本題に入ります。

It might be easier if we said our names each time we speak.

話す時に名前をそれぞれ言ったほうがわかりやすいですね。

The purpose of this conference meeting is to share the plan for the upcoming annual sales meeting.

この電話会議の目的は、次回の年次営業会議の計画をシェアすることです。

We are here today to discuss our travel policy.

今日は旅費規程を話す目的でここに集まりました。

I would like to make sure that we cover everything on the agenda.

アジェンダにあるすべてをカバーするようにしたいと思います。

Mike, would you mind taking notes today?

マイク、今日ノート（議事録）をとってもらえますか？

Let's make sure we finish in one hour.

1 時間で終わるようにしましょう。

We'll have to keep each item to 15 minutes.

各トピックは 15 分です。

Otherwise we'll never get through.

そうしないと、いつまでも終わりませんからね。

First, let's start by going over what we discussed in the last conference call.

まず、前回の電話会議で議論したことを見ていきましょう。

Just to make sure, I would like to remind you of the ground rules for our conference call, one at a time when speaking.

念のため、私たちの電話会議の基本ルールの確認をします。話す時は一人ずつお願いします。

We have participants from 3 different countries today.

今日は 3 ヶ国からの参加者がいます。

I would like you to speak clearly and slowly so that everyone understands.

皆が理解しやすいように、はっきりゆっくり話すようにしてください。

Now, let's begin with the first topic on the agenda.

では、アジェンダの最初の話題から始めましょう。

I'm sharing my screen right now.

今、私の画面をシェアしています。

Can everyone see it?

皆さん見えますか？

We should see this document while we talk. Let me email this to you right now.

話しながらこの資料を見たほうがいいですね。今すぐメールで送ります。

The first item on the agenda is to share each progress for our next new product launch.

アジェンダの最初のトピックは当社の次の新製品発売についてのそれぞれの進捗を共有することです。

I suggest we go around the table first, starting with Mr. Sato.

佐藤さんから始まって、全員に話してもらいます。

Ken, could you update us on the marketing plan?

ケン、マーケティングプランについてアップデートをお願いできますか？

Tom, what are your thoughts?

トム、どう思いますか？

David, how is the ABC project coming along?

デービッド、ABC プロジェクトの進捗はどうですか？

This is Tom in Tokyo. Could I say something?

こちらは東京のトムです。発言してよろしいですか？

Could you speak more slowly, please?

少しゆっくり話してもらえる？

Could you repeat that, please?

もう一度、言ってもらえる？

I'm afraid I didn't get that.

すみません、理解できないです。

Could you explain that in another way, please?

違う方法で説明してもらえるかな？

John in New York, do you have anything you would like to add?

ニューヨークのジョン、何か付け足すことはない？

Sorry Tom, could we let Mike finish, please?

すみませんトム、マイクの話を最後まで聞くようにしよう。

Lisa, I just want to clarify what you have mentioned.

リサ、今あなたが言ったことを確認するよ。

Sorry would you mind if I asked a question?

質問してもいいかな？

Let's leave this item for now.

とりあえず、この件は後にしましょう。

I think we should cover that topic at the next conference call.

その件は次の電話会議で話すことにしよう。

So far, I think we have all had our say on this topic.

ここまでで、この件についてはみんな言いたいことは言いましたね。

Let's move on to the next topic.

次の話題に移りましょう。

4. オンライン会議特有の問題（技術的問題など）や 状況に対処する　　　　　　　　Track 16

I think there's a problem with the line.

回線に問題あるようです。

The line keeps breaking up.

回線が途切れ途切れになります。

We're looking into it now.

今確認しています。

Please give us a moment.

少々待ってください。

Just hold on one second.

ちょっと待ってください。

Let me reboot the system.

システムを再起動します。

The sound quality is not good today. Please, can everyone speak up?

今日は音質が良くないようです。皆さん、はっきり話すようにお願いね。

I'm afraid we can't hear you very well.

申し訳ないけど、よく聞こえません。

Will you be able to turn the volume up?

ボリュームを大きくしてもらえますか？

Can you please speak up?

もう少し大きな声で話していただけますか？

Excuse me, I am hearing a lot of noise from your background. Could you find out what's going on?

すみません、背後から雑音が聞こえます。何が起きているか確認してもらえますか？

Unfortunately, we can't hear you very well.

あいにく、あなたの声がよく聞こえません。

Could you check the connection on your end?

そちらの回線をチェックしてもらえますか？

I can hear background noises.

後ろの雑音が聞こえます。

Shall we hang up the phone once and try to connect once again?

電話を一度切って、もう一度接続してみますか？

Could you put yourselves on mute when you are not talking?

話していない時はミュートにしてくださいますか？

One moment please, everyone. Mr. Sato, the HR manager has just joined us.

皆さん、ちょっと待ってください。人事マネージャーの佐藤さんが今参加しました。

Sorry. Who was that just now?

すみません。今話したのは誰ですか？

There are three people speaking.

3人が話していますよ。

May I remind you to speak one at a time?

話す時は1人ずつでお願いします。

Sorry, who's speaking please?

すみません、誰が話していますか？

Could you say your name before speaking?

話す前に名前を言ってもらえますか？

Sorry everyone, we're looking for the PowerPoint slides.

皆さん、すみません、今パワーポイントのスライドを探しています。

Please give us a second.

少々待ってください。

I won't keep you long.

長くはかかりません。

May I remind everyone that we have to finish by 5 pm?

午後5時までには終わらないといけなかったですよね？

I will keep my explanation brief.

私の説明は短くするようにします。

I need to leave for 10 minutes due to some urgent matters.

10分間、急用で会議から抜けなければなりません。

Would you continue the discussion without me?

私なしで議論を続けていてくださいますか？

Ken, please lead the discussion while I am away.

ケン、私がいない間、議論をリードしてください。

I'm back on the line again.

会議に戻りました。

That covers everything we had to discuss today.

本日お話したいことはすべてカバーしましたね。

Is there anything else to discuss?

何か他に話すことはありますか？

Now are there any questions?

では、何かご質問はありますか？

That is a really good question.

とても良い質問です。

Let me get back to you on that.

その点については、後日ご連絡します。

Before we close today's meeting, let me just summarize the main points.

今日の会議を終える前に、主要ポイントをまとめます。

If there are no other comments, I'd like to wrap this meeting up.

他にコメントがなければ、この会議を終わりにしたいと思います。

We're running out of time, let's wrap it up for today.

時間がなくなりました。本日はここまでにしましょう。

Let's set the date for the next conference call.

次の電話会議の日程を決めましょう。

Shall we schedule a follow-up call in three weeks?

3週間後にフォローアップの電話会議をスケジュールしましょう。

Can we agree on the next meeting to be on June 5, from 3 pm Eastern Time?

次の会議は6月5日、イースターンタイムの午後3時からで、皆さん大丈夫ですか？

Please mark on your calendar that we will have a regular conference call from 4 pm, Japan Time on the first business day of the month.

毎月の最初の営業日、日本時間午後4時からの電話会議を定期的に開催しますので、カレンダーに入れておいてください。

Thanks for your participation.

ご参加ありがとう。

I would like to thank you all for your contributions today.

本日のご協力に感謝します。

That's it for today, speak to you soon.

今日はこれで終わります。またお話ししましょう。

4 雑談、スモールトーク

1. 同僚との何気ない雑談 Track 18

How's it going?
調子どう？

Pretty well.
とても良いよ。

Great.
良いです。

I'm okay.
まあまあかな。

Not too bad.
結構良いです。

How about you?
君はどう？

This weather is crazy, isn't it?
今日の天気はひどいね。

Yes, it's horrible.
まったく、ひどい天気だね。

It's a beautiful day, isn't it?
良い天気ですね。

Yes, it's fantastic.

うん、すばらしいね。

It looks like it's going to snow.

雪になるそうだよ。

Really?

本当に？

It's terrible.

それは嫌だな。

It's a bit cold for this time of year, isn't it?

今年は例年より少し寒いようだね。

It's a bit warm for this time of year, isn't it?

今年は例年より少し暖かいですね。

Hi Ken, how are you doing?

やあケン、元気ですか？

I'm doing great. How are you doing?

元気だよ。君はどう？

I'm doing well myself.

私も元気だよ。

It's been a while.

久しぶりだね。

When was the last time we saw each other?

最後に会ったのはいつ頃だっけ？

What have you been up to lately?

最近はどう？

Well, I just started to work on a new project, so I'm a bit busy.

えっと、ちょうど新しいプロジェクトに取りかかったところで、ちょっと忙しくしてるよ。

Do you do anything fun these days?

最近は何か楽しいことをしていますか？

I've been playing the guitar a lot lately.

最近はギターを弾くことにはまっています。

That's cool.

かっこいいね。

How did you become interested in playing the guitar?

何をきっかけにギターを弾くことに興味を持ったの？

How was your weekend?

週末はどうだった？

Did you watch the Super Bowl last night?

昨夜のスーパーボールを観た？

What did you think of it?

どう思った？

Could you tell me about Major League Baseball?

メジャーリーグの野球について教えてくれる？

I don't know much about Major League Baseball.

メジャーリーグの野球には詳しくないんだ。

Do you have a favorite team?

応援しているチームはあるの？

How are they doing this year?

彼らの今年の調子はどう？

What are you up to this weekend?

今週末はどんな予定？

What was the best part of your weekend?

週末で一番良かったことは何だった？

Did you go somewhere for the weekend?

週末はどこかへ行ったの？

Do you have any plans for this summer?

この夏は何か予定があるの？

Have you been there before, or will this be your first time?

そこには行ったことがあるの？　それとも初めて？

How was your break?

休みはどうだった？

What was the best part of your trip?

旅行で一番楽しかったのはどんなこと？

Are you working on anything exciting these days?

最近は何かエキサイティングな仕事をしてる？

Have you seen any interesting movies these days?

最近、何かおもしろい映画を観ましたか？

What are you working on these days?

最近はどんな仕事をしているの？

How is your current project going?

今やっているプロジェクトの調子はどう？

2. ビジネス交流会などでの初対面の人との雑談　Track 19

Do you mind if I ask your name?

お名前を伺えますか？

No problem. My name is Mike.

大丈夫です。マイクです。

My name is Kentaro, but please call me Ken.

私の名前はケンタロウですが、ケンと呼んでください。

How did you meet the host?

主催者とはどこで知り合いましたか？

Are you enjoying yourself?

楽しんでいますか？

How do you like Japan?

日本はどうですか？

How do you like Japanese food?

日本食は好きですか？

Is there any place you would like to visit while you are here?

ここにいる間にどこか行きたい所はありますか？

Why would you like to visit Shinjuku?

なぜ新宿に行きたいのですか？

Have you had any interesting trips this fall?

この秋には何か楽しい旅行をしましたか？

Do you travel a lot?

旅行はたくさんしますか？

What are some of your favorite cities?

気に入った都市はどんなところですか？

Have you been to any great new restaurants lately?

最近、どこか新しい良いレストランに行きましたか？

I'm looking for a good summer read.

今夏に読む、良い本を探しています。

Have you read anything good lately?

何か良い本を最近読みましたか？

What do you do?

お仕事は何をしていますか？

I work in the sales department at a construction company.

建設会社の営業部で働いています。

What company are you with?

どこの会社で働いていますか？

What company do you work for?

どちらの会社にお勤めですか？

What position do you hold?

どんな役職をお持ちですか？

What are you doing here?

こちらで何をされていますか？

What brings you here?

なぜここに来ましたか？

I am on a business trip.

出張で来ています。

I'm here for the conference.

会議に出るためにここにいます。

Do you like your job?

仕事は好きですか？

What do you like about it?

どんなところが好きですか？

I have opportunities to travel abroad and attend a great conference.

海外に旅行し、すばらしい会議に出る機会があります。

That sounds challenging.

とても良いですね。

Where are you from?

どちらから来ましたか？

This is my first visit to New York.

今回初めてのニューヨーク訪問です。

How do you like living in New York?

ニューヨークに住むのはどんな感じですか？

Where are you from originally?

元々のご出身はどちらですか？

Is there anything that you would like to do while you are here?

ここに滞在中に何かなさりたいことはありますか？

Where do you recommend for me to visit while I am here?

ここに滞在している間、どこに行ったらいいと思いますか？

Is there anything that you would recommend in your town?

あなたの町で何かおすすめのものはありますか？

Will you have time for some sightseeing?

観光する時間はありますか？

I need to run to the airport right after the conference.

会議の後、すぐに空港に向かわなければなりません。

3. 会合や商談の前や休憩中での雑談　　Track 20

It is great to meet you at last after all those emails.

メールのやり取りだけでしたが、遂に初めてお会いできてうれしいです。

I am sorry to keep you waiting.

お待たせしてすみませんでした。

I had an urgent phone call to deal with.

緊急の電話に対応しなければなりませんでした。

Is this your first trip to Tokyo?

東京には初めてですか？

How do you like Tokyo?

東京はどうですか？

Will you have any time to visit outside of Tokyo during your business trip?

出張中に東京以外を訪れる時間はありそうですか？

Your office is spacious.

広々としたオフィスですね。

Can you see Mount Fuji when the weather is good?

天気が良い時は富士山が見えますか？

This office location is amazing.

このオフィスの場所はすばらしいです。

Is it convenient for the commute?

通勤に便利ですか？

You have great pictures.

すてきな写真ですね。

May I ask who they are with you?

一緒にいるのはどなたか伺ってよろしいですか？

Are there any nice restaurants nearby?

近くにすてきなレストランはありますか？

What's the weather like in your hometown?

あなたのホームタウンの天気はどんな感じですか？

I come from the northern part of the US.

アメリカの北のほうから来ました。

So, it's a bit colder than here.

ですので、ここより少し寒いです。

What fun activities do you do on the weekends there?

そこでは週末にどんな楽しい活動をしていますか？

How did you get here?

こちらにはどうやって来ましたか？

Did you have any problem to find this place?

この場所を見つけるのは大変ではありませんでしたか？

Did you have any trouble getting here?

こちらに来るのに何か問題はありませんでしたか？

I took the subway.

地下鉄に乗りました。

It was convenient, and I found this place easily.

地下鉄は便利で、この場所も簡単に見つかりました。

I didn't have any problems.

問題はありませんでした。

I found directions on the internet.

ネットで方向を確認してきました。

However, the traffic was not that great.

しかし、ちょっと混んでいました。

Traffic is never good around here.

この辺はいつも混んでいます。

You have a nice watch.

すてきな時計ですね。

Where did you get it?

どこで手に入れたのですか？

You always wear an attractive tie.

いつもすてきなネクタイをお召しですね。

What are your favorite stores?

どこがお気に入りのお店ですか？

I got this as my birthday present.

これは誕生日プレゼントでもらいました。

What inspired you to become a lawyer?

何をきっかけ弁護士になろうと思いましたか？

How did you get into accounting?

どのようなきっかけで経理の仕事に就きましたか？

Have you worked here long?

ここでは長く働いていますか？

Have you always been in IT, or have you worked in other industries?

IT 業界でずっと働いてきましたか？　それとも他の業界でも働いてきましたか？

How long have you worked for this company?

この会社には何年働いていますか？

I spent about five years working for a major company before starting my own business.

自分のビジネスを始める前、5年くらい大手の会社に勤めていました。

What do you like about working in the big company?

大会社で働くのはどんなところが良いですか？

What is the scope of your responsibilities?

あなたの責任範囲はどこまでですか？

I heard you recently transferred from the sales department.

最近、あなたは営業部門から異動してきたと聞きました。

How is the transition going for you?

異動はうまく行っていますか？

What do you think of the new conference room?

新しい会議室はどうですか？

What do you think of the conference so far?

ここまでの会議をどう思いますか？

Has this training been helpful for you?

このトレーニングは役に立っていますか？

What did you like about the presentation?

プレゼンテーションの何が良かったですか？

I found it very useful.

とても有意義です。

You look tired a bit.

少しお疲れのようです。

Why don't we go together to have some coffee?

一緒にコーヒーブレークに行きましょう。

What are your interests outside of work?

仕事以外、どのようなことに興味がありますか？

How did you develop an interest in it?

どのように、それに興味を持ったのですか？

I've never been to Los Angeles.

ロサンゼルスには行ったことがありません。

What would you suggest I do if I visit?

もし行く機会があれば、何がおすすめですか？

Have you thought about living abroad?

海外に住んでみたいと思ったことはありますか？

In my spare time I enjoy reading.

時間がある時は、読書を楽しみます。

One of my favorite things to do on weekends is jogging.

週末に私がよくやることの１つがジョギングです。

Generally, how is the economy in New York?

一般的に、ニューヨークの景気はどうですか？

Is unemployment a big problem in your country?
失業はあなたの国では大きな問題ですか？

Well, it is an issue, but it's not as bad as a few years ago.
そうですね、問題ですが、数年前ほど悪くはありません。

I found out your head office is in London.
御社の本社はロンドンにあるのですね。

My sister lives there.
姉がそこに住んでいます。

Do you like sushi?
寿司は好きですか？

In fact, there's a great sushi restaurant near here.
実は、この近くにとても良い寿司屋があります。

We should get together for lunch sometime.
いつかランチをしましょう。

Yes, that would be great.
ええ、ぜひお願いします。

How's your meeting going?
会議はどうですか？

May I set up a meeting to follow up on this conversation?
この話の続きをしたいので、ミーティングを設定してもいいですか？

It's nice to meet someone from the same school.

同じ学校出身の人に会うのはうれしいです。

Your comments about this market are very insightful.

この市場についてのあなたのコメントはとても洞察力があります。

What's your plan this long weekend?

この長い週末のご予定は？

Do you expect a busy week again?

今週も忙しそう？

How has your week been so far?

今週は今のところどうですか？

I hope it hasn't been too stressful.

あまりストレスのない週だといいのですが。

It's been a while.

久しぶりですね。

When was the last time we talked with each other?

最後に話したのはいつ頃でしたか？

What have you been up to lately?

最近はどうですか？

What is your opinion on this topic?

この話題についてはどう思う？

What's been going on at work since the last time we talked?

最後に話してから、仕事のほうはどうですか？

What have you been working on lately?

最近取りかかっている仕事は何ですか？

How is your current project going?

今携わっているプロジェクトの進捗はどうですか？

Have you had any interesting projects?

何か楽しいプロジェクトに携わっていますか？

What's your industry like right now?

今、あなたの業界はどうですか？

Why have you come to be interested in sales?

なぜあなたは営業に興味を持つようになったのですか？

What do you enjoy most about your work?

仕事で一番楽しんでいることは何ですか？

What is the biggest challenge your company is facing now?

あなたの会社が今直面している課題について教えてください。

What advice would you give students who are interested in your industry?

あなたの業界に興味を持つ学生にはどんなアドバイスをしますか？

What's the most difficult part of your job?

あなたの仕事で最も難しいことは何ですか？

How has AI impacted your company?

あなたの会社は、AIでどのような影響を受けていますか？

4. 気の利いた相づちや沈黙を埋めるフレーズ Track 21

Sure.

もちろん。

I see.

なるほど。

Exactly.

確かに。

Really?

本当ですか？

Is that so?

そうなのですか？

That's true.

その通りです。

That's great.

いいですね。

That's too bad.

それは残念です。

I feel the same way.

同感です。

No kidding.

本当ですか？

I wish I could do that.

うらやましいです。

I wish I could be there.

私もそこに行きたかったです。

I am happy for you.

それは良かったですね。

That makes sense.

そういうことですか。

Well ~

そうですね～

Let me see.

そうですね。

I mean,

つまり、

Something like that.

そのような感じです。

So,

それで、

How do I say?

なんて言うのだろう？

5. 会話が聞き取れなかった時　　Track 22

Sorry?

すみません。

Excuse me?

すみません。

Could you repeat that for me?

もう一度、言っていただけますか？

I am afraid I am not following you.

すみません、お話の意味がわかりません。

Sorry, I couldn't catch it.

すみません、聞き取れませんでした。

Could you speak a bit slower?

少しゆっくり話していただけますか？

Could you say it again?

もう一度、言っていただけますか？

Come again?

もう一度、言ってくれる？〔カジュアル〕

Are you with me?

伝わっていますでしょうか？

Does it make sense to you?

意味がわかりますか？

Am I making myself clear to you?

わかっていただけましたでしょうか？

Can we move on to the next topic?

次の話題に行っていいですか？

By the way,

ところで、

Anyway,

ところで、

Speaking of ~

～と言えば

6. スマートに雑談を終了する　　　　Track 23

Excuse me, I need to find my friend.

すみません、友人を探さなければなりません。

Well, I need to go to a meeting.

では、会議に行かなければなりません。

It's been nice talking to you.

あなたとお話しできて良かったです。

It was a pleasure meeting you.

あなたにお会いできてうれしかったです。

Let me give you my business card before I go.

出発する前に名刺をお渡しします。

Enjoy your time here!

ここでの滞在を楽しんでください！

Thank you for the delightful conversation.

楽しい会話をありがとうございます。

Now, I need to say hello to some of my old colleagues.

そろそろ、かつての同僚に挨拶しなければなりません。

I would love to chat more, but let's get down to business now.

もっとおしゃべりしたいのですが、そろそろ仕事の話に移りましょう。

You must tell me more about that later, but shall we get started?

その件については後でもっとお話を聞くとして、仕事に取りかかりましょうか。

We have a lot to cover today, so now, let's move on to business.

今日はお話ししなければならないことがたくさんあるので、そろそろ仕事を始めましょう。

Column ❶

オンライン英語会議の攻略法

　リモートワークが増える中、自宅からオンライン会議に参加することが増えています。Zoom や Google Meet などでのオンライン会議は、利便性もあらためて認識され、今後も増加していくでしょう。

　一方、オフィスで同僚と一緒に、海外のビジネスパートナーとのオンライン会議に出席する場合は、助け合うこともできますが、自宅で一人の場合はそうはいきません。一人でもオンライン英語会議に貢献（＝意見を出すこと）ができるよう、戦略的な準備が必要です。

　本書でご紹介している、オンライン会議用のフレーズを覚えて活用できるようになっていただくほか、いくつか攻略の秘訣があります。

　まずは**事前にアジェンダのチェックと入念な準備**です。自分の職責として発言すべき内容や、確認しなければならない質問事項などを、簡潔に言えるように準備しましょう。

　自宅からオンライン会議に参加する場合、**会議中に必要になるかもしれない資料や過去のメールなど、すぐに出せるようにしておくこと**も役立ちます。こういった情報は、いざ必要になって探し出すと、焦ってしまってなかなか見つからないものです。備えあれば憂いなし。事前に準備しておけば、余裕をもって会議に臨むことができます。

　ビジネスシーンでのコミュニケーションには、**瞬発力**が大事です。

　複数名が参加しているオンライン会議の場合は、話したい、質問したいという雰囲気を読み取ってもらうことが難しいものです。ここで絶対発言したい、質問したいという場面では、ひと呼吸を置きすぎず、話し出す勢いが大事です。誰かと被ってしまうことがあるかもしれませんが、遠慮せずに発言の意思表示をしましょう。

　私が英語の電話会議を初めて経験してから 20 数年が経ちます。どんなに経験しても、話しながら考えても何とかなる、日本語のオンライン会議とは異なるテンションがあります。

　事前に考えをまとめる、いざという時に発言できるように集中する。意外にのどが渇きますので、お気に入りの飲み物の準備もお忘れなく。

Chapter 2

人を育てるための
最強フレーズ

競争の激しい欧米社会では、優秀な人材を採用するために候補者に様々な質問を投げかけます。また、候補者からも会社に対して踏み込んだ質問をすることも可能で、面接はお互いにベストマッチであるかを確認する過程でもあります。採用後は新卒、中途採用ともに、最良の成果を出すために上司は適切なフィードバックを行い、人事考課にも細分化された評価システムを導入しています。

1 優秀な人材の採用（面接）

1. 相手を知る雑談（自己紹介）　　　　Track 24

Thanks for coming here today.

今日は来てくれてありがとう。

....

Thank you for taking the time to meet with us today.

本日はお時間をいただき、会いに来てくれてありがとうございます。

....

It's a beautiful afternoon, isn't it?

良い天気の午後ですね。

....

Please make yourself comfortable.

どうぞ、くつろいでください。

....

Sorry to keep you waiting.

お待たせして申し訳ない。

....

I trust we haven't kept you waiting too long.

長くお待たせしていないですよね。

....

I'm John Smith, the head of HR, and this is my colleague, Mr. Tanaka.

私は人事部長のジョン・スミスです。こちらは同僚の田中さんです。

....

Please take a seat.

どうぞ座って。

....

How is your day going today?

今日はどうですか？

Are you familiar with Marunouchi?

丸の内界隈は詳しいのかな？

Is this your first time in Tokyo?

東京には今回が初めて？

Did you have any problems with your journey?

旅はどうでしたか？

Did you have any trouble getting here?

ここはすぐに見つかった？

Did you have any problem finding this place?

ここには迷わずに来られましたか？

Would you like a coffee before we start?

始める前にコーヒーはどうですか？

We are excited to learn more about you today.

今日は君のことをもっと知る機会を楽しみにしています。

I would like to let you know that this is a follow-up interview.

これはフォローアップインタビューです。

The interview will last about one hour.

面接は約１時間です。

As you know, this is a final interview.

ご存知の通り、今回は最終面接です。

I would like you to meet our Department Head and HR Director for interviews.

部門長と人事部長と面接をしていただきます。

Let me tell you a little about our company before we start.

始める前に、私たちの会社について少しお話ししましょう。

Now, tell me a little about yourself.

では、自分自身のこと、少し話してください。

Can you make a brief introduction about yourself?

簡単に自己紹介してくれますか？

How would you describe yourself in one word?

自分自身をひとことで言うとどう表現しますか？

Can you tell me about your educational background?

どんな勉強をしてきたか話してくれますか？

Why did you choose your major?

専攻を決めた理由は？

Why did you choose your mathematics major?

なぜ数学を専攻したの？

What work experience do you have?

実務経験はどんなものがありますか？

What skills have you got from your work experience?

実務経験からどのようなスキルを得ましたか？

2. 志望動機を聞き出し、深掘りする　　Track 25

Why are you interested in this job?

この仕事に興味を持ったのは何ですか？

How did you hear about this position?

このポジションについてはどうやって知りましたか？

Have you done this kind of work?

同じような仕事をやったことがあるのかな？

What were your key roles at your prior job?

あなたの前職での主な役割はどんなことでしたか？

What do you like about working in marketing?

あなたはマーケティングの仕事の何が好きですか？

What do you know about us and our industry?

我社やこの業種について、どんなことを知っていますか？

What kind of job opportunities are you currently looking for?

現在はどのような仕事の機会を探していますか？

How is your prior experience relevant to this job?

あなたのこれまでの経験はこの仕事にどう役立ちますか？

What is the most important thing for you in this new job opportunity?

この新しい仕事の機会で、最も重要なことは何ですか？

How do you keep up with your latest technical skills required for this kind of job?

このような仕事に必要な、最新の技術的スキルはどのように学んでいるの？

Why do you think you are qualified for this position?

あなたはなぜ自分がこのポジションに適任であると考えていますか？

Do you believe that you have all the skill sets required for this position?

このポジションに必要なスキルは全て持っていると信じていますか？

What can you offer us if we hire you?

あなたを採用したら、何を提供できますか？

Why did you choose to work in the marketing field?

なぜマーケティング分野で働くことを選んだのですか？

3. 長所や短所を聞き出し、深掘りする　　　Track 26

What are your strengths?

あなたの長所（強み）はどんなこと？

What are your greatest professional strengths?

仕事に生かせるあなたの最大の強みは何ですか？

What are your main weaknesses?

あなたの主な短所（弱み）はどんなこと？

Tell me about your strength.

あなたの長所を教えてください。

May I ask you what your greatest weakness is?

あなたの最大の短所は何ですか？

What do you consider to be your professional weaknesses?

仕事において、自分のどんなところが弱みだと思いますか？

How would your colleagues describe you?

同僚はあなたをどんな人だと言うでしょう？

Please tell me how you think your current supervisor would describe you.

今のあなたの上司は、君のことをどのような人と言うか、話してください。

4. これまで達成したこと・人生に影響を与えた経験について　　Track 27

What is one important lesson you have learned at work in the past few years?

過去数年間にあなたが職場で学んだ、重要な教訓を1つ挙げると何ですか？

What professional accomplishment are you most proud of?

仕事で達成したことで最も誇りに思うことは何ですか？

Could you tell me the experience when you took your leadership?

リーダーシップを発揮した時の経験を教えてくださいますか？

Could you tell us about the most challenging environment you've ever worked in?

あなたが今まで働いた中で最も大変だった環境について教えてくださいますか？

Could you tell me about the toughest decision you had to make in your life?

あなたがこれまでの人生で下した最も難しい決断は何ですか？

What was the best team experience for you?

最高のチーム経験は何ですか？

When are you most satisfied in your job?

仕事で一番満足感を感じるのはどんな時ですか？

What do you see as a major success in your life?

あなたの人生において、大きな成功は何ですか？

What are three of your major accomplishments in your life?

これまでの人生で達成した、大きな成果を３つ挙げると何ですか？

Could you tell me about your work experience that didn't go as well as expected?

あなたが期待したほどうまく行かなかった仕事の経験について教えてくださいますか？

How did you manage it?

それにどう対処しましたか？

What were the most memorable accomplishments in your last position?

あなたの最後の仕事で、最も記憶に残る偉業は何ですか？

Please describe a situation where you convinced someone to accept your proposal.

誰かにあなたの提案を受け入れるよう説得した状況を説明してください。

What steps did you take?

どのようなステップを踏みましたか？

Could you share your experience when you participated in any volunteering activities?

ボランティア活動に参加した時の経験を教えてくださいますか？

How have you worked to expand your knowledge at work?

仕事で知識を広げるためにどのようにしていますか？

Do you have any example that a decision you made created a competitive advantage for your company?

あなたが下した決定があなたの会社に競争上の優位性をもたらした例はありますか？

How would you work with someone who is difficult to get along with?

仲良くするのが難しい人とどのように仕事をしますか？

What would motivate you to make a move from your current role?

現在の仕事から転職する動機は何ですか？

Please share one example of overcoming difficulties at work.

職場での困難を乗り越えた例を 1 つ教えてくれるかな。

What skills have you learned in your prior jobs?

以前の仕事でどんなスキルを学んできた？

Tell me about a conflict you've faced at work, and how you dealt with it.

職場で対立した経験についてと、それにどう対処したかについて教えてください。

5. 今後の夢やキャリア展望を聞く　　　Track 28

What are your short-term goals?

あなたの短期的な目標は何ですか？

What are your long-term goals?

あなたの長期的な目標は何ですか？

What are your lifelong dreams?

あなたの人生の夢は何ですか？

Where do you see yourself in five years?

5 年後には自分はどうなっていると思いますか？

What are your professional ambitions?

あなたの仕事をする上で、どんな野心がある？

How do you see the opportunity fitting into your long-term career objective?

この機会があなたの長期的なキャリアの目標にどのように合致すると思いますか？

Why should we hire you?

我々はなぜあなたを採用すべきだと思いますか？

Why should we choose you for this position?

なぜ私たちはこのポジションにあなたを選ぶべきですか？

6. 転職の理由を聞き出す　　Track 29

Why do you want to leave your current job?

なぜ今の仕事を辞めたいのですか？

Why are you looking for a new job?

新しい仕事を探しているのはどうしてですか？

Can you tell me why you resigned just in one year?

たった1年で辞めた理由は何ですか？

Why has there been a gap in your employment?

仕事をしていない期間がある理由は何ですか？

How do you expect this job to be different from your previous jobs?

この仕事は以前の仕事とどう違うのでしょう？

Could you explain why you would like to change your career path?

なぜキャリアの方向性を変えたいか説明してもらえますか？

7. 価値観や大切にしていることを聞く　　　　Track 30

What type of work environment would you prefer?

どのような職場環境を望みますか？

What advantages do you see with a global workplace like us?

私たちのようなグローバルな職場ではどのような利点がありますか？

How do you organize your schedule when you have multiple urgent tasks?

複数の緊急案件がある場合、どのようにスケジュールを立てますか？

How would you handle it, if you were on a team that is not performing well?

あなたがうまく行ってないチームにいる場合、どうやって対処しますか？

Do you work well under pressure?

プレッシャーがある中で働くのは大丈夫ですか？

How do you react to criticism?

批判に対してどのように反応しますか？

How well do you work under pressure or tight deadlines?

プレッシャーや厳しい期日がある環境で働くのは大丈夫ですか？

Can you work under strict deadlines on a regular basis?

定期的に厳しい期限が求められる仕事は大丈夫ですか？

How do you manage your work stress?

仕事上のストレスをどのように管理しますか？

Are you a risk taker or do you like to stay away from risks?

あなたはリスクをとるタイプですか、それともリスクを避けるタイプですか？

What's your leadership style?

どんなリーダーシップをとりますか？

How do you balance both your family and your job?

家族と仕事のバランスはどう取りますか？

What's the most important thing I should know about you?

私があなたについて知っておくべき最も大事なことは何でしょう？

Could you tell me what you're most passionate about in the work you do?

あなたの仕事で最も情熱を注いでいるものを教えてくださいますか？

What absolutely excites you right now?

今あなたを本当に興奮させるものは何ですか？

Do you see yourself as a leader?

自分にリーダーシップがあると思いますか？

Are you a team player?

あなたはチームプレイヤーですか？

What do you think of working in a group?

あなたは集団で働くことをどう思いますか？

Do you prefer working independently or in groups?

あなたは単独で働くことを好みますか、それともグループで働くことを好みますか？

What qualities do you feel a successful manager should have?

あなたは成功するマネージャーにはどのような資質が必要だと思いますか？

Can you describe your management style?

あなたのマネージメントスタイルはどのようなものですか？

Are you comfortable with working in a diversified group?

多様なグループで働くことは大丈夫ですか？

Are you comfortable with leading a global project in English?

英語を使ってグローバルプロジェクトをリードすることは大丈夫ですか？

How do you motivate team members if you became a leader of a project?

プロジェクトのリーダーになった場合、チームのメンバーのモチベーションをどう上げますか？

What do you do when you have a problem with a co-worker?

同僚との間で何か問題が起きた時、どうしますか？

How would you resolve it, when you have any conflicts with co-workers?

あなたは同僚と衝突した場合、どのように解決しますか？

How do you react if your manager requests an unreasonable task beyond the scope of your responsibility?

上司があなたの責任範囲を超えて、不合理な仕事を要求してきたら、どう対応しますか？

How would you handle it, if the company changes priorities in the middle of a major project?

大きなプロジェクトの進行中に会社が優先順位を変更した場合、どのように対処しますか？

Have you ever experienced any significant organizational change?

あなたは今までに大きな組織変更を経験したことがありますか？

8. 質問を促し、真摯に答える　　　Track 31

What is your salary in your current job?

現在の仕事での給料はいくらですか？

What are your compensation requirements?

報酬はどのくらい望んでいますか？

How do you feel about moving abroad for your job in the future?

将来海外転勤することはどう思いますか？

Will you be able to relocate?

転勤できますか？

Do you have any limitations for travelling?

出張に何か制限がありますか？

That's all the questions we have for today.

本日こちらから伺いたいことは以上です。

Do you have any questions?

何か質問はありますか？

Have you got any questions for us?

ここまでで何か疑問に思うことはありますか？

Is there anything else you'd like us to know about you?

あなたについて他に知っておくべきことはありますか？

I will be the direct supervisor for this position.

このポジションの直属の上司は私です。

Are there any other questions I can answer for you?

他に私が答えられる質問はありますか？

What do you like to do outside of work?

仕事以外、どんなことが好きですか？

What kind of books do you enjoy reading?

どんな本を読みますか？

What are your interests?

何に関心がありますか？

What do you like to do in your spare time?

時間がある時はどんなことをしたいですか？

What is your favorite memory from your school days?

学生時代の楽しい思い出は何ですか？

Do you do any sports?

何かスポーツをしますか？

Is there anything you do for your health?

健康のために何かやっていることはありますか？

Is there anything you are passionate about outside of work?

仕事以外で情熱を注いでいるものは何かありますか？

We may contact you again to get additional information about your experience.

あなたの経験に関する追加情報を得るために、再度連絡する場合があります。

We will get back in touch with you within one week.

1週間以内にご連絡します。

We will let you know our next steps in a week.

1週間以内に次のステップをお知らせします。

Are you considering any other offers right now?

今、他のオファーを検討していますか？

What other companies are you planning to interview with?

他にインタビューを受けようとしている会社はありますか？

When are you able to start?

いつから始められそう？

How quickly would you be able to work if we give you an offer?

オファーを出したら、どれくらいすぐに始められますか？

I haven't any further questions to ask you.

これ以上の質問はありません。

Is there anything else you would like to ask before we finish?

終える前に、他に聞きたいことはありますか？

We plan to finish interviewing all candidates by the end of this week.

今週末までに全ての候補者へのインタビューを完了する予定です。

We hope to make our decision in the next couple of weeks.

次の数週間で決定を下すことを期待しています。

After that, we'll be contacting everyone to inform our decision.

その後、全ての人に連絡して決定を通知します。

Does that work for you?

大丈夫ですか？

Are you still interested in this position?

あなたはこのポジションにまだ興味がありますか？

Thanks again for coming to see us today.

今日は来てくれてありがとう。

Have a great rest of your day.

良い一日を。

2 部下を育てるためのフレーズ

1. 部下の不安を取り除く日頃の声かけ　　Track 32

I am excited to welcome you to our team!

チームにようこそ！

I am very pleased to have you on board.

来てくれてとてもうれしいよ。

This is our new organization chart.

これが新しい組織図です。

When you need help, please come to see me at any time.

助けが必要な時は、いつでも私のところに来てね。

Please come to talk to me directly with any issues.

どんな問題でも私に直接話しに来るように。

I suggest you get familiar with your new environment first.

まずは新しい環境に慣れるようにね。

Please refer to your position description if you have any questions about the scope of your responsibility.

責任範囲に質問があれば、職務記述書で確認するようにね。

Please review the operational manual then bring me your questions.

まず業務マニュアルを見て、それから質問してね。

You can also ask your senior colleague whenever you have any questions.

質問があればいつでも先輩に聞いていいよ。

The procedure manual for this department will be a great source of information for you.

この部門の手順書にいろいろ情報があるからね。

The best time to reach me is first thing in the morning most of the time.

私と話すのに一番良いタイミングはたいてい朝一番だよ。

Let's plan to have regular morning meetings once every three days.

3日に1回、定例の朝ミーティングをしよう。

Please give me a quick update at the end of your day for the first three months.

最初の3ヶ月は、退社前に簡単な報告をお願いするよ。

2. 部下のモチベーションを上げる　　　Track 33

I have high expectations of you.

君に期待しているよ。

I am counting on your experience and perspective.

君の経験や見識に期待しているよ。

I trust your judgment.

君の判断を信じるよ。

I always value your opinion.

君の意見はいつも貴重です。

You're learning fast!

覚えが早いね！

After the first three months, I expect you to make decisions about daily works without consulting me.

最初の３ヶ月後、私に相談せずに日々の仕事について判断することを期待しているよ。

After six months of training, I expect you alone to visit our customers.

６ヶ月のトレーニングの後には、一人でお客さんのところに行ってもらうからね。

This is a more common mistake than you might think.

この間違えはあなたが思う以上によくあることですよ。

I can show you how I avoided any mistakes.

私がどうやって間違いが起きないようにしたか、教えますね。

You did an outstanding job to prepare the meeting on such a short notice.

短時間で会議のためにすばらしい準備をしましたね。

I can't tell you how much your extra efforts have helped our team.

君のさらなる努力がどれほどチームのためになっているか、お伝えすることもできないくらいです。

You were instrumental in solving the issues yesterday.

昨日の問題解決はすばらしかったです。

I expect you to keep up the good work.

良い仕事を続けてください。

I guess you are on the right track.

良い調子だと思うよ。

I couldn't have done it better myself.

私だけじゃこんなにうまくできなかったよ。

You are getting better every day.

毎日成長しているね。

What do you think of this problem?

この問題についてはどう思う？

I would like to hear your opinions first.

まずは君の意見を聞きたいな。

You are always so creative.

いつもとてもクリエイティブですね。

Your expertise has made a tremendous difference since you joined our team.

あなたがチームに参加してくれてから、あなたの専門知識には本当に助かっています。

Your positive attitude has made this place a significantly better place for work.

君の前向きな姿勢で、ここをとても働きやすい環境にしてくれているよ。

3. 部下の仕事の進捗を確認する Track 34

I would like to get an update on Project X.

プロジェクト X の進捗を教えてくれるかな。

Please update me on how things are going by the end of this week.

今週末までに、進行状況を私にアップデートしてください。

Would you like to get my feedback on your report?

君のレポートについてのフィードバックをしようか？

I would need you to send me a weekly update by email to share your progress.

毎週、君の進捗報告のメールを私に送るようにお願いするよ。

I would like you to update me of this progress to keep me in the loop.

情報共有のために、私に進捗の報告をしてね。

Do you have any update on whether you'll be able to complete the project on time?

プロジェクトを予定通りに完了できるかどうかについて、何か最新情報がありますか？

How are you coping with the deadline?

締切、大丈夫そう？

Could I assume everything is under control?

全て問題ないと考えていて大丈夫そう？

When do you think you'll get this assignment completed?

この仕事はいつ完了しそう？

When can I have the sales report for the last month?

先月の営業報告書はいつになりそう？

4. 困っている部下を助ける　　　　　Track 35

What can I do to help?

どんな助けができるかな？

Is there anything I can do to help?

何か助けられることはない？

I'm seeing some delays with your report submission.

レポートの提出に遅れが見られます。

I would be happy to help to prioritize your workload.

仕事の優先順位づけを助けるよ。

I know you can do better.

もっとできるはずだよね。

Let's make a plan to discuss the priorities.

優先順位を確認する時間を作ろう。

Let's work together to make it happen.

一緒に実現しよう。

Are you comfortable to finish the report by the end of this week?

今週末までにレポートは完成しそう？

Should I take a look when your draft is ready?

ドラフトが完成したら確認しようか？

Please ensure that there will be no errors in the report as we send this to clients.

クライアントに送るので、レポートに間違いがないように確認してね。

I might have overlooked your workload this week.

今週の君の仕事量を見落としていたかもしれないね。

How can I remove any of your workloads with low value?

価値の低い仕事の量を減らすにはどうすればよいかな？

Let me talk to other members to share this workload.

この仕事量を分担してもらうように、他のメンバーと話します。

I will let you concentrate on your project this week.

今週はこのプロジェクトに集中してください。

I will handle all the other workloads this week.

今週は私が他の仕事を全部やるからね。

5. 部下のキャリアアップを助ける　　　Track 36

I have a project that is outside your regular work.

君の通常の仕事以外のプロジェクトがあるんだ。

I am sure that you will enjoy the project and learn a lot from this opportunity.

プロジェクトは楽しいと思うし、この機会から多くのことを学ぶと思うよ。

Are you willing to take this assignment?

この課題をやってみてはどうかな？

What can we do to make your responsibility more challenging for your advancement?

君の成長のために、責任範囲をよりチャレンジングにするにはどうしたらいいだろう？

This is a learning experience and I would like you to master leadership skills.

これは良い経験になると思うし、君にはリーダーシップスキルをマスターしてほしいと思っているよ。

What kind of training would you need to advance your technical skills?

技術力を磨くためにどのようなトレーニングが必要？

I encourage you to take external training to gain accounting expertise.

会計の専門知識を身に付けるために、外部トレーニングを受けるといいよ。

I suggest you challenge a bigger role next year.

来年は、より大きな役割にチャレンジしたらどうかな。

I encourage you to take leadership development courses sometime soon.

近いうちにリーダーシップ育成コースをとるのがいいね。

Why don't you find coaching to advance your career?

キャリアに役立つコーチングを見つけてはどうだろう？

3 日頃のフィードバックに使えるフレーズ

1. 良かったことをこまめに伝える　　Track 37

Great job, thanks.

すばらしい、ありがとう。

I'm glad you did a great job.

すばらしい仕事をしてくれてうれしいよ。

It was very impressive.

すごかったよ。

Tell me how you did it.

どうやってやったのか教えてほしい。

Great progress!

大進歩！

That was awesome.

すばらしい。

That's very helpful insight.

それはとても役に立つ洞察だ。

I knew you could do it.

君ならできると思っていたよ。

I am sure that's the right way to do it.

正しい方法だと思うよ。

I couldn't have done it without you.

君なくしてはできなかったよ。

It's really great to have you on our team.

君がチームにいてくれて、本当に良かった。

Could I have your perspective regarding this issue?

この問題についての君の意見をもらえる？

I like how you handled the difficult customer.

難しい顧客をうまく扱ったね。

I appreciate your commitment.

一生懸命やってくれてありがとう。

I am very impressed with your quality.

質の高さに感心しているよ。

I'm convinced that your results show your hard work.

結果は君の努力のおかげだね。

I like the way you handled this tough situation.

この厳しい状況、うまく対応したね。

I appreciate your extra work to make it happen.

実現のために余分に頑張ってくれてありがとう。

Your leadership brought success to the team.

チームの成功は君のリーダーシップのおかげだよ。

Your valuable input always helps me to make the right decision.

君の貴重な意見は、いつも正しい決断をするのを助けてくれるよ。

We couldn't have done it without you.

あなたがいなかったら達成できなかったよ。

I always appreciate your suggestions before making an important decision.

大事な決断前の君の提案、いつも感謝してるよ。

You are a great asset to my team.

君がチームにいてくれて助かるよ。

Thank you for your frequent status updates of the project.

プロジェクトの進捗を頻繁に教えてくれてありがとう。

I admire your communication styles as they are effective and clear.

君のコミュニケーションスタイルは効果的で明確ですばらしいね。

2. 改善点をポジティブに伝える　　　　Track 38

I have noticed that you have failed to meet sales targets three months in a row.

３ヶ月連続で君は販売目標を達成できていないよね。

Are you getting the resources you need?

必要なリソースはあるのかな？

You were unable to submit the monthly report on time again this month.

今月もまた期限に月報を提出することができなかったよね。

Are you aware of how this will affect the other team members?

これが他のチームメンバーにどのように影響するか理解しているかな？

I know how busy you are.

君が忙しいのはわかっているよ。

Are you ok with your workload?

仕事量は大丈夫？

Are you aware that this report was due yesterday?

このレポート、昨日が締切だったのはわかっている？

I would request you to meet the deadline next time.

次回からは締切を厳守してほしい。

Please give us a warning in advance, if you find it difficult to meet the deadline.

期限を守ることが難しい場合は、事前に教えてください。

Are there obstacles to perform your job on time?

時間通りに仕事を遂行するのに障害があるのかな？

I notice that you have been taking too much time on the marketing analysis.

マーケティング分析に時間がかかり過ぎているんじゃないかな。

I respect your deep understanding of the analytical method.

分析手法についての君の深い知識には感心するよ。

Why don't you review the content to accelerate the entire process?

全体のプロセスを早くするために、内容を見直したらどうかな？

Let's focus on what we can do now.

今何ができるか考えてみよう。

I encourage you to try new approaches.

新しいアプローチを試すことをすすめるよ。

What can we do to support your work?

君の仕事をサポートするには何ができるかな？

What do you think we should do differently next time?

次回はどう違うやり方をしたらいいと思う？

I am happy to clarify your priorities if it helps you to meet our expectations.

君に期待されていることを理解するのに役立つなら、君の優先事項について説明するよ。

If you need my guidance on your daily priority, please set up a brief meeting every morning.

日々の優先事項について私の指導が必要なら、毎朝短いミーティングをしよう。

If you have any conflicts in your assignments, please let me know.

もし仕事で悩んでいるなら、教えてほしい。

Why don't you break the process into three steps?

プロセスを3つのステップに分けてみませんか？

Please make sure to give this assignment priority.

必ずこの仕事を優先してください。

We have to handle multiple tasks at the same time.

複数のタスクを同時に処理する必要があります。

However, this task is our top priority now.

ただし、このタスクが現在、最優先事項です。

3. 現状の問題点について　　　　　　Track 39

I notice that you have not adequately shared information as a leader to your team members.

リーダーとして、チームメンバーとの状況共有が足りてないのではないかな。

I encourage you to timely notify team members about critical information.

重要な情報については、タイムリーにチームメンバーに知らせるべきだよ。

Is there any reason why you didn't copy your subordinate on this e-mail?

部下にこのメールをコピーしなかったのには何か理由があるの？

I notice that you have been doing too many tasks yourself.

多くのタスクを自分でやろうとし過ぎてないかな。

I assume that your team members would appreciate more autonomy on projects.

君のチームメンバーは、プロジェクトでもっと自主性を持たされることを望んでいるじゃないかな。

It might be better for you to delegate some of your responsibilities to your subordinates.

責任の一部を部下に任せてみてはどうだろう。

It could be a better way for you to develop your leadership skill.

君のリーダーシップスキルを伸ばすのに、そのほうがいいよ。

I am always here to support your leadership development.

君がリーダーとしての指導力を伸ばすのをいつも支援してるよ。

If you have any issues that require immediate advice, please send a quick e-mail.

すぐにアドバイスが必要な問題があったら、短いメールを送ってください。

If you need any urgent help from me, my assistant will tell you how you can get hold of me.

緊急に私のヘルプが必要場合は、アシスタントが私にどうやったら連絡がつくかを教えます。

Please remember that even if everything didn't go as planned, we can learn from it.

全てが予定通りに行かなかったとしても、そこから学ぶことがあるからね。

I would like to talk with you privately to discuss your recent performance.

あなたの最近のパフォーマンスについて、1対1で話しましょう。

Do you have remaining concerns about your current role?

現在の役割についてのまだ懸念していることはあるのかな？

What questions remain?

まだ残っている質問は？

I understand your frustration about your current position.

現在のポジションで不満があるのは理解しています。

Can you tell me more about the goals you are trying to achieve in this quarter?

この四半期に達成したい目標を教えてくれる？

What's on your mind now?

今、何を考えている？

How can we focus on our goals?

我々のゴールのためには、どうしたら集中できるかな？

I need your commitment to the timely execution of our project.

我々のプロジェクトをタイムリーに実行するのに君のコミットメントが必要なんだ。

I would like to remind you that our daily works are contributing to our company achieving its goals.

私たちの日々の仕事は、会社の目標達成に貢献していることを忘れないで。

Can I count on that?

頼りにして大丈夫？

Is there anything that might cause you to delay this task?

この仕事を遅らせる原因が何かあるのかな？

What have you done so far?

これまでに試したことは？

Please update me on how things are going by the end of this week.

今週末までに、進行状況を私にアップデートしてください。

I would need you to send me a weekly update by email to share your progress.

毎週、君の進捗報告のメールを私に送るようにお願いするよ。

Does that work for you?

できそう？

If you have a question about my decision, I would like to know now.

私の決定に質問があるなら、今教えてほしい。

Please be prepared to update us on this project in our next monthly meeting.

次回の月例会議でこのプロジェクトの進捗を報告するようにしてください。

I would like you to understand that this project takes the highest priority.

このプロジェクトが最優先事項だからね。

I am a bit disappointed that you took that action without consulting me.

私に相談せずに、その行動をとったことにちょっとがっかりしているよ。

I would request you include me in all your future communications.

これから全ての連絡メールに私を入れてください。

Today, I need to communicate clearly the implications of your continued poor performance.

今日、君の継続的な業績不振の影響を明確に伝える必要があります。

I suggest you schedule your work in advance.

前もって仕事のスケジュールを立てるように。

As a next step, I have decided to initiate a performance improvement plan for you.

次のステップとして、君の業務改善計画を立てることにしました。

We will assess your progress based on the agreed goals and deadlines defined in the plan.

計画で合意された目標と期限に基づいて、君の進捗状況を評価していきます。

Are you on board?

わかりましたか？

I appreciate your input in this matter.

この件について意見ありがとう。

I appreciate your enthusiasm.

熱意に感謝します。

I make the final decision about this as a manager.

私はマネージャーとして、これについて最終決定を下します。

Let's talk about how we can make it work.

うまく進める方法について話しましょう。

Please take a moment and review your next steps.

ちょっと時間をとって、次のステップを確認してください。

I expect you to follow this procedure.

この手順に従ってください。

I would like to make sure whether I communicated clearly my expectations to you.

あなたに期待することを、明確に伝えられたか確認したいです。

1. 年初に目標設定を促す　　　　　　　　Track 41

I would like to have a meeting to set performance goals for the new year.

新年の業績目標を設定するための会議を持ちましょう。

You need to set up SMART goals, which are specific, measurable, achievable, relevant, and time-bound.

具体的で、測定可能で、達成可能で、関連性があり、そして期限がある、SMART 目標を設定してください。

We will measure achievements by setting a specific target.

具体的な目標を設定して業績を測定していきます。

The goals of the new year should help you to define your focus and motivation.

新年の目標は、あなたが集中すべきことと、モチベーションになることを明らかにするべきものです。

Let me remind you that goals need to be clear as well as reasonably challenging.

目標は明確で、かつ適度にチャレンジングなものにしてくださいね。

Please make sure to create clear goals that align with the company's mission.

会社のミッションと一致する、明確な目標を作成するようにしてください。

Let's set specific goals for each quarter.

四半期ごとに明確な目標を立てよう。

Please report your progress on a regular basis for my review.

定期的に見直しするために進捗を報告してほしい。

Your goals might be too aggressive.

君の目標、アグレッシブすぎないかな。

Why don't you set more attainable goals?

もっと達成可能な目標を立ててみてはどうだろう？

I encourage you to get some input from your team members before finalizing your goals.

目標を確定する前に、チームメンバーからの意見も聞くといいよ。

How can I help you do even better next year?

来年さらに良いパフォーマンスをあげるには、どんな助けができるかな？

Are these performance goals in line with your expectation?

これらの目標は期待通り？

Could I have your commitment to these goals?

これらの目標にコミットできますか？

2. スキルアップを目指す　　　　Track 42

What skills would you like to further develop next year?

来年さらに伸ばしたいスキルはどんなこと？

What strengths do you want to develop?

君の得意分野でさらに伸ばしたいところは何？

What weaknesses do you want to overcome?

克服したい弱点は何？

It is recommended that you improve your English language skills to stay competitive in this industry.

この業界で競争力を維持するには、英語力を向上することをすすめるよ。

What training would you like to get to advance your expertise?

専門知識を向上させるためにどのようなトレーニングを受けたいですか？

Where would you like to be in five years?

5年後にはどうなっていたい？

Are you comfortable with these goals to be met by the end of the year?

年末までに達成すべきこれらの目標に満足していますか？

What guidance do you need from me to achieve these goals?

これらの目標を達成するために私からどのような指導があればいいですか？

I am impressed that you have very clear and long-term goals.

非常に明確な長期目標をもっていますね。

What training would you like to get to advance the required skills?

求められるスキルを向上させるためにどのようなトレーニングを受けたいですか？

3. 達成度合いを客観的に伝える　　Track 43

Before our performance review meeting, please take some time to review your objectives for this year.

パフォーマンスレビュー会議の前に、今年の目標をゆっくり見直してください。

Please bring your self-assessment to the meeting.

ミーティングには自己評価を持って来てください。

I would like to talk about where you did very well and where you could further improve.

あなたが非常にうまく行ったところと、さらに改善することができるかについて話したいと思います。

This meeting is an opportunity for us to discuss your continuous development and how I can support you.

このミーティングは、あなたの継続的な発展と私がどのようにサポートできるかを話す機会です。

What do you think of your overall performance this year?

今年の業績は全体的に見てどう自己評価していますか？

I would like to review the progress of your current year objectives.

今年度の目標に対する進捗状況を確認しよう。

Let's review each objective and your achievements one by one.

各目標と達成度を1つずつ確認しましょう。

Shall we compare each note?

それぞれのメモを比較しましょうか？

In what areas do you think you have been doing well this year?

今年はどの分野で順調に推移していると思いますか？

In what areas do you think you have successfully improved this year?

今年はどの分野で改善したと思いますか？

You have met the expectations except for one area. You missed opportunities to do 〜.

あなたは1つの分野を除いて期待に応えました。その分野とは〜です。

You have successfully exceeded performance standards by 10%.

業績基準を10％上回りました。

I regard your performance as exceptional.

あなたの業績はすばらしいと評価します。

I am generally pleased with your performance.

あなたの業績には概ね満足しています。

Your extensive expertise in Marketing is highly appreciated.

君のマーケティングに関する後半な専門知識を高く評価しています。

With your contribution, we have managed to achieve our sales target this year.

あなたの貢献により、今年の販売目標を達成することができました。

I appreciate you always demonstrate the value of respecting people.

いつも周りの人に敬意を払ってくれてありがとう。

I would like to let you know that everyone on the management team celebrates your success.

管理職のみんな、君の成功を喜んでいるよ。

We are so proud of you.

君を誇りに思うよ。

You have excellent skills to hold yourself accountable for the department objective.

部門の目標に対して責任を負う優れたスキルがあります。

You demonstrated an incredible contribution to the project.

プロジェクトへの信じられないほどの貢献をしてくれました。

You came up with a great marketing plan to support our product launch.

製品発売をサポートするための優れたマーケティング計画を立案してくれました。

You initiated proactive plans to beat our competitors.

競合他社に勝つための積極的な計画を開始しましたね。

You effectively communicated our objectives and goals to the entire team.

目的と目標をチーム全体に効果的に伝えてくれました。

You always approach things in a professional and reasonable manner.

あなたは常に専門的かつ合理的な方法で物事にアプローチしますね。

You have successfully kept the team focused on the main goal.

あなたはチームを主要な目標に集中させることに成功しました。

You have carefully chosen suitable duties for every project member.

全てのプロジェクトメンバーに適切な職務を慎重に選択してくれましたね。

I am impressed with your professionalism.

あなたのプロ意識に感銘を受けています。

You always work toward team goals without considering your personal interests.

個人的な興味を考慮することなく、常にチームの目標に向かって働いてくれていますね。

You keep very good track of your progress this year.

今年の進捗状況を非常によく把握していますね。

I appreciate your efforts to clarify how your individual goals align with company long-term objectives.

あなたの個人目標が会社の長期目標とどのように一致するかを明確してくれてありがとう。

What do you think of my feedback so far?

これまでの私のフィードバックはどうですか？

Are you satisfied with this review?

このレビューに満足していますか？

Did I overlook anything?

何か見逃していますか？

Is there anything unclear about your review?

レビューについて不明瞭な点がありますか？

4. 良かった点・達成できなかった点を効果的に伝える
Track 44

I am glad to see your steady progress.

あなたの着実な進歩を見てうれしいです。

I must say you fell short of your goals in this area.

この分野では目標に足りなかったと言わなければなりません。

There is one area that you can do much better.

もっとよくできるはずのところが 1 つあります。

Let's talk about the areas for improvement.

では、どこが改善できるか話しましょう。

What area would you like to further improve?

さらに改善したいと思っていることはどの分野ですか？

I noticed you seem a bit distracted these days.

最近、少し集中できてないようですね。

Are there any problems that make it difficult for you to concentrate on your work?

仕事に集中することを難しくする問題でも何かありますか？

Are there resources you need to perform your duties?

職務を遂行するために必要なリソースはありますか？

Please share with me any concerns.

どんな懸念でも私と共有してください。

I would like to clarify the situation.

状況を明らかにしたいと思います。

We all are optimistic about your future.

みんな君のすばらしい未来に期待しているよ。

Let me know any information I am missing here.

私が見逃している情報があれば教えてください。

It is critical for everyone to comply with the performance standard.

パフォーマンス基準を順守することは、全ての人にとって非常に重要です。

I would request you to follow my advice.

私のアドバイスに従ってください。

Unfortunately, you have missed your sales targets for the eight months during the year.

残念ながら、年間の8ヶ月間、売上目標を達成できませんでしたね。

If you are late on the delivery of your task, it slows down the rest of the project.

タスクの実行が遅れると、プロジェクトの残りが遅くなります。

I must say that you have fallen short of expectations recently.

最近、期待を下回っていると言わなければなりません。

I would like to understand why your performance has dropped lately.

なぜあなたのパフォーマンスが最近落ちたのか理解したいのですが。

Was there any confusion about what the requirements were?

求められていることが何かについて、混乱していることがありますか？

Let's identify the source of the problem.

問題の原因を特定しましょう。

If there is anything I can help, please let me know.

もし私が助けられることがあれば、教えてください。

What can we do to improve your performance?

パフォーマンスを上げるには、何ができるでしょう？

Are there any resources you would like to get?

必要なリソースはありますか？

I expect you to improve your performance in three months.

私はあなたが3ヶ月以内にあなたのパフォーマンスを向上させること
を期待します。

What is your understanding of what we just talked?

私たちが今話したことについて、あなたの理解は？

I must say you failed to elaborate action plans for achieving
your goals.

あなたは目標を達成するための行動計画を練ることに失敗しました
ね。

You should have made achievable goals.

達成可能な目標を作成する必要があります。

I suggest you develop your objectives to be more measurable
and achievable.

より測定可能で達成可能な目標を開発することをおすすめします。

You are not motivated to achieve your stretched goals.

少し高い目標を達成する意欲がないのですね。

I understand that your performance is not so bad.

あなたのパフォーマンスはそれほど悪くないことを理解しています。

However, you failed to achieve your objectives.

ただし、目標を達成できませんでした。

What do you think the major reason for this is?

この主な理由は何だと思いますか？

I would like to remind you that objective settings and progress checks are important for all employees.

目標設定と進捗チェックが全ての社員にとって重要であることを思い出してください。

I suggest not to blame others for your failure to meet the objective.

あなたが目標を達成できなかったことを他人のせいにすることはおすすめしません。

Could we discuss whether you could stay focused on the key objectives throughout the year?

年間を通して、主要な目標に集中できるかどうか話せますか？

I assume you had difficulty to give clear directions or goals when delegating tasks to your team members.

チームメンバーにタスクを委任する際、明確な指示や目標を与えるのが難しかったのではありませんか。

I suggest you stretch out of your comfort zone.

私はあなたが心地良いエリアから抜け出す必要があると思います。

Let's make the due dates for each task more specific next time.

次回、各タスクの期日をより具体的にしましょう。

You should assign appropriate due dates when setting goals.

目標を設定する時は、適切な期日を割り当てる必要があります。

You need to show your initiative in setting your own professional goals.

自分の専門的な目標を設定する際にはイニシアチブをとる必要があります。

It is important to adhere to company goals.

会社の目標を遵守することが重要です。

How can I help you do better next time?

次回の改善をどう助けられますか？

Is there anything you need to perform your duties?

職務を遂行するのに必要なことはありますか？

What would you really want to improve on?

実際、どこを改善したいと考えていますか？

You did great work on sales report last month.

先月の営業レポートは良い仕事をしましたよね。

How can you transfer that skill to the rest of your tasks?

あのスキルを、どうやったら他の仕事に転用できますか？

All of our us were impressed with your last presentation.

我々は皆、前回のあなたのプレゼンテーションに感動しました。

Would you put in more energy to make the plan happen?

計画を実現するために、もっとエネルギーを注げませんか？

You have missed your sales target for this quarter.

あなたは今四半期の販売目標を逃しました。

Do you have additional ideas to get back on track?

軌道修正するための追加のアイデアはありますか？

I know you missed your target for this quarter, but it's still the first quarter.

今四半期は目標を逃しましたが、まだ第一四半期ですよ。

I would suggest you improve your knowledge of our products.

当社の製品知識を伸ばすことをすすめます。

That will be critical for you to be successful as a customer relationship manager.

顧客リレーションシップマネジャーとして成功するには重要なことです。

I ran into a similar problem when I started here.

実際、私が始めた頃も同じような問題にぶつかりましたよ。

Here's what I learned.

私が学んだことは以下です。

This is a more common challenge than you might think.

これはあなたが思うより共通なチャレンジですよ。

Let's develop a good plan how we can do better.

どう改善できるかプランを話し会いましょう。

I understand that you work under time pressure.

時間のプレッシャーがある中で働いていますよね。

However, I would strongly suggest you do double-check your calculations before the submission.

しかしながら、提出前には計算をダブルチェックすることを強くすすめます。

You fell behind on some deadlines this year.

今年、何度か期日を逃しましたよね。

How can we get your process to run a bit faster?

どうしたら少し早く仕事を進めることができますか？

5. 部下からの質問・反論に対する適切な回答をする
Track 45

How do you feel about my suggestion?

私の提案についてどう思いますか？

Let me know if I was not clear enough for you.

十分に明確でなかったら教えてください。

I understand that you don't agree with some of my evaluations.

私の評価のいくつかの点にあなたが同意しないことは理解しています。

I suggest you review what you have accomplished this year.

あなたが今年達成したことを確認することをおすすめします。

Let's clarify one by one.

一つひとつ確認しましょう。

I need you to identify the objectives you achieved and you did not achieve.

達成できた目標と、できなかった目標を確認してほしいのです。

Is that clear enough for you?

十分に明確でしょうか？

I would like to make sure that my guidance is clear.

私の指導が明確に伝わったか、確かめたいです。

Let's see where we see differences in each evaluation.

それぞれの評価でどこに違いがあるか確認しましょう。

I would like to remind you that I am committed to your success.

あなたの成功に私がコミットしているということをご理解ください。

How can I help you do better next year?

来年の改善に私は何ができますか？

Could I confirm you are clear with our next step?

次にやるべきことはクリアーですか？

I appreciate your candid opinion about my feedback.

私のフィードバックに対して、率直な意見をありがとう。

Let's resume our discussion next time.

次回、議論を再開しましょう。

May I suggest that we meet again next week?

来週またお会いしましょうか？

May I arrange for another meeting at a time most convenient for you?

あなたの都合が一番良い時に再度ミーティングを設定しましょうか？

Let's meet in two weeks again to discuss this future.

さらにこれを議論するために、2週間以内にまた会いましょう。

6. 部下との誤解を解消してフォローする　　Track 46

We need to sit down and talk about this topic.

この件に関して、時間を見つけてじっくり話し合おう。

We need to talk about what happened this morning.

今朝起きた件について、話さなければならないな。

Could you tell me more about how you felt?

どう感じていたか、もっと教えてくれる？

Now I have a better understanding of your feeling.

今は君の気持ちをよりよく理解できます。

I had no idea that this has been disturbing you a lot.

この件で君をとても悩ませているとは思いもしなかったよ。

I did not realize that this was a big issue for my team.

チームにとってこれが大きな問題になったとは気づかなかったです。

I did not know the team took this matter that way.

チームがそのように感じていたとは思いも寄りませんでした。

Is everyone feeling the same way?

みんなも同じ気持ち？

I appreciate your sharing your concerns with me.

懸念点をシェアしてくれてありがとう。

What else do I need to know?

他に知っておくべきことはあるかな？

Is there anything else you need to update me on this matter?

この件で私のアップデートすること、他にもある？

Please continue what you would like to say.

言いたいこと、続けて言ってください。

What else concerns you?

他に何が心配ですか？

I am open to hearing any feedback.

私はフィードバックを聞くことにはオープンだから。

I have understood now that I caused some confusion among the team.

チームに混乱を引き起こしてしまったようだね。

I had no intention to ignore your comments.

君のコメントを無視するつもりはまったくなかったんだ。

Due to the urgency, I missed an opportunity to come back to your questions sooner.

急を要していて、君の質問に早く答えられなかったんだ。

Let me talk to everyone to clarify my intention.

私の意図を明確にするため、みんなと話します。

I appreciate your suggestions about what should be changed.

何を変えればいいか、提案を頼むよ。

I had no idea that I made an unreasonable request to the team.

チームに不当なリクエストをするつもりはなかったんだ。

Let's work together to come up with a solution that works for everybody.

みんながうまく行く解決策を一緒に考えよう。

I need your help to get everyone to work together on this again.

みんながこの件に再び取り組んでくれるには、君の助けが必要だ。

Can I count on you?

頼りにできる？

Let me summarize what you have mentioned.

君が言ったことをまとめさせてね。

I would like to understand the issue exactly.

問題を正確に理解したいんだ。

Can I ask your commitment to making it happen?

これを実現するためのコミット、お願いできる？

Let's have a meeting with all members to talk face to face.

メンバー全員と顔を合わせて打ち合わせしよう。

I suggest putting our discussions and agreements in writing.

みんなが話したことと合意したことを書いておこう。

I would like to make sure that we are on the same page.

みんなが同じ理解でいるようにしたいんだ。

This will help me to avoid surprises later.

これで将来驚くようなことが起きるのを避けられると思う。

We can refer to our agreements in case a situation arises that we did not anticipate.

予期していないことが発生したら、合意していたことを見直そう。

We will review our earlier discussions if unexpected things happen in the future.

将来、想定外のことが起きたら、先に話し合ったことを見直そう。

Will this approach solve your concern?

この方法で懸念していることは解決しそう？

Can I assume this solution is satisfactory for you?

この解決で満足できそう？

Can we live with this option?

みんなこのオプションで大丈夫かな？

Your bright attitude has a positive impact on everybody.

あなたの明るい態度はみんなに良い影響を与えるね。

You always allocate appropriate tasks to your teammates.

君はいつもチームメイトに適切に仕事を割り振るね。

I highly appreciate your work collaboration to finish the assignment faster than expected.

予想よりも早く課題を完了するために、みんなで協力してくれてありがとう。

I am so impressed that you always deliver more than you promise at the beginning.

初めに約束した以上の成果をいつも出してくれることに感銘するよ。

I appreciate your leadership to help colleagues who are outside your direct responsibility.

君の直接の責任外にいる同僚を助ける君のリーダーシップはすばらしいね。

I appreciate that you always take care of all the team members that they get an appropriate allocation of the works.

チームメンバー全員が常に適切に仕事を割り当てられるように配慮してくれていますね。

I admire your wide skill set and practical advice.

幅広いスキルと実践的なアドバイスに感心します。

You always seek help from appropriate senior colleagues when needed.

必要に応じて、常に適切な先輩に助けを求めますね。

You tackle all assigned jobs enthusiastically.

割り当てられた仕事全てに熱心に取り組みますね。

Thank you for your willingness to take on additional tasks.

追加のタスクを快く引き受けてくれてありがとう。

You work hard to get the job done ahead of your own interests.

自分の利益より先に仕事を成し遂げるために一生懸命働いてくれますね。

You are regarded as a proven team player.

あなたはチームプレイヤーとしての実績があります。

You always have great time management to get the job done.

仕事を成し遂げるための時間管理がいつもすばらしいですね。

I noticed that you made some significant improvements in your proposal from the last time.

前回から提案でいくつかの重要な改善を行ってくれましたね。

They are very convincing now with clearer sentences.

より明確な文章で非常に説得力があります。

Your arguments are well supported.

あなたの議論はよくサポートされています。

Thank you for working hard to resolve all the errors in the report.

レポート内の全てのエラーを解決するために一生懸命働いてくれてありがとう。

I am sure that our client will find this report very useful.

クライアントにとって、このレポートが非常に役立つものになると確信しています。

The prior version was a bit difficult for me to understand the details.

以前のバージョンは、詳細を理解するのが少し困難でした。

The revised version was dramatically simplified to focus on the key issues and the solution for them.

更新版は、主要な問題とそれらの解決策に焦点を当てて劇的に簡素化されましたね。

This will help them improve their productivity significantly.

これにより、彼らの生産性が大幅に向上しますよ。

I am impressed by how well you assessed the clients' needs and developed great recommendations.

あなたがクライアントのニーズをよく分析し、すばらしい推奨をしたことに感銘を受けました。

8. 改善点をポジティブに伝える Track 48

I'm a little concerned about the completion of your sales report.

君の営業報告書の完成について少し心配しています。

I want to make sure we are doing everything we can to help you.

君を助けるためにできる限りのことをしていることを確認したいんだ。

As you are aware, the due date is this Friday.

わかっていると思うけど、期日は今週の金曜日です。

From what I see, you seem to need at least a few days to complete.

私が見るところ、完成までには少なくとも数日を必要なんじゃないかな。

If we miss the deadline, that will be a problem for the sales team who are relying on this report.

期限に間に合わないと、このレポートを頼りにしている営業チームにとって問題になるよ。

What do you think about this delay?

この遅れについて、どう思っている？

What resources do you need to complete this assignment on time?

この課題を期限通りに完了するには、どのようなリソースが必要？

Let's consider the alternatives before deciding on the best solutions for this problem.

この問題の最良の解決策を決める前に、代替案も検討しよう。

Sometimes you need to admit your mistakes and work to correct them.

間違いを認め、それを修正するために努力する必要がある場合もあるよ。

It does not matter how slowly you make progress as long as you keep working on it.

努力を続けている限り、ゆっくり進んでもかまわないよ。

The only way to continuously do great work here is to collaborate with your team members.

ここで継続的にすばらしい仕事をする唯一の方法は、チームメンバーと協力することです。

I really appreciate the way you handled the urgent request from the customer yesterday.

昨日、お客様からの緊急のリクエストを処理してくれて本当にありがとう。

The one thing I would like you to remember next time is that you check with your supervisor before extending the payment deadline.

1つ覚えておいてほしいんだけど、次回からは、支払期限を延長する前に上司に確認するようにしてね。

The overdue payment is relatively small this time and the extension wasn't a problem.

期限を過ぎている支払いは今回は比較的少なくて、延期しても問題はなかったね。

However, that will not be always the case.

ただ、いつもそうとは限らないから。

Please ensure to check with your supervisor next time.

次回からは上司に確認するのを忘れないでね。

Have you noticed that your behavior is sometimes a bit unprofessional?

あなたの行動が時々少し職場で適切でないことがあるのに気づいていますか？

I am happy to offer professional assistance either from myself or someone outside.

私自身または外部の誰かから専門的なアドバイスを提供できますよ。

9. 改善が見られない部下に一歩踏み込んだ指導をする
Track 49

We agreed at the beginning of this month that you would immediately inform me if any problem occurred.

今月初めに、問題が発生した場合はすぐに私にお知らせくださいと同意しましたよね。

If you had told me this earlier, I could have let other members help you sooner.

もっと早く私に伝えてくれていたら、他のメンバーにあなたを助けるように指示できました。

If we could do that, we would have avoided this situation.

それができれば、この状況を回避できたでしょう。

I would like to see your immediate improvement in communication.

すぐにコミュニケーションが改善されることを期待しています。

Otherwise, I need you to understand that we may have to reconsider your role in my team.

さもなければ、チームでのあなたの役割を考え直さなければならないことを理解ください。

Please understand that it's against company policy to allow exceptions for you.

例外を認めることは会社のポリシーに違反していることを理解してください。

We might be able to accept your request for flexible work hours if you could commit to attending these meetings.

これらの会議に出席できるとコミットできるなら、あなたのフレックス勤務のリクエストを受け入れられるかもしれない。

For an immediate solution, I will take over the second part of this process.

早急な解決策として、このプロセスの後半部分を引き継ぎます。

We will allocate one more person to help your data analysis for this critical project.

この重要なプロジェクトのデータ分析を支援するために、もう１人を割り当てます。

Please take the time to fully understand what we discussed today.

今日議論したことを十分に理解してください。

Let's resume our conversation tomorrow so that you can clarify any questions you may have.

君の疑問点を明確にするために、明日も会話を再開しましょう。

Please feel free to share any concerns with me.

懸念事項があれば気軽に私とシェアして。

If this help is not sufficient, we can think about an alternative together.

このヘルプが十分でない場合、一緒に代替案について考えよう。

Please remember that it is important to me that you succeed in my team.

あなたが私のチームで成功することが私にとって大切であるということを覚えておいてください。

For your success, you need to make a commitment to what we agreed upon in advance.

あなたが成功するためには、事前に合意した内容にコミットする必要があります。

It is important to listen well to what your colleague has to say.

同僚の発言をよく聞くことも大事ですよ。

The bottom line is that we all are expected to meet deadlines for any tasks.

大事なことは、どんな仕事でも締切には間に合わせることが期待されているということだよ。

I recommend you learn from your senior colleague, Mike who is an expert in sales.

セールスのエキスパートである先輩、マイクから学んだらどうだろう。

I want you to shadow him through his next customer visit.

彼の次の顧客訪問について行って、彼がどうやっているか学んでください。

After that, please email me what you learned and the things you are going to adopt.

その後、あなたが学んだことと採用しようとしていることを私にメールしてください。

We will be able to offer you some time off if you think it helps.

助けになるなら、少し休みをとってもいいよ。

Let me make sure I got your point.

君の言いたいことを私が理解できているか確認させてもらうね。

I understand that you have several concerns about your personal matters.

個人的なことでいくつか心配ごとを抱えているのは理解しています。

Let's find a solution for how you can balance work and personal matters.

仕事と個人の問題のバランスを取る方法の解決策を見つけましょう。

Would you like to discuss alternative career paths in the organization?

組織内の別のキャリアパスについて議論しますか？

Could you tell me how you feel about stepping down from the current leadership role?

今のリーダー職から降りることをどう思いますか？

We could offer you an independent position which is less demanding.

仕事量の少ない、独立したポジションをあなたに提供することはできます。

I think this is the best we can do for you right now.

これが今できる、最良のことではないかと思う。

However, we need you to understand that your compensation will be adjusted accordingly.

ただし、それに応じて報酬が調整されることは理解ください。

Would you summarize what we agreed on today?

今日合意したことについてまとめてもらえますか？

I just want to make sure we are on the same page for the next step.

次のステップについて、双方が同じ理解でいるか確認したいと思います。

I will summarize the main points of today's discussion in writing so that both of us have fully aligned.

今日話したことを書面で要約して、双方理解を確認しますね。

I prefer working together to overcome this problem, rather than I make a decision for you.

私があなたのための決断を下すよりも、協力してこの問題を乗り切ることを好みます。

Can I expect your commitment to getting this right?

これを正すためのコミットを期待できますか？

An overly negative attitude will not be left overlooked in my team.

私のチームでは、過度に否定的な態度が見落とされることはありません。

I will do everything to keep every behavior aligned with the success of the whole team.

私は全ての行動がチーム全体の成功を導くようになるよう、全力を尽くします。

I will be monitoring your behavior and improvement for the next few months.

今後数ヶ月間、あなたの行動と改善するのを見ていきます。

If you are unable to continue working effectively with other members, it will begin to influence your performance review.

他のメンバーと効果的に仕事を続けることができない場合、パフォーマンスのレビューに影響を与え始めます。

Your contribution is appreciated, however, your current attitude toward others is contrary to the team's value.

あなたの貢献は高く評価されますが、他者に対するあなたの現在の態度はチームの価値に反しています。

If your behavior won't change in the next three months, I must say there will not be a position available for you in my team.

今後３ヶ月以内にあなたの行動が変わらない場合は、私のチームにあなたの役職がないと言わなければなりません。

Your performance has been deteriorating despite my continuous feedback.

私の継続的なフィードバックにもかかわらず、あなたのパフォーマンスは悪化しています。

Your job has not been up to standard quite some time.

あなたの仕事は長い間、満足の行くものではありません。

I wonder if you are planning to leave the company.

会社を辞めるつもりなのかしら。

10. キャリア・デベロップメントを話し合う　Track 50

We would like to discuss your long-term career objectives.

あなたの長期的なキャリア目標について話し合おう。

Have you ever considered to assume a different role in the organization?

組織内での別の役割を検討したことがある？

Have you considered moving into a different department to broaden your expertise?

専門分野を広げるために別の部門に移ることを検討したことはある？

Do you have the desire to learn the skills needed to move into a different role?

別の役割に移行するために必要なスキルを習得したいと考えている？

Are you willing to move into a leadership role?

あなたはリーダーシップの役割につく希望はある？

Are you willing to take on more responsibility in the future?

今後、より多くの責任を引き受けたいと思いますか？

I would encourage you to challenge a sales manager role in the next five years.

今後 5 年間でセールスマネージャーの役割に挑戦することをおすすめします。

In order for you to assume a new role, you need to learn people management skills.

新しい役割を引き受けるには、人事管理スキルを学ぶ必要があるね。

If you would prefer to lead the global project, you need to learn project management skills.

グローバルプロジェクトをリードする希望があれば、プロジェクト管理スキルを学ぶ必要があります。

Let's develop a plan to bridge the gap between your current skill set and skill set needed for the manager.

あなたの現在のスキルセットとマネージャーに必要なスキルセットのギャップを埋める計画を立てましょう。

I will investigate the possibilities of your transfer to a new role and get back to you at our next meeting.

新しい役割への異動の可能性を調査し、次のミーティングで連絡しますね。

If you are willing to invest your time to take outside professional courses, we can talk about company scholarships and the application process.

あなたが時間を投資して外部の専門コースを受講する意思がある場合は、会社の奨学金と応募プロセスについてお話しします。

It would be of great value to the organization if we could develop your talent to promote you to a managerial role.

管理職に昇進するために君の才能を伸ばすことができれば、組織にとって大きな価値があると考えているよ。

I would like to let you know that we are creating a great career path for everybody in the organization.

我々は組織の全ての人に、すばらしいキャリアパスがあるようにしているからね。

I am happy with your progress working hard to seize the opportunity.

機会をつかむために一生懸命に頑張っている君の成長にはうれしく思っているよ。

Please let me know anytime if you need any help to advance your skills.

スキルアップのためのサポートが必要な場合は、いつでも知らせてね。

We are keen to retain top talent like you.

君のような優秀な人材にはずっといてほしいと考えているよ。

I commit to putting my time and effort into your development.

君の成長のために私の時間と努力を注ぐことを約束します。

瞬発力を鍛えることを意識しよう

　ビジネスシーンの英会話では、相手が言ったことに対して、黙っていないで **"とりあえず" 何か反応すること**が必要です。また、発言すべき状況、質問を挟みたい時は、躊躇せずに切り出す覚悟をしてください。そんな瞬発力が大切です。

　気の利いたコメントをしようとか、うまくまとめてから意見しようとモジモジしていると、タイミングを逃します。あまり難しく考えず、とりあえず反応すればいいくらいに考えましょう。

　例えば、相手が何かを提案していたら、

　　That's a great idea.（いい考えですね）

　　Sounds interesting.（興味深いです）

といった、簡単なものでも大丈夫です。

　私たちは、すぐに口を挟むのは失礼だから、しばらくは黙って聞いておこうと考えがちですが、外国人ビジネスパーソンは反応を求めます。英語のコミュニケーションはキャッチボールのようなやり取りが大事です。

　もう一つとても大事なのが、**いざという時の意見や質問は "我先に"** の意識で切り出すことです。

　英語の会議では、意見するタイミングを逃していたら、別の人の発言をきっかけに、議論が別の方向に行ってしまうということがよくあります。こうなってしまうと、話題を軌道修正して再チャンスを狙うのは至難のわざです。リーダーだからといって、自分がコメントする番が最後に回ってくると考えるのも間違いです。

　とりあえず自分の言いたいことは遠慮せずに、先手必勝で言ってしまいましょう。**積極的に意見を出す姿勢を見せること**は、英語の流暢さがどうであれ、前向きな姿勢を印象づけることにもつながります。

Chapter 3

チームを率いるための
最強フレーズ

　リーダーの立場にいる人は、日頃からチームメンバーや部下の人たちと仕事の進行状況や問題点などを把握しておくことが必要です。プロジェクトがうまく行った時はともに喜び、また、苦境にいる時はなんとか乗り越えることができるよう励まし、部下を指導して育てて行くリーダーシップが求められます。

1 チームを作る

I always work hard to expand my current skills and learn new things.

私はいつも自分の現在のスキルを伸ばし、新しいことを学ぶために意欲的です。

I am good at learning new concepts and practices quickly.

私は新しい概念ややり方をいち早く習得するのを得意としています。

I have strengths to lead the team to focus on goals and drive them for results.

チームをリードして、目標に焦点を合わせ、そして結果を出す力があります。

I believe the most important qualities for successful people is having integrity.

成功する人々にとって最も重要な資質は誠実さを持っていることだと信じています。

I am willing to let you take on new and even difficult challenges.

皆さんには新しく、さらに難しい挑戦をしてほしいと思っています。

I will provide you the best practices when you do something new.

新しい仕事をする時には、皆さんにベストプラクティスを提供できるようにします。

I'm decisive as well as flexible.

私は決断力があると同時に、柔軟です。

You can count on me when you need to handle urgent matters.

緊急案件を対処する必要がある時は、私に頼ってください。

If you have two urgent matters and only the time to do one, please ensure to ask for my help.

緊急案件が2つあって、1つだけしか取り組む時間がない時、必ず私の助けを求めてください。

I am result-oriented and very energetic.

私は結果指向で、とてもエネルギッシュです。

I always actively listen to your concerns and plan to resolve issues as quickly as possible.

私はいつもあなたの懸念に積極的に耳を傾け、できるだけ早く問題を解決する計画を立てます。

Because of my extensive experience in negotiation, I am good at drafting persuasive presentations.

交渉の経験が豊富なので、説得力のあるプレゼンテーションをドラフトするのが得意です。

I am happy to share my tips.

喜んで秘訣を共有します。

I am honored with this opportunity to lead a diversified group with different backgrounds.

様々なバックグラウンドを持つ多様なグループを率いるこの機会に光栄に思います。

One of my strengths is connecting people.

得意なことの1つは、人々をつなげることです。

I will help you expand your network.

みんなのネットワークを広げるお手伝いをします。

I'm a self-motivated and creative marketer with five years of experience in a global organization.

私はグローバルな組織で5年の経験がある、自発的でクリエイティブなマーケターです。

I'm a highly trained project manager at a leading Japanese pharmaceutical company.

私は日本の大手製薬会社で高度な訓練を受けたプロジェクトマネージャーです。

I am willing to share my expertise as well as learning from all of you.

私は、私の専門知識を共有し、皆さんから学んでいきます。

I am highly confident with my communication skills both in Japanese and in English.

私は日本語と英語の両方のコミュニケーションスキルにとても自信を持っています。

Please use the language which you are more comfortable with.

より使いやすい言語を使ってください。

I would like you to be reliable to get the assignment done on time.

業務を時間通りに遂行し、信頼を得るようにしてください。

I would like you to be flexible to put extra work during the busy season.

繁忙期には、柔軟に対応していただきたいと思います。

I welcome your outside-of-the-box thinking.

独創的な考え方を歓迎します。

I would like to make the most memorable accomplishment with you through this project.

このプロジェクトを通して、あなた方と一緒に最も思い出深い成果を上げたいと思います。

I will ensure to successfully lead this project from the beginning to the end.

このプロジェクトを最初から最後まで首尾よく成功裏にリードしていきます。

This will be a major milestone for all of you.

皆さんにとって、これは大きな節目になるでしょう。

I would like you all to have the leadership to execute this project successfully.

このプロジェクトを成功させるために、皆さんにリーダーシップを発揮していただきたいと思います。

I would like you to be highly productive at work, while you keep your work-life balance.

仕事と生活のバランスを大切にしながら、仕事の生産性を高めてほしいと考えています。

Outside of work, I encourage you to enjoy various activities with your families or friends.

仕事以外でも、家族や友達といろいろな活動を楽しんでください。

I highly value time management skills as we all have multiple responsibilities for work, families and personal developments.

仕事、家族、そして個人の成長という複数の責任を負っていますから、時間管理スキルを高く評価します。

I would like you to enjoy your work and challenge various things in your life.

仕事を楽しんで、人生の様々なことにチャレンジしてほしいです。

I strongly suggest you develop technical abilities to be successful in your job.

仕事で成功するための技術的な能力を開発することを強くおすすめします。

Please learn different areas of the business to expand your career.

ビジネスの様々な分野を学び、キャリアを拡大してください。

2 チームを一段ワンランクアップさせる

1. チームワークを強固にする Track 52

I expect everyone to have a positive attitude in my team.

私のチームでは全員が前向きな姿勢でいてほしいと思っているよ。

I encourage open communication, so please talk to me anytime.

コミュニケーションはオープンにしたいから、いつでも話しに来てね。

I would like to have an environment where you can feel comfortable and productive.

皆が働きやすく、生産的でいられるような環境を持ちたいと思っています。

Being a good teammate to help each other is my biggest expectation for you all.

お互いに助け合う、良いチームメイトであることをみんなに一番期待しています。

I expect you to have self-respect and respect for others.

自尊心を持ち、他者を尊重するようにしてください。

I expect you all to respect your colleagues and work together for a common goal.

同僚を尊重し、共通の目標のために協力して働いてください。

Please make sure to treat your junior colleagues fairly and provide your help whenever they need it.

後輩を公平に扱い、必要な時にはいつでも助けるようにね。

I encourage you to disagree with me candidly, whenever you need to.

必要な時は、いつでも率直に私に反対意見を言うように。

I highly appreciate your friendship and honest opinion.

あなたの友情と正直な意見にとても感謝しています。

I would like you to work hard and play hard.

働く時も遊ぶ時も一生懸命やってほしいよ。

Once I make a commitment, I will be sure to fulfill my commitment to the end as a leader.

私はリーダーとして、一度コミットしたことは、最後まで確実にやり遂げます。

If you make a commitment, you are expected to stand by that commitment.

皆さんも一度コミットしたことは、やり遂げてください。

My goal as a new manager is to be respected and relied upon by all of you.

新しいマネージャーとしての私の目標は、皆さんから尊敬され、信頼されることです。

I am not going to tell you what to do or how to do it for small things.

細かいことに対して何をすべきか、どのように行うべきかの説明はしません。

I believe you all have the experience to figure out solutions.

皆さんには解決策を見つけるための十分な経験があると信じています。

I encourage you to trust your instincts.

直感を信じたらどうでしょう。

Please do not expect that I always have an answer for you.

私がいつもあなたに答えを持っていると期待しないでください。

I always trust your judgment and suggestions.

私はあなた方の判断と提案を常に信頼しています。

Please tell me how you solved this issue and made this decision.

この問題を解決し、この決定を行った方法を教えてください。

What does the team think about this issue?

チームのみんなはこの問題についてどう思いますか？

I think we discussed all the issues in depth this time.

今回は全ての問題を詳細に議論したと思います。

Shall we move on to make it happen?

実現するために進みましょうか？

Let's do this.

やりましょう。

Let's take this option.

この選択をしましょう。

Let's look at situations more holistically.

状況をより全体的に見てみましょう。

175

We need to review situations from all perspectives.

全ての観点から状況を検討する必要があるようだ。

I would like you to help each other to overcome any tasks.

どんな課題でも克服できるように助け合ってほしい。

Let's challenge ourselves to come up with more creative solutions.

より創造的な解決策を思いつくようにチャレンジしよう。

I am sure that we can get through this.

私たちはこれを乗り越えることができると確信しています。

We can rely on your sharp ideas and critical thinking to solve any issues.

あらゆる問題を解決するために、鋭いアイデアと批判的思考に頼ることができますね。

Let's become a great team to be a good example for others to follow.

他の人が従うべき良い例となる、すばらしいチームになりましょう。

2. チームメンバーの成長をさらに促す　　　Track 53

I need to promote cooperation throughout the organization to succeed in the project.

プロジェクトを成功させるには、組織全体で協力を促進する必要があります。

I expect you to make a commitment to reach our most important goal for the company.

会社にとって最も重要な目標を達成するためのコミットメントを期待しています。

With your dedication to the project, I strongly believe that we will find a way to overcome this challenge.

みんなのプロジェクトへの献身で、この課題の克服方法を見つけると強く信じています。

I need to remind you to cooperate well to meet deadlines.

締切に間に合うように協力してください。

Let's work together to achieve a team goal.

チームの目標を達成するために協力しましょう。

I would like you all to understand clearly that completing this project on time is our primary goal.

このプロジェクトを期日通りに完了することが私たちの主な目標であることを、皆さんに明確に理解していただきたいと思います。

My priority is to create a team-work environment.

私の優先事項は、チームワークの環境を作ることです。

I would like to ensure that everybody coordinates the work to meet deadlines.

みんながしっかり協力して、締切を守るようにお願いするね。

I am confident with our thorough study.

私は、私たちの徹底的な研究に自信を持っています。

Let's emphasize our analytical outcome at the next presentation.

次のプレゼンテーションで分析結果を強調しましょう。

I always highly value our comprehensive report of our business results.

業績に関する包括的なレポートをいつもありがとう。

I would like to stress that the management cannot make the right decision without your contribution.

経営陣は君たちの貢献なしには正しい決定を下すことができないということを敢えて言います。

Let's go through the priorities of our team once again in the next meeting.

次の会議でチームの優先事項をもう一度見てみましょう。

Could everyone think about how you can contribute to achieving the department objective?

みんな、部門の目標の達成にどのように貢献できるか考えてきてくれる？

I would also like to hear any suggestions for improvements at this opportunity.

また、この機会に改善のための提案を聞きたいと思う。

Let's think about what we can further improve and what we can do to advance our business.

ビジネスを前進させるために、さらに改善できることを考えてみよう。

I suggest we have an offsite meeting to brainstorm our objectives next year.

来年の目標をブレーンストーミングするためのオフサイトミーティングをしたらどうかな。

I would like to hear everybody's opinion on how to improve our work environment.

私たちの職場環境を改善する方法について、みんなの意見を聞きたいな。

I am open to any suggestions on how we can work better.

より良い仕事ができるための提案を歓迎するよ。

I suggest you not stop thinking about how to overcome any challenge.

チャレンジをどう克服するか、考え続けるようにね。

As we all know, it's always important to keep challenging.

みんなも知っているように、挑戦し続けることは常に大事だよ。

I would like to allow everybody the freedom to decide the best way to perform your work.

みんなが仕事を遂行するための最良の方法を、誰でも自由に決定できるように任せます。

Unless commitment is made by every member, there is little chance to accomplish this project.

全てのメンバーがコミットメントを行わない限り、このプロジェクトを達成する機会はほとんどないよ。

I prefer not to end up going with my idea but appreciate new ideas from a different perspective.

私は自分のアイデアで終わるのは好まず、別の視点から新しい考えを期待するよ。

Chapter 3

Maybe we can combine our ideas to come up with a better solution.

アイデアを組み合わせて、より良い解決策を考え出すことができるかもしれませんね。

It will be a great learning opportunity for everybody to share candid feedback.

率直なフィードバックを共有することは誰にとってもすばらしい学びの機会になるね。

3. 交渉力を高めるための指導的なフレーズ　　Track 54

You need to learn how to be persuasive when selling an idea to others.

自分の考えを他人にわかってもらうためには、説得力を高める方法を学ぶ必要があるね。

I strongly believe that collaborative relationships with all stakeholders are the most important thing for our success.

全ての利害関係者との協力関係は、私たちの成功にとって最も重要だと確信しています。

I would like to emphasize that good relationships build trust with each other and help get the job done.

良好な関係がお互いに信頼を築き、あなたが仕事を成し遂げるのを助けることを強調しておくよ。

The quality of our work will be further improved if we build strong relationships within the company.

社内で強い関係を築けば、仕事の質はさらに向上します。

4. 社内交渉を円滑に進めるための準備を話し合う
Track 55

We need to plan realistic approaches.

現実的なアプローチを計画する必要があります。

Now let's talk about the next steps.

それでは、次のステップについて話しましょう。

Which departments do we need to ask for cooperation?

どの部門に協力を求める必要がありますか？

I will raise this topic at the next manager's meeting.

このトピックを次のマネージャー会議で取り上げます。

Let me handle this issue.

この問題の処理は私に任せて。

I will separately consult with the HR manager.

HR マネージャーと個別に相談します。

Let's assume we can clear up the resource problem.

リソースの問題を解決できると仮定しましょう。

Shall we move on to the next to-do list?

次のやることリストに移ろうか？

I understand that the budget is something we need to discuss with the accounting team.

予算は会計チームと話し合う必要があるね。

But before we do, I would like to make sure we completely identify all the requirements required for this project.

でもその前に、このプロジェクトに必要な全ての要件を完全に特定したいと思います。

Let's work with everybody to make this project as valuable as possible for the company.

このプロジェクトを会社にとってできるだけ価値のあるものにするために、みんなと協力しましょう。

We should spend some time to hear any questions which other departments may have.

私たちは、他の部門が抱く可能性のある質問をじっくり聞かないとね。

We should clearly explain the benefits of the entire company by completing this project.

このプロジェクトを完了することによる、全社へのメリットを明確に説明する必要があります。

How about we focus on project goals for now?

まずはプロジェクトのゴールにフォーカスしてみてはどうだろう？

Let's go over every issue in detail before presenting it to other departments.

他の部門に提示する前に、全ての問題を詳しく調べてみましょう。

We need to talk about the estimated cost of our proposal.

提案の概算コストについて話す必要があります。

Can you walk me through all the steps we need?

必要な全ての手順を説明してもらえますか？

We should make this proposal comprehensive as much as we can.

この提案はできる限り包括的にすべきです。

Can you help me understand how this initiative helps administrative matters once again?

このイニシアチブが管理上の問題にどのように役立つかを、もう一度教えてもらえますか？

I don't have the authority to exceed the budget.

私には予算を超過する権限はありません。

But I can certainly talk to the head of the department.

しかし、部長と掛け合うことはできますよ。

Have we reached a consensus here what to propose?

ここで何を提案するかについて合意に達しましたか？

The finance team may not be open to negotiation.

財務チームは交渉を受け入れないかもしれません。

We should come with a counterproposal to avoid deadlock.

行き詰まるのを避けるために、対案を準備する必要があります。

We don't have a lot of leverage this time.

今回はあまり影響力がなさそうだね。

So, we should carefully review potential questions and concerns in advance.

それでは、予想される質問や懸念点を事前にしっかり見直しておこう。

Let's discuss how we can develop a win-win relationship with the Sales department.

営業部門と win-win の関係をどう構築できるか話しましょう。

I would like to identify potential disagreements from the Marketing team first.

まず、マーケティングチームが合意できないであろう箇所を確認しよう。

It will be helpful if we could prepare counter-arguments to convince them to accept our proposal before we meet them.

彼らに会う前に、提案を受け入れてもらう説得をするために反論を準備しておくと助かりますね。

We should also listen well to their viewpoints and concerns.

彼らの考え方や懸念によく耳を傾ける必要もあります。

3 部下を指導する

1. 会社の閑散期に部下のモチベーションを維持する
Track 56

Since our business is currently in a low season, let's discuss how we can use our time more efficiently.

現在は忙しくない時期ですから、より時間を効率的に活用する方法を話し合いましょう。

Now is a great opportunity to reflect on our accomplishments and plan ahead for next year.

今は私たちの業績を振り返り、来年に向けて計画を立てる絶好の機会です。

I would like to talk about a stretched goal for the team and how we can make it happen.

私は、チームのより大きな目標と、それを実現する方法について話したいと思います。

I would like to use our extra time for your professional development.

皆さんの専門能力開発のために余分な時間を使いたいと思います。

Please think about how to identify knowledge and skill gaps.

知識とスキルのギャップを特定してください。

Then we will develop in-house training so that you acquire additional skills to help your future career.

その後、社内トレーニングを開発して、将来のキャリアに役立つ追加スキルを習得しましょう。

Now, we can fully focus on what we need for personal development.

今は、個人の成長に必要なことに完全に集中できますね。

I will facilitate the tracking progress toward each learning objective.

各学習目標に向けた進捗状況を追えるようにしておきます。

Let's regard this slow time as a great opportunity for us to finish up any work we have been avoiding.

忙しくないこの時期を、私たちが避けてきた仕事を終わらせる絶好の機会ととらえよう。

Taking this opportunity, shall we update our internal documents, such as policy procedures?

この機会を利用して、ポリシー手順などの内部文書を更新しておきませんか？

Let's review all the information on our website to be current.

当社のウェブサイト上の全ての情報が最新のものであることを確認しましょう。

I am looking forward to seeing our upgraded presence on the internet.

ネットで私たちのより良いサイトが見られるのを楽しみにしています。

We would like to offer the opportunity to work flexible hours as an exception next month.

来月は例外として、柔軟な勤務時間を提供する機会を提供したいと思います。

I would encourage you to spend more time with your families or do personal things which we have been unable to do during our busy season.

ご家族ともっと時間を過ごすか、忙しい季節にはできなかった個人的なことをすることをおすすめします。

This is an appreciation for what we all have achieved during the demanding season.

これは、厳しい季節に私たち全員が達成したことに対する感謝です。

Please take this opportunity to recharge yourself to be energized again.

この機会を利用して、エネルギーを再充電してください。

2. 厳しい状況、緊急事態の時   Track 57

We have to be prepared to face the most devastating economy in a decade.

10年間で最も破壊的な経済に直面する準備が必要です。

I would like to remind you that we can expect the economy to recover in the second half of the year.

今年の下半期には景気回復が期待できると思います。

I would like to assure you that we have a contingency plan in place.

我々には緊急時の対応計画があるので安心してください。

We have prepared a crisis management plan in case of an emergency.

緊急時の危機管理計画を策定してあります。

I am ready to help you to keep your morale and motivation during the crisis.

危機的な状況下で、皆さんの士気やモチベーションを保つようにサポートしていきます。

I would like to do whatever to mitigate your fears and concerns.

恐れや懸念点を和らげるために何でもしたいと思っています。

We have gone through hard times several times before.

私たちは以前も何度か厳しい状況を経験してきました。

I would like to remind you that we have always managed to survive.

私たちはいつも乗り越えてきたことを念頭においておきましょう。

I would like to emphasize that the management is aware of this issue and diligently working on this.

経営陣はこの問題を認識しており、これに熱心に取り組んでいることを強調しておきます。

While we manage this crisis, we need to remember that many people are relying on our services.

この危機を管理する一方で、多くの人々が私たちのサービスに依存していることを私たちは覚えておく必要があります。

As you know, we hold a strong responsibility in the local economy.

ご存知のように、私たちは地域経済において強い責任を負っています。

We would like you to stay focused on whatever you have to do today.

今日あなたがしなければならないことに集中してください。

I will make sure to create a supportive environment that motivates all of you.

皆様のやる気を引き出す環境作りに努めます。

We would like to ask for your continuous dedication and commitment to your work.

あなたの仕事への継続的な献身とコミットメントをお願いしたいと思います。

I would like to assure you that your compensation will stay the same and you will keep your jobs.

今後もあなたの報酬は変わらず、仕事があり続けることを保証します。

I would encourage you to come up with any new ideas and suggestions to change the way we do business.

私たちのビジネスのやり方を変えるための新しいアイデアや提案を考えてください。

I will make timely communication of the progress at the weekly staff meeting when possible.

毎週のスタッフ会議で、可能な限り進捗状況をタイムリーに伝えます。

I will ensure that the top management will be transparent in communicating any critical decisions to employees.

トップ経営陣が透明性を持って重要な決定事項を社員に伝えるようにします。

Here are the steps I am taking to overcome this situation.

この状況を克服するために私が取っている手順は、次の通りです。

I would appreciate your feedback and any opinion.

フィードバックとご意見をお願いします。

Please talk to me whenever you have any concerns.

懸念がある場合は、いつでも私に相談してください。

I always keep my door open so that you can talk to me individually.

常にオープンにしていますので、いつでも個別に話しに来てください。

I am not able to answer all of your questions.

全ての質問に答えられる訳ではありません。

Please understand that there are things we can't discuss until the management decides to make a broader announcement.

経営陣がより広範な発表を決定するまでは、議論できないことがあることを理解してください。

I would like to assure that you are not going through this tough time alone.

皆さんがこの厳しい時間を 1 人で乗り越えるわけではありません。

I need you all to take care of each other.

皆さん全員がそれぞれ助け合ってほしいと思います。

We are all united and will work hard to overcome the challenges we are facing now.

皆が一致団結しており、現在直面している試練を克服するために頑張りましょう。

I expect you to contribute to fulfilling our mission.

私たちの使命を果たすために貢献してください。

I encourage you to find ways to manage your pressure and stress.

プレッシャーとストレスを管理する方法を見つけるようにしてください。

Please take some time to find the things that help you stay pleasant during tough times.

困難な時期を元気に過ごすために役立つことを見つけるようにしてみてください。

We expect to hear an important management decision at a company-wide meeting this afternoon.

今日の午後の全社会議では、重要な経営判断を聞くことになります。

To prepare for the emergency, everyone should be prepared to work from home remotely.

緊急事態に備えるために、誰もが自宅でリモートで作業する準備をする必要があります。

We will adjust our objectives along with the organizational mission under the current economy.

現在の経済状況下、組織の使命に沿って、目標を調整します。

We will modify our group objectives in the face of unexpected market changes.

予想外の市場の変化に直面して、グループの目標を変更します。

I would like to welcome your input in implementing new initiatives.

新しい取り組みを実施する上での意見をお願いします。

I have to inform you that the decision was made to cut the budget dramatically and eliminate a few positions in this department.

予算が大きく削減され、この部門のいくつかのポジションがなくなる決定が下されたことをお知らせしなければなりません。

Let me clarify the priorities for the immediate three weeks.

直近3週間の優先順位を明確にしましょう。

This is one of the hardest things I have to face in my career.

これは私のキャリアの中で直面する最も厳しい状況の1つです。

I am deeply sorry but I have no power to change the decision by the management.

本当に申し訳なく思いますが、経営陣の決断を変える力は私にありません。

Some of our jobs need to be eliminated, despite our efforts to avoid having to do so.

そうしなくて良いように努力してきましたが、我々のいくつかの仕事はなくなることになります。

Affected employees will be offered another position in the organization.

影響を受ける社員は、社内の別のポジションをオファーされます。

Alternatively, you are entitled to receive a severance package and look for opportunities outside of the company.

または、退職パッケージを受け取り、社外の機会を探す権利もあります。

HR will help you to clarify the process.

人事がプロセスの理解を助けてくれます。

Please feel free to talk to me anytime.

いつでも話しに来てください。

Although I am not in a position to change the decision, I would listen and understand your feeling.

決定を変えることができる立場ではありませんが、あなたの気持ちを聞いて理解することはできます。

I am happy to provide any support for you to find a new position.

新しいポジションを見つけるためのサポートは何でもします。

Please let me know anytime if you need a reference for your next move.

次の異動のためにレフェレンスが必要な場合はいつでもお知らせください。

I am impressed with the way you handled the urgent request from the management.

経営陣からの緊急のリクエストの処理の仕方に感心しました。

You showed great leadership for this project.

このプロジェクトですばらしいリーダーシップを発揮しましたね。

Which part of this project was most difficult for you?

このプロジェクトのどの部分があなたにとって最も難しかったですか？

What could we do to make your role more challenging?

あなたの役割をよりチャレンジングにするために私たちは何ができるかな？

Are you getting the help you need to meet the due date of the report?

レポートの期日を守るための必要な支援を受けていますか？

I have noticed that you have not completed your marketing report on time.

マーケティングレポートが予定通りに完了していないようだね。

As you know, the sales department has requested us to provide timely information.

営業部がタイムリーな情報を必要としているのは知っているよね。

Are there any ideas on how you can speed up preparing the report?

レポートの作成を早める方法、何かアイデアある？

You were not attending our department weekly meeting.

君は部門のウィークリーミーティングに出席していなかったね。

Shall I give you a quick update on the important things?

大事な点について、簡単に話そうか？

The numbers on your report this month seem to have some discrepancies from the last one.

今月の君のレポートの数値には、前回の数値といくつかの矛盾があるよ。

Will you be able to check where you got those numbers?

これらの数字をどこから入手したか確認できる？

Please share your findings if you found any issue with our database.

データベースに何か問題あるようだったら教えてね。

I really appreciate that your reports are always easy to understand.

君のレポートはいつも理解しやすくて、本当に助かるよ。

Thank you for being flexible to accommodate this urgent request the other day.

先日は急なリクエストに柔軟に対応してくれてありがとう。

Was there any impact on your regular work?

通常の仕事に何か影響はあった？

I am grateful for your support on this special matter.

この特別な案件をサポートしてくれてありがとう。

Shall we revisit your work schedule?

君の仕事のスケジュールを見直そうか？

Let's identify the source of the problem.

問題の原因を特定しましょう。

Shall we list all the obstacles and discuss how to resolve them one by one?

全ての障害をリストアップし、それらを1つずつ解決する方法について話し合いましょう。

I would like to make sure that you won't fall behind any of your key responsibilities.

主な仕事には遅れないようにしてほしいんだ。

Could you tell me more about the situation?

状況について詳しく教えてくださいますか？

What do you think is most important for the client?

クライアントにとって、何が最も重要だと思いますか？

What other ways do you think you can take?

他にどのような方法があると思いますか？

What are your views on this matter?

この件についてはどう思っている？

You really have a great scheduling skill.

スケジューリング管理がすばらしいね。

I would like everyone on our team to learn from you.

チームのみんなに君から学んでほしいよ。

Have you noticed any area for improvement during this preparation?

これを準備している間、何か改善したほうが良い点は見つかった？

Which part of this assignment did you find the most time consuming for you?

この課題のどの部分に一番時間がかかった？

Do you have any suggestions about whether we should change the process?

プロセスを変更する必要があるかどうかについて、何か提案はある？

Please tell me the best part and the worst part you experienced during this project.

このプロジェクトで経験した、最高の部分と最悪の部分を教えてください。

How do you proceed if you are requested to do the same task again?

同じタスクを再度行うように要求された場合、どのように進めますか？

What did you learn from this experience?

この経験から何を学びましたか？

What is your takeaway from this challenging project?

このやりがいのあるプロジェクトから得たものは何ですか？

What part of this project has been the most exciting for you?

このプロジェクトのどの部分があなたにとって最もチャレンジングでしたか？

You are always very creative.

いつもとてもクリエイティブですよね。

Have you tried a new approach to that problem?

その問題に対して、新しいアプローチを試みましたか？

How much overtime did you have to work to do this part of your job?

仕事のこの部分を行うためにどれだけ残業しなければなりませんでしたか？

I am generally pleased with your report, except that you passed the due date by a week.

納期が１週間を過ぎたことを除いて、私は一般的にあなたの報告に満足しています。

Are there any disruptions that make it difficult for you to concentrate on your work?

仕事に集中するのを難しくするような混乱はありますか？

Are there any difficulties for you to get information from other departments?

他部門から情報を入手するのに何か困難はありますか？

Have you experienced a lack of resources to do this job?

この仕事をするためのリソース不足はありましたか？

Could you help me have a better understanding of this matter?

この問題を私がよりよく理解できるように助けてもらえますか？

Could you tell me what happened as a result of the delay?

遅延の結果として何が起こったのか教えてくださいますか？

What steps could you take to complete this assignment on time?

この課題を時間通りに完了するには、どのような手順を踏むことができますか？

What are you going to do if you receive a similar request again?

同じようなリクエストを再度受け取った場合、どうしますか？

What actions can you think of for helping other departments?

他の部門を支援するためにどのような行動が考えられますか？

I encourage you to see this problem as an opportunity for further growth.

この問題をさらなる成長の機会とみなすことをお勧めします。

Once you fix this problem, you will gain the confidence to do a bigger project.

この問題を修正すると、より大きなプロジェクトを行う自信が得られます。

Let me know if I should step into this situation to assist you.

あなたを助けるためにこの状況に私が足を踏み入れるべきだったら教えてください。

I respect your preference not to talk about your personal matters.

私は、あなたが個人的な問題について話すことを好まないことを尊重します。

If there is anything I can do to help, please let me know.

何か私ができることがあれば、教えてください。

I am ready to do whatever I can do to support you.

私はあなたをサポートするためにできることは何でもする準備ができています。

If you need to adjust your goals for a while, we can discuss it together.

しばらく目標を調整する必要がある場合は、一緒に話し合うことができます。

Would you be interested in learning a new function of the system?

システムの新しい機能を学ぶことに興味がありますか？

Would you like to discuss your objective for personal development this year?

今年の自己啓発の目標について話しますか？

What do you think of your freedom to do the job in your way?

自分のやり方で仕事をする自由をどう思いますか？

Are your current responsibilities sufficient to motivate you?

現在の責任はあなたのやる気を出させるのに十分ですか？

Is the amount of discretion you have enough to motivate you?

あなたが持っている裁量はあなたをやる気にさせるのに十分ですか？

What could we have done differently?

我々は他に何ができただろう？

What difference might it have made if we had changed the schedule?

予定を変更していたら、どんな違いがあっただろうか？

Can you think of any ideas about how we can reduce turnaround time?

所要時間を短縮する方法についてのアイデアを考えてもらえる？

How do you think we can streamline the process?

プロセスを効率的にするにはどうしたらいいだろう？

Which part of the skills would you like to further develop?

スキルのどの部分をさらに発展させたいですか？

Please think about further training to help your growth in the marketing field.

マーケティング分野での成長を支援するための、さらなるトレーニングをご検討ください。

I am particularly impressed by the way you lead your junior colleague.

私はあなたが後輩を指導するやり方に特に感銘を受けました。

I just want to mention that your results show your hard work.

結果があなたの努力を示していますよね。

I would like to let you know that the management appreciated the new reporting format you initiated.

経営陣は、あなたが始めた新しいレポート形式を高く評価していますよ。

4. 自信のない部下を励まして力を発揮させる　Track 59

I just want to mention that you did a great job meeting the tight deadline for this project.

このプロジェクトの厳しい締切に間に合うように、すばらしい仕事をしてくれたね。

I believe you're ready to assume a bigger assignment next time.

次回はもっと大きなプロジェクトを引き受けることができるね。

I would like you to develop your own schedule to complete the assignment.

課題を完了するために、独自のスケジュールを作成してもらうよ。

As long as you can meet the timeline, I am happy to leave this to your judgment.

期限を守ってもらう限り、これを君の判断に任せるよ。

I am always impressed with your analytical skills and detail works.

君の分析スキルと詳細な仕事にはいつも感銘を受けます。

You have the best technical skills in our teams.

君はチームで最高の技術スキルを持っているよね。

Could you do a training session for other members to share your advanced knowledge?

他のメンバーも君の高度な知識が学べるようにトレーニングをしてもらえる？

As you have extensive knowledge about this market, I would like you to lead the next presentation.

君はこの市場に関する幅広い知識があるので、次のプレゼンテーションをリードしてもらうね。

Your spreadsheets are always very easy to follow and well structured.

君の作るスプレッドシートはいつも非常にわかりやすくて、構成もいいよね。

I would like to ask you to develop the department budget this time.

今回は部門予算の策定を君に任せるよ。

You can refer to the prior excel sheets to understand how the budget is developed.

以前のExcelシートを参照すると、予算の策定方法がわかると思います。

However, please use your expertise to modify the sheet where needed.

ただし、必要に応じて、君の専門知識を活用してシートを修正してくださいね。

Please check with the accounting team about the exchange rate we need to use for overseas purchases.

海外からの購入に使用する為替レートについては、会計チームにご確認ください。

If you need to talk to me, I will be available anytime.

あなたが私と話す必要があるなら、私はいつでも対応できます。

5. 自信過剰な部下をコントロールする　　Track 60

I appreciate your blunt opinion at our team meeting.

チームミーティングでの君の率直な意見には感謝するよ。

I would like to remind you that listening to a different opinion is also an effective way to show respect to others.

異なる意見を聞くことは、他人への敬意を示す効果的な方法だということを思い出してね。

You sometimes have to put yourself in their shoes.

時には相手の立場になって考えてみないといけないよ。

I am afraid that your uncooperative behavior sometimes works against your goals.

君の非協力的な行動は、自身の目標達成に時々反する恐れがあるよ。

I would like to talk about the benefits of balancing working alone and working collaboratively with the team.

一人で働くこととチームと協力して働くことのバランスを取ることのベネフィットを話したいと思います。

We have highly regarded your technical skills and potentials.

君の技術的なスキルと可能性については高く評価しているよ。

We also expect you to be accountable for acting with our company value, collaborative culture.

我々の企業価値、協力的な文化に沿うことにも責任があるからね。

Your interactions with other people are critical to your success.

他の人とのやり取りは、あなたの成功にとって重要です。

I see you have strong confidence in your job.

あなたが仕事に強い自信を持っているのはわかります。

I suggest you develop self-confidence and assertiveness.

自信をもって主張するようにしてください。

Please be mindful not to speak in a manner that sounds arrogant to others.

他人に対して傲慢に聞こえるような話し方はしないように。

6. 困難な状況にいる部下を励ます　　Track 61

Let's get over this situation.

何とか乗り越えましょう。

You need experience of overcoming challenges yourself.

自分で乗り越える経験が必要だ。

Let's not give up and move forward.

あきらめず前へ進んで行こう。

We will eventually get there if we never give up.

あきらめなかったら、いつかうまく行く。

Nobody is perfect.

何でもできる完璧な人はいない。

We learn valuable lessons from any failures.

どんな挫折でも次に活かすことができます。

Tough situations always bring opportunities.

ピンチがあってもチャンスはきっとやって来る。

Failure is a crucial path for success.

失敗は成功のプロセスの一部です。

We should take things in a positive way.

物事を前向きにとらえましょう。

We should find out every possibility.

どんな可能性があるのか考えていこう。

Teamwork will be critical to go through a crisis.

危機の時こそチームワークが重要だ。

Why don't we develop a long-term strategy?

長期的な戦略を立てましょう。

If you get lost in your own way, I suggest you go back to the original.

自分のやり方に迷った時は原点に立ち戻りましょう。

Let's ignore negative comments and just keep going.

雑音は無視して前に進みましょう。

Our achievements will blow off any bad rumors.

悪い噂を吹き飛ばすにはやってみせるしかない。

I am sure a bright future is waiting for us.

この先いいことが起きるかもしれない。

4 社内とチームの関係を調整する

1. 社内交渉を円滑に進める　Track 62

I see that your points are valid.

おっしゃることはごもっともだと思います。

I appreciate your feedback on our proposal.

提案についてのフィードバックありがとうございます。

Let me provide you further details on why we strongly encourage you to accept our suggestion.

提案を受け入れることを我々が強くお勧めする理由について詳しく説明します。

As we have built strong partnerships, I am confident that we can work together to resolve any internal dispute.

私たちは強力なパートナーシップを築いてきましたので、協力して内部の対立を解決できると確信しています。

After all, we all are working for the same goal, to further the growth of the company.

結局のところ、私たち全員が同じ目標、つまり会社のさらなる成長のために働いているんですよ。

Shall we have a break-out session to brainstorm solutions?

解決策をブレーンストーミングするためのブレイクアウトセッションを開催しますか？

I would like to suggest having a luncheon meeting so that all of us get to know each other well.

私たち全員がお互いをよく知ることができるように、昼食会を開催しましょう。

You can count on my team as we always deliver what we promise.

私たちは常に約束したことを提供するので、私のチームを信頼いただけます。

I would like to emphasize that we need an aggressive plan to win the competition.

競争に勝つためには積極的な計画が必要であることを強調したいと思います。

We should try unprecedented initiatives to impress our clients.

前例のないイニシアチブを試みて、クライアントを感動させる必要があります。

With all due respect, I must say you have underestimated my team.

お言葉ですが、私のチームを過小評価されていると言わざるを得ません。

It will never be our intention that we create any problem for your department.

あなたの部署に問題を引き起こすことは決して私が意図していることではありません。

What I would like to propose today is that we work together to find the best solution for both of us.

今日提案したいのは、協力して双方にとって最良の解決策を見つけることです。

We will support your additional campaign, as long as you manage your spending within the budget.

予算内で支出を管理している限り、追加のキャンペーンをサポートします。

I would like your team to ensure to meet the submission deadline.

提出期限を確実に守れるよう、あなたのチームにお願いします。

We would like to have your understanding that the due date of this request is critical for the organization.

このリクエストの期日は組織にとって重要であることをご理解ください。

I would like to emphasize that all of us are required to commit to this project.

私たち全員がこのプロジェクトにコミットする必要があることを強調したいと思います。

Once each department delivers what they are supposed to do on time, we can meet the tight deadline.

各部門が予定通りにやるべきことができれば、厳しい締切に間に合わせることができます。

Shall we jointly resolve these issues before they become too serious?

これらの問題が深刻になりすぎる前に、共同で解決しませんか？

I will not be able to support your proposal as this seems not to be aligned with our company's goal.

これは会社の目標と一致しないので、あなたの提案をサポートすることはできません。

We should proceed with this project with a sense of urgency.

私たちはこのプロジェクトを緊急に進める必要があります。

I don't agree with your suggestion as this sounds to be unethical from my point of view.

私の考えでは、あなたの提案は倫理的ではないと思いますので、合意できかねます。

I have the impression that you have not disclosed all the information you have.

持っている情報を全て開示していただいていないのではないかとの印象ですよ。

We should be transparent about the current problem with each other.

私たちはお互いの現在の問題について透明でなければなりません。

I would like you to follow up on this matter as soon as possible.

この問題について、できるだけ早くフォローアップしていただきたいと思います。

Otherwise, I will have no choice but escalate this matter to the management team.

さもなければ、この問題を管理職にエスカレートする選択をするしかありません。

What can I do next time to make this more efficient for both of us?

双方にとってこれをより効率的にするために、次に何ができますか？

I will talk with my team to improve communications so this kind of issue won't happen again.

この種の問題が二度と起こらないように、コミュニケーションを改善するためにチームと話します。

I need to talk with my team to come up with alternatives.

私はチームと話し合い、代替案を考え出す必要があります。

I will incorporate your requests, which we agreed on today, and update our plan.

本日同意したお客様のリクエストを組み込み、プランを更新します。

5 チームの仕事環境

1. 自分のチームに必要なリソースを勝ち取るための フレーズ Track 63

Today I would like to explain our requirements clearly why we need an additional headcount for my team.

本日は、チームに人員を追加する必要について明確に説明したいと思います。

I am convinced that additional resources help the success of the organization.

追加のリソースが組織の成功に役立つと確信しています。

An additional headcount will help us to boost our bottom-line profit.

一人の人員を増やすことで、私たちの最終利益を押し上げます。

Based on my business plan, financial benefits will exceed the costs of hiring.

私のビジネスプランに基づくと、経済的利益は（追加の社員を）雇うコストを超えます。

I would like to ask your budget approval to advance our team skill set.

チームのスキルセットを向上させるための予算承認をお願いします。

Due to the rapidly changing technological advancement, we should add an expert in this field to my team.

急速に変化する技術の進歩により、この分野の専門家をチームに加える必要があります。

I must say we are significantly behind the competition in enhancing our internal resources.

私たちは、内部リソースの強化において、競争に大きく遅れていると言わざるを得ません。

Considering the importance of social media, we need someone who has cutting-edge expertise in this area.

ソーシャルメディアの重要性を考えると、この分野で最先端の専門知識を持つ人が必要です。

Because of expanding our business overseas, we need additional bilingual staff to support our operation.

海外で事業を展開するため、業務を請け負うバイリンガルスタッフの増員が必要です。

I understand that we have limited financial resources.

財源が限られていることを理解しています。

However, I would like to present the reasons why this investment in our team will bring significant benefits to the organization.

しかしながら、私たちのチームへのこの投資が組織に大きな利益をもたらす理由をご説明させていただきます。

I would like to cover what exactly we need and how this will work as the best interests for the organization.

実際に何が必要で、これが組織の最善の利益としてどのように働くのかをお話しします。

You will be convinced how my proposal is aligned with the organization's strategic goals.

私の提案が組織の戦略的目標とどのように一致しているかを納得していただけます。

My team has successfully implemented a series of innovative processes to be productive.

私のチームは一連の革新的なプロセスを導入し、生産性を向上させてきました。

We have been always proactive to bring new ideas to make significant contributions to the organization.

私たちはいつでも新しいアイデアを積極的に提案し、組織に大きく貢献してきています。

I am confident that we can make further contributions to the future of the company with additional resources.

追加のリソースで、会社の将来にさらに貢献できると確信しています。

I am sure that you are fully aware of the importance of investing in people.

人材に投資することの重要性は十分にご理解いただいていると思います。

Our people are always looking for opportunities for their professional growth.

彼らはいつでも専門的な成長のためのあらゆる機会を探しています。

Based on my research, our competitors provide multiple training opportunities for their employees.

調べてみたところ、競合他社が社員にたくさんのトレーニングの機会を提供しています。

As you know, it will be a huge loss if we lose some of our talented and experienced employees.

ご存知のように、才能のある経験豊富な社員を失うと、大きな損失になります。

It will cost a lot for us if we have to hire replacements and provide basic training to them.

後任を雇って基本的なトレーニングを提供しなければならなくなると、かなりの費用になってしまいます。

I would like to provide reasonable development opportunities to my team so that they continue to be highly motivated working with us.

私のチームに彼らの成長のための適切な機会を提供して、引き続き私たちと一緒に働く彼らの意欲を高めたいと思います。

2. チームを過剰な仕事量から守る　　　　Track 64

I need to check on a few things before accepting this unexpected work.

予定していなかったこの仕事を受ける前に、いくつか確認しなければなりません。

As you know, my team is working on three projects.

ご存知の通り、私のチームは３つのプロジェクトに取り組んでいます。

I need to check whether they can squeeze this task into their workload.

このタスクを彼らがなんとかできるかどうか確認する必要があります。

I wish we could say yes on the spot.

この場でお引き受けできれば良いのですが。

Let me get back to you.

またお知らせします。

Which project would you like us to set aside to do this new project?

この新しいプロジェクトを実行するために、どのプロジェクトを先に延ばしますか？

Am I correct to understand that this assignment is more important than outstanding projects?

この課題が現在進行中のプロジェクトより重要だと理解して間違いありませんか？

Could you help me to draw the priority lists for the next few weeks?

今後数週間の優先リストの作成を手伝っていただけませんか？

Firstly, I would like to check with my team to see whether they have extra capacities to do this job at this moment.

まず、チームに現在この仕事を引き受ける余裕があるかどうかを確認したいと思います。

Let me talk to my team to find out the resources they need.

彼らがどのようなリソースを必要とするかをチームと話したいと思います。

I need to share this unexpected request with my team to get their support.

この予期しないリクエストをチームと共有して、彼らのサポートを得る必要があります。

I appreciate your higher expectations of my team's capabilities.

私のチームの能力に、より高い期待をいただいて感謝します。

I'm honored that you thought of my team for this challenging task.

この難しいタスクに、私のチームを思い出していただいて光栄です。

However, we have been overwhelmed with new projects.

しかしながら、新しいプロジェクトでいっぱいの状態です。

Our circumstances make it impossible to take over this work at this moment.

現状、この仕事を今引き受けることはできません。

Would it be an option to put this project postponed to the next month?

このプロジェクトを来月に延期することは可能でしょうか？

While my team can't accept a new project now, I will be able to provide some advice.

新規のプロジェクトを私のチームが今引き受けることはできませんが、アドバイスすることは可能です。

We have exceeded your expectations to meet the challenging deadlines.

厳しい締切に間に合わせるため、我々は期待を超えてきました。

I need to give you a warning that part of our regular workload will be compromised because of this.

この件のために通常業務の一部を妥協しなければならない可能性があります。

I prefer not to put too much pressure on my team constantly.

チームに過度なプレッシャーを継続的にかけないようにしたいです。

My team has constantly been working overtime to meet the regular workload.

私のチームは、通常業務をこなすのに常に残業しています。

After the reorganization last year, we have been managing to meet the responsibilities with reduced headcount.

昨年の組織再編後、人員を削減しながらなんとか責任を果たすことができています。

We have been stretching ourselves to meet the standards.

私たちは求められる仕事をするために頑張っています。

This relates to what we don't have any expertise.

これは、私たちが専門知識を持っていないことに関連するものです。

I am not sure whether we are the right team to do this job.

私たちがこの仕事をするのにふさわしいチームかどうかわかりません。

Have you considered assigning this task to other teams?

このタスクを他のチームに依頼することを検討しましたか？

I would like my team to do uncompromised work for this important task.

私のチームには、この重要なタスクのために妥協のない仕事をしてもらいたいと思います。

Could I ask you to extend the due date by one month?

納期を1ヶ月延長してもらうことは可能でしょうか？

Alternatively, would you consider transferring part of the task to other teams?

または、タスクの一部を他のチームに移行することは可能でしょうか？

I will put this new assignment as the highest priority for my team.

私はこの新しい任務を私のチームの最優先事項と位置づけます。

This means we won't be able to complete Project A on time.

ということは、プロジェクトAを予定通りに完了することができません。

Is that acceptable for you?

それは許容いただけますか？

One of my senior team members will be on annual leave next week.

私のチームのシニアメンバーの1人が来週、年次休暇予定です。

Would it be possible to start this project after his return?

彼が戻ってからこのプロジェクトを始めることは可能でしょうか？

I understand the urgency of this request and will work hard on this with my team.

このリクエストの緊急性を理解しますので、チームと一緒に懸命に取り組みます。

I would highly appreciate it if you could share the workload well in advance next time.

次回は事前に作業負荷を共有していただければ幸いです。

I would like you to understand the workload to complete all the works.

全ての作業を完了するための作業負荷を理解していただきたいです。

I am going to draft our work-schedule on how to accommodate all of your requests.

全ての要求にどのように対応するかについて私たちの作業スケジュールをドラフトしてきます。

Would that work for you?

それでよろしいですか？

My team is accustomed to working based on the advance schedule.

私のチームは事前のスケジュールに基づいて作業することを習慣としています。

My team members are highly experienced and appreciate to work independently based on the agreed assignment.

私のチームメンバーは非常に経験が豊富で、合意された仕事を独立して進めることを好んでいます。

I have confidence that this approach is a better use of all of our resources.

このアプローチが私たちの全てのリソースのより良い活用方法であると確信しています。

I need to provide sufficient reasons why we need them to suddenly change their priorities.

彼らの優先順位を突然変更する必要がある理由をしっかりわかってもらう必要があります。

I am afraid that changing priorities during the middle will demotivate my team.

途中で優先順位を変更すると、チームがやる気を失うのではないかと心配です。

We have specific objectives that we agreed at the beginning of the new year.

新年の初めに合意した具体的な目標があります。

Sudden additional requests beyond the agreed objectives could confuse my team.

合意した目標以外の、突然の追加の要求は、チームを混乱させる可能性があります。

Chapter 3

6 チームの結果に責任をもつ

1. チームの失敗をかばう　　　　　　　　　Track 65

I have the responsibility for what happened this time.

今回の出来事には私が責任を負っています。

My team worked hard to make it happen.

私のチームは実現するために一生懸命働きました。

The only reason for the failure is that I underestimated the resources we need.

失敗の唯一の理由は、必要なリソースを私が過小評価していたことです。

My instruction for the team was not sufficient for them to deliver their work on time.

チームに対する私の指示が、彼らが仕事を予定通りに行うのに不十分でした。

I will do a thorough review to find out the reasons why things did not go well this time.

今回はうまく行かなかった理由を徹底的に見直します。

I will come back to you with my action plans on how to avoid similar issues in the future.

今後、同様の問題を回避するための行動計画をお伝えします。

It is not my team's problem that we could not meet your expectations.

期待に応えられなかったのは、私のチームの問題ではありません。

I will take full responsibility for the delay.

遅れたことについて、私が全責任を負います。

I appreciate your understanding that they made their best efforts.

彼らが最善を尽くしたことをご理解いただきたく存じます。

I will have brainstorming with my team on how we can improve our process.

プロセスを改善する方法について、チームとブレーンストーミングを行います。

I have sat down and talked with my team about plans to improve the accuracy of our works.

作業の正確さを向上させるための計画について、チームとじっくり話しました。

I have already reviewed the workload among the team and shuffled some responsibilities.

私はすでにチーム間のワークロードを確認し、いくつかの責任を移行しました。

I understand that you have relied on our great track record to meet the deadline.

締切に間に合う私たちの優れた実績に頼っていただいていたと思います。

I apologize for not meeting your expectations this time.

今回はご期待に添えなかったことをお詫び申し上げます。

I would like to take this experience as an opportunity to review and improve our process.

この経験を、プロセスを見直して改善する機会としたいと思います。

This experience told me that I should not rely too much on my team for their over-time work.

この経験から、私はチームの時間外勤務についてチームに頼りすぎないようにすべきであることがわかりました。

I will ensure to talk to you for any extra resources we need to meet expectations next time.

次回の期待に応えるために必要な、その他のリソースについては、必ずお話しいたします。

I will make sure to cover any resource gaps in my team in the future.

将来的には、チーム内のリソースのギャップを確実にカバーします。

2. チームの功績をたたえる　　　　　　　　Track 66

I would like to give credit to my team.

チームの功績です。

My team deserves all of your compliments.

お褒めのお言葉は私のチームが受けるべきです。

I could never do this alone.

これを 1 人では絶対にできません。

I could not deliver this task without my team's help.

私のチームの助けがなければ、このタスクを実行できませんでした。

I owe my team a lot for the success of this project.

このプロジェクトが成功したのは、チームのおかげです。

It is my team who did most of the difficult work.

難しい作業のほとんどをやってくれたのは私のチームです。

I will pass your appreciation onto my team.

感謝のお言葉、チームに伝えます。

Thank you very much for the nice compliment.

すてきな賛辞をありがとうございます。

I will pass along your message to my team.

チームにあなたのメッセージを伝えます。

My team worked hard to make this happen.

私のチームはこれを実現するために一生懸命働きました。

I could not do this alone.

これは一人ではできませんでした。

3. ふり返る（評価、反省） Track 67

I didn't realize that this has not been timely communicated to you.

これがタイムリーにあなたに伝えられていないことに気づきませんでした。

Could you tell me more?

もっと教えてもらえますか？

I am open to listening to your perspectives.

あなたの視点に耳を傾けます。

Could you go through your points one by one?

あなたのポイントを１つずつ確認できますか？

We appreciate your views but we see it differently.

ご意見に感謝いたしますが、見方が異なります。

I will make sure to incorporate your needs next time.

次回もあなたのニーズを取り入れるようにします。

I suggest we take some time to find out the best solution for both sides.

双方にとって最善の解決策を見つけるために、少し時間をかけましょう。

Let's specify the issues we have at this time, so we won't repeat them in the future.

今回、私たちが抱えている問題を特定してみましょう。そうすれば、今後それらを繰り返すことはありません。

Call it a day and come back with a fresh mind tomorrow morning to resume our conversation.

今日はこのくらいにして、明日の朝、新たな気持ちで会話を続けましょう。

We should sit down and talk about how we can work more efficiently next time.

次回はもっと効率的に仕事ができるようにじっくり話し合いましょう。

Let's brainstorm how we can improve our communication.

コミュニケーションを改善する方法をブレインストーミングしましょう。

7 チーム、部下を守る

1. 会社の上層部とのちょっと難しい局面でのやり取り

Track 68

Could I assume you are generally satisfied with our team's performance?

私たちのチームのパフォーマンスに概ね満足していると考えてよろしいですか？

Chapter 3

Sometimes it is hard for me to understand the priorities of the management team.

経営陣の優先順位を理解するのが難しい場合があります。

Please help me to explain to my team how the management team reached the conclusion.

経営陣がどのように結論に達したかをチームにどう説明したら良いか助けてください。

I wonder if you had sufficient information to make this conclusion.

この結論を出すのに十分な情報があったのでしょうか。

I wish you consulted with us first before accepting this offer.

この申し出を受け入れる前に、まず相談していただけたらと思います。

There is one thing I need to clarify with you before moving to the next step.

次のステップに進む前に、明確にしたいことが1つあります。

227

I must say that we are rather uncomfortable with this decision.

私たちはこの決定にかなり不快だと言わざるを得ません。

Is there any chance that you would reconsider this decision?

この決定を再考する余地はありますか？

We feel that the direction is too short-sighted.

方向性が短絡的すぎるのではないかと思います。

We feel this is a rushed decision without considering long-term value for the company.

これは、会社の長期的な価値を考慮せずに急いだ決定だと感じています。

Have you considered all the negative consequences because of this?

これによる全ての悪影響を考慮しましたか？

I am concerned that we could easily get over budget if we continue at this pace.

このペースで続ければ、予算を簡単に超過してしまうのではないかと心配しています。

Some of the assumptions are overly optimistic, compared with our histories.

いくつかの仮定は、これまでの実績と比較して、過度に楽観的です。

We should evaluate this matter not only from the legal but also from the ethical point of view.

私たちはこの問題を法律だけでなく倫理的な観点からも評価すべきです。

Have you considered a long-term impact on the team by this decision?

この決定によるチームへの長期的な影響を考慮しましたか？

I have a responsibility to update my team with the management decision.

私はチームに経営陣の決定をアップデートする責任があります。

Would you copy me on critical emails, so that you can keep me in the loop?

私が情報共有してもらえるように、重要なメールに CC で送ってもらえませんか？

If possible, I would like to be involved in this decision-making process for this matter.

できれば、この問題に関するこの意思決定プロセスに参加したいと思います。

Could you have a meeting with me at least once a week?

少なくとも週に一度、私と面談していただけませんか？

I would like to have a better understanding of the progress on a timely basis.

タイムリーに進捗状況をより理解したいと思います。

I would like to be informed of any decision timely so that my team can align our priorities with management expectations.

私のチームが優先事項を経営陣の期待に合わせることができるように、決定はタイムリーにお知らせください。

I must say that my team was extremely disappointed with this unexpected decision.

私のチームはこの予想外の決定に非常に失望したと言わざるを得ません。

We feel our efforts have not been appreciated by the management team.

私たちの努力は経営陣に評価されていないと感じています。

Could you consider providing a further explanation to help our understanding?

私たちが理解できるように、さらに説明することを検討していただけませんか？

I strongly request your decision will be fair to everybody in my team.

決定が私のチームの誰にとっても公平であることを強く要請いたします。

I would like to update you on what my team has concerned with this matter.

私のチームがこの件に関して懸念していることをお知らせしたいと思います。

We don't think the strategy will not be financially viable from the long-term view.

長期的な観点からは、この戦略は財政的に実行可能ではないと思います。

I would highly appreciate your understanding.

何卒ご理解を賜りますようお願い申し上げます。

We think we need to have a sense of urgency to keep up with competitors.

競争相手に追いつくには、切迫感が必要だと思います。

We should pay more attention to what our customers are saying.

私たちは顧客が言っていることにもっと注意を払うべきです。

We should never underestimate what is happening on site.

現場で起こっていることを過小評価すべきではありません。

We strongly feel that this proposal is unethical and not aligned with our long-term value.

この提案は非倫理的であり、長期的な価値と整合していないと強く感じます。

We would like to bring to your attention what our employees are concerned about in the field.

社員が現場で気にかけていることに、ぜひ注目していただきたいと思います。

I have to check with my team whether we can meet the deadline.

期限に間に合うかどうかをチームで確認する必要があります。

Let me get back to you by the end of today after confirming with my team.

チームに確認した後、今日中にご連絡いたします。

As you know, my team is working hard to meet the growing demand from the customers.

ご存知のように、私のチームは顧客からの高まる需要に応えるために一生懸命に働いています。

It will be difficult to add additional tasks until the peak workload stabilizes in the next weeks.

今後の数週間で仕事量のピークが安定するまで、タスクを追加するのは困難です。

The originally set due-date has been already challenging to meet.

最初に設定された期日は、すでに達成するのが困難です。

I must say that pulling forward the timing is totally unrealistic.

タイミングを早めることは完全に非現実的だと言わなければなりません。

I would suggest postponing this project until next year to avoid putting an additional burden on the team.

チームに追加の負担をかけることを避けるため、このプロジェクトを来年までに延期することを提案します。

Based on our records, the average overtime this year has been 20% higher than the last year's.

私たちの記録に基づくと、今年の平均残業時間は昨年よりも20％増加しました。

I would like to recover the work-life-balance for everybody before they burn out.

全員が燃え尽きる前に、ワークライフバランスを回復したいと思います。

I understand that the new initiative became the company's top priority.

新しいイニシアチブが会社の最優先事項になったことを理解しています。

We will work hard to meet the requirements.

リクエストに答えるために努力します。

However, I would like you to be aware that we have already been stretched in our workload before this initiative.

ただし、このイニシアチブの前に、仕事量がすでに拡大していることに注意してください。

Meeting all the milestone timing of this project will be extremely challenging for us.

このプロジェクトの全てのマイルストーンのタイミングを満たすことは、私たちにとって非常に困難です。

I believe cutting off the IT budget would bring a huge negative impact on our future.

IT 予算を削減することは、私たちの将来に大きな悪影響をもたらすと思います。

I must say reducing the headcount in my department would be a mistake from the customer satisfaction point of view.

顧客満足度の観点から、部門の人員削減は間違いだと言わざるを得ません。

Could I come back to you with alternative ideas to reduce our department costs?

部門経費削減のための別のアイデアを持ってきてもいいですか？

Cost reduction by reducing the headcount may work to lower the cost in the short term.

人員削減によるコスト削減は、短期的にはコスト削減に役立つ可能性があります。

However, this will bring a significant disadvantage to our competitive advantage in the future.

ただし、これは将来の競争上の優位性に大きな不利益をもたらします。

It is my responsibility that my team could not deliver what you expected.

私のチームが期待通りのものを提供できなかったのは私の責任です。

Please allow me a couple of days to find out how we can recover the project delay.

プロジェクトの遅延を回復する方法を見つけるのに数日お待ちください。

With our great track record, I am confident that we can accelerate our work to meet the final deadline.

我々のこれまでのすばらしい実績からしても、最終期限に間に合うように作業を加速できると確信しています。

I must say that we had underestimated the workload for this assignment.

この仕事の作業負荷を過小評価していたと言わざるを得ません。

Let me talk to my team to find out what went wrong and what we learned from this experience.

チームと話をして、何が間違っていたのか、この経験から何を学んだのかを確認します。

Chapter 3

Column ③

単語を覚える時は連想ゲームの発想で

社会人になって久しぶりに英語をやり直す方から、新しい単語が覚えられないというお悩みをよく聞きます。

やみくもに単語を一つひとつ覚えようとするのではなく、実際に使う可能性の高いものから集中して覚える、関連性のある単語をまとめて覚えるというアプローチがおすすめです。

マインドマップなどを活用するのも役立ちます。下記の例では、「緊急な（urgent）」という単語を覚えると同時に、想定される「緊急な〜（urgent〜）」を一緒に覚えるようにしています。

もう一つのおすすめは、**コロケーション（collocation）**と言われる、よく使われる定番の組み合わせを一緒に覚えることです。

ビジネスでよく使うconsider（考慮する）の後に続く単語を見てみましょう。

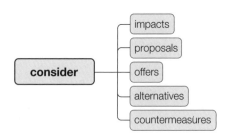

いずれの勉強法も、自分が明日使う可能性のある単語を軸に、関連性のある単語をまとめて覚えることがポイントです。単語を覚えたら、例文を作って覚えていくようにしましょう。

Chapter 4

キャリアアップのための
最強フレーズ

即戦力を求める傾向が強い欧米企業では、中途採用の機会も多いです。また、社内で異動や昇進の機会に、本人自ら名乗り出ることが可能な企業も多く、そういった機会を利用するために自己アピールの方法を身につけておくことは非常に大切です。

1. 自分が達成してきたことを効果的に伝える　　Track 71

I am a finance professional with ten years of experience.

私は 10 年の経験を持つ金融専門家です。

I have extensive experience in the consumer marketing area.

私は消費者マーケティング分野で豊富な経験を持っています。

I have contributed to the growth and success of the company for the last ten years.

私はこの 10 年間、会社の成長と成功に貢献してきました。

I am highly motivated to contribute to a great organization that aligns with my values.

自分の価値観に沿った、すばらしい組織に貢献することに、私は大変意欲的です。

I always work hard to expand on my current skill set and learn new things.

私はいつも自分の現在のスキルを伸ばし、新しいことを学ぶために一生懸命働いています。

I am good at learning new concepts and practices quickly.

私は新しい概念ややり方を早く習得するのを得意としています。

I have strengths in focusing on goals and driving for results.

私は目標に集中し、結果を追求することに強みがあります。

I am confident that I have all the skills you need to contribute to the growth of the company.

御社の成長に貢献するために必要な、全てのスキルを持っていると確信しています。

With my expertise, I can provide a lot of value to the company.

私の専門知識で、私は会社に多くの価値を提供することができます。

I believe the most important qualities for a leader to excel is having integrity.

私は、優れたリーダーになるための最も重要な資質は誠実さを持っていることだと考えています。

I am willing to take on new and even difficult challenges.

私は新たな、そして難しくもある挑戦に挑むことを厭いません。

I always find out any best practices for doing a new task.

新しい仕事をする時には、常にベストプラクティスを学んでいます。

I always try to learn proven approaches from team members.

私は常にチームメンバーから実証済みのアプローチを学ぼうとしています。

I am good at handling urgent priorities.

私は緊急の優先事項の処理を的確に判断します。

If I have two urgent matters and only time to do one, I would ensure to ask co-workers to help.

緊急の問題が2つある中、1つだけしか実行する時間がない場合は、同僚に助けを求めます。

My colleagues always say I am results-oriented and very energetic.

私の同僚はいつも私が結果を重視し、エネルギーにあふれていると言います。

If someone asks for my help for any issue, I actively listen to their concerns and make a plan to resolve the issue as quickly as possible.

誰かが私の助けを求める問題があれば、私は積極的に彼らの懸念に耳を傾け、できるだけ早く問題を解決するための計画を立てます。

I received the best sales award for two years in a row for the past two years.

過去2年間で、2年連続で最優秀セールス賞を受賞しました。

Because of my experience in PR, I have more confidence about speaking in public.

PRの経験から、私は人前で話すことにはさらに自信があります。

I am quite good at connecting people.

特に得意なことは、人々をつなげることです。

I received the best-team-player award three years running.

3年連続で最優秀チームプレイヤー賞を受賞しました。

In my annual review, my supervisor is always grateful for my leadership skills.

年次レビューでは、上司からいつも私のリーダーシップに感謝されています。

I am proud of organizational abilities with the diversified group.

多様化したグループをまとめる組織力に誇りを持っています。

I'm a self-motivated and creative marketer with five years of experience in a global organization.

グローバルな組織で5年の経験がある、自発的でクリエイティブなマーケターです。

I'm a highly trained project manager at a leading Japanese pharmaceutical company.

私は日本の大手製薬会社で高度な訓練を受けたプロジェクトマネージャーです。

I'm decisive as well as flexible.

私は柔軟性があると同時に、決断力があります。

I am highly confident with my communication skills both in Japanese and English.

日本語と英語の両方のコミュニケーションスキルに大いに自信を持っています。

I'm always reliable and make sure to get the assignment done on time.

私は常に信頼でき、時間通りに課題を完了させるようにします。

I am flexible to put in extra work until the project is completed.

私は、プロジェクトが完了するまで余計に働く柔軟性を持ちます。

I like to think outside the box and adapt to challenging circumstances.

枠を超えて考え、困難な状況に適応するのが好きです。

Chapter 4

The most memorable accomplishment at the trading company was closing a global acquisition deal.

商社で働いていて、最も思い出深い成果は、グローバルな買収契約の締結でした。

I once successfully led the due diligence process from beginning to end.

私はかつてデューデリジェンスプロセスを最初から最後まで成功裏に導いたことがあります。

＊due diligence：投資やM&Aなどの取引に際して行われる、対象企業や資産などの調査活動のこと。文章ではDDと略すこともある。

This was a major milestone of my accounting career.

これは私の経歴の大きな節目でした。

I have successfully led an accounting team for the last five years.

過去5年間、経理チームを率いてきました。

I am ready to take the next step by taking on bigger responsibilities.

より大きな責任を引き受けることで、次のステップに進む準備ができています。

I am highly productive at work while I value the work and life balance.

私は仕事と生活のバランスを大切にしながら、仕事で非常に生産的です。

Outside of work, I engage in my personal activities such as volunteering.

仕事以外では、ボランティア活動のような個人の活動に従事しています。

I have an excellent time management skill with multiple responsibilities at work, family and personal development.

私は仕事、家庭、そして自己成長と複数の役割を持ち、時間管理能力に優れています。

I really enjoy being busy and managing multiple things in my life.

忙しくて複数のことを管理するのが人生において本当に楽しいです。

I have the technical abilities to be successful in my job.

私は自分の仕事で成功するための技術的な能力を持っています。

Now I want to learn the different areas of the business to expand my career.

これからはビジネスの異なる分野を学び、キャリアを拡大したいと考えています。

2. 長所をどのように生かしたか具体的な事例を伝える

I enjoy working with different types of people.

私は異なるタイプの人たちと働くのを楽しみます。

I like to challenge myself for my personal development.

私は自分の成長のために自分自身にチャレンジするのが好きです。

One of my strengths is to help others grow.

私の強みの1つは、他の人の成長を助けることができることです。

I see myself as a person with relatively high emotional intelligence.

私は自分自身を比較的高い感情的知性を持つ人だと思っています。

Because of my experience as an instructor, I have confidence about speaking in public.

講師の経験のおかげで、人前で話すことに自信を持つようになりました。

I can stay calm even under a tough environment.

厳しい環境下でも、落ち着いて対応することができます。

I'm a hard worker and I like to take on a variety of challenges.

私は一生懸命に働き、いろいろチャレンジするのが好きです。

I majored in Psychology at university because I was interested in studying how the mind works.

私はどのように心理が働くのかを勉強したくて、大学では心理学を専攻しました。

I found it useful because it helped me to work better with people.

その知識によって（他者の考え方の違いを理解して）人々と一緒により良く働くことができています。

I could be a more effective leader by understanding differences in others.

他人をよく理解できることで、より効果的なリーダーとなっています。

I've always been a great team player.

私はいつも非常に良いチームプレイヤーです。

I'm good at keeping a team together to deliver high-quality work in a team environment.

チーム一丸になって、チームの環境で、質の高い仕事を達成することが得意です。

My strongest trait is in customer service.

私の最大の強みは顧客サービスです。

I always listen and pay close attention to my customer's needs.

私はいつも顧客のニーズをよく聞いて、注意を払うようにしています。

I make sure they are fully satisfied.

顧客に十分に満足してもらうようにしています。

I enjoy working under pressure.

私はプレッシャーがある中でも働くのが楽しいです。

I use pressure to help me work more efficiently.

プレッシャーがあると、より効率的に働くことができます。

I work well under pressure because I don't panic.

私はプレッシャーがあってもパニックにならないので、よく働くことができます。

I maintain self-control and work as efficiently as possible.

自分を律し、可能な限り効率的に働くことができます。

I am good at finding a solution for conflicts by listening well to the different points of view.

私は、異なる観点によく耳を傾け、紛争の解決策を見出すのが得意です。

As an IT manager, implementing a workflow process was my biggest contribution to the company.

IT マネージャーとして、ワークフロープロセスの導入は、会社への私の最大の貢献でした。

I like to lead people to work in groups.

私はグループで働くように人々をリードするのが好きです。

I can say that I am a natural leader.

私は、自分は生まれながらのリーダーだと思います。

I am good at developing highly skilled and diverse individuals.

私はスキルが高く、多様な人材を育てることが得意です。

I am proud of my communication skills both in Japanese and English.

私は日本語と英語の両方でのコミュニケーション能力に自信を持っています。

I am willing to build on my leadership skill whenever I have an opportunity.

機会があればいつでも、リーダーシップのスキルを強化したいと思っています。

I'm very collaborative.

私はとても協力的です。

I'm a compassionate person and listen well to others at any occasion.

私は思いやりのある人であり、いつでも他の人の話をよく聞きます。

I have extremely strong writing skills.

私には非常に強力なライティングスキルがあります。

I have worked as a journalist earlier in my career and developed the skills.

私はキャリアの初期にジャーナリストとして働き、スキルを磨きました。

I know how to develop a well-balanced sales letter to customers.

顧客へのバランスの取れた販売レターを作成する方法を知っています。

I'm thorough and persistent.

私は徹底的で根気強い性格です。

I keep track of the details of complicated tasks and complete them on time.

複雑なタスクの詳細を追跡し、期日通りにタスクを完了します。

I'm highly organized by nature.

私は本質的にまとめるのが得意です。

I have used this skill in organizing people and projects at work.

私はこのスキルを使用して、職場の人々やプロジェクトをまとめてきました。

I am reliable to keep the deadline for any tasks.

私はどんな仕事の締切も守るので安心ください。

From past failure, I have learned the importance of scheduling all to-do lists in advance.

過去の失敗から、全ての予定リストを事前にスケジュールすることの重要性を学びました。

I have always good communication with all stakeholders to timely inform any upcoming problems.

今後の問題をタイムリーに知らせるために、全ての利害関係者と常に良好なコミュニケーションをとっています。

I am passionate about training young professionals.

私は若手プロフェッショナル人材の訓練に情熱を注いでいます。

I am very patient to develop subordinates.

部下を養成することに、非常に辛抱強く臨んでいます。

I am very creative to think out of the box.

私は非常に創造的で、独創的な考えをすることができます。

I am an action-oriented leader.

私は行動指向のリーダーです。

I have an entrepreneurial spirit and like to challenge new business.

私には起業家精神があり、新しいビジネスに挑戦するのが好きです。

I am quite a detail-oriented person.

私はかなり詳細な人です。

Once I determined something, I commit myself to make it happen.

いったん何かを決定したら、それを実現するためにコミットします。

I am respectful of people with different backgrounds.

私は異なるバックグラウンドを持つ人々を尊重しています。

Chapter 4

I am strongly disciplined to do the right things.

私は正しいことをするように強く規律を正してきました。

I am always dedicated to the ethical behaviors.

私は常に倫理的な行動をするようにしてきました。

I am a result-driven person and highly motivated to achieve a goal.

私は結果重視の人間であり、目標を達成するために非常にやる気があります。

I am quite flexible to adjust myself to the new environment.

私は新しい環境に順応するために非常に柔軟です。

Integrity is one of my strengths.

誠実さは私の強みの1つです。

I have strong financial literacy as I started my career at a bank.

銀行でキャリアを始めたので、高度な金融リテラシーを持っています。

I am trilingual and speak Japanese, English, and Spanish.

私は３ヶ国語を話し、日本語、英語、そしてスペイン語を話します。

I am a hard worker but like humor as well.

私は働き者ですが、ユーモアも好きです。

I would say that the broad perspectives to analyze issues is my greatest strength.

問題を分析する際、幅広い視点を持ってするのが私の最大の強みだと思います。

As a leader, I am not afraid of confronting any problem we have to face.

リーダーとして、私たちが直面しなければならない問題と対峙することを恐れません。

I am always happy to cover my co-worker's jobs whenever needed.

必要な時はいつでも、同僚の仕事を喜んで引き受けます。

I always properly delegate jobs to my team members.

私は常にチームメンバーに仕事を適切に任せるようにしています。

My supervisor always relies on me a lot and delegates important tasks.

私の上司は常に私を非常に頼りにしていて、重要な仕事も任されます。

I am very calm and never express too much frustration at work.

私はとても冷静な性格で、職場で過剰にフラストレーションを出すことはありません。

I have lots of experience speaking in front of people.

私は人前で話す経験が豊富です。

I am confident in presenting to large groups.

大勢の人の前でプレゼンをすることに自信があります。

I have extensive experience with public speaking.

私は人前で話すことに関して豊富な経験を持っています。

I have developed my ability to learn from mistakes throughout my career.

私は自分のキャリアの中で、間違いから学ぶ能力を身につけてきました。

I am very good at prioritizing multiple tasks.

複数の仕事の優先順位づけが非常に得意です。

As a marketer, I have developed my creative thinking.

マーケターとして、私は創造的な思考を育成してきました。

With my CPA background, I have strong analytical skills.

私は公認会計士のバックグラウンドがあるので、強力な分析スキルを持っています。

＊CPA（certified public accountant）「公認会計士」

I am energetic and a well-rounded person.

私はエネルギッシュで、バランスの取れた人物です。

One of my strengths is an interpersonal skill.

私の強みの1つは対人スキルです。

I am comfortable working with people from different backgrounds.

私は、様々なバックグラウンドの人々と一緒に仕事をするのが得意です。

I have extensive office management experiences and have strong organizational skills.

私は広範なオフィス管理の経験があり、強力な組織をまとめるスキルを持っています。

I have the ability to do multi-tasks with high qualities.

私は質の高い複数の仕事を行う能力を持っています。

I am good at quickly adapting to a new environment.

私は新しい環境をすぐに採用するのが得意です。

I am quick to learn new things.

私はすぐに新しいことを学びます。

I am very reliable in performing a confidential assignment.

機密性の高い任務を遂行することに十分信頼していただけます。

I always get my team to meet critical deadlines.

私は常にチームに重要な期限を守らせます。

3. 短所をうまく伝え、長所ともとれるように伝える
Track 73

I am a hard worker and always try to do things as perfectly as I can.

私はハードワーカーで、常にできる限り完璧に物事をやろうとしてしまいます。

I tend to focus too much on the details of any assignments.

どんな課題でも細かいところまで集中しすぎる傾向があります。

Because of this, I have had a hard time giving tasks to more junior colleagues.

このため、後輩に仕事を回すことがなかなかできません。

I regard my weakness as not asking for help.

私の短所は助けを求めないことです。

I always try to solve my own problems instead of asking someone for help.

誰かに助けを求めず、いつも自分で問題を解決しようとしてしまいます。

Now, I have realized that it's far better to work as a team, as we could be more productive and enjoyable.

今は、チームとして働くことがより良く、私たちはより生産的で楽しむことができるということに気づきました。

I should ask for more help so that I could be more efficient.

より効率的になるために、もっと助けを求めるべきだと考えています。

I sometimes put too much pressure on myself to exceed expectations.

期待を超えるために、自分にプレッシャーをかけすぎることがあります。

It has been somewhat difficult for me to work with low performers.

パフォーマンスの低い人たちと仕事をすることは、私にとってやや困難でした。

Now, I have learned how to listen to their concerns and provide effective advice.

今では、私は彼らの懸念に耳を傾け、効果的なアドバイスを提供する方法を学びました。

I could get impatient when my team members are behind the deadline for a critical task.

チームメンバーが重要なタスクの締切に遅れていると、イライラすることがあります。

I am now trying to check the progress to make sure they are on track.

現在は進行状況をチェックして、順調に進んでいるかどうかを確認するようにしています。

I have found it difficult to say no from time to time.

時々ノーと言うのは難しいと感じることがあります。

I try to make sure to align my priorities and organizational requirements as a leader.

私は、リーダーとしての優先事項と組織の要求を一致させるようにしています。

In the past, I have been uncomfortable with uncertainties.

過去に、私は不確実な環境が心地良くありませんでした。

I have now gained sufficient experience to proceed with limited information.

今では限られた情報でも進めることができるような十分な経験をしてきました。

I feel my weakness is not being detail-oriented enough.

私の短所は、十分に細かい点に注意しないところであると感じています。

I am actively working on the improvement of my weakness.

私は自分の弱さの改善に積極的に取り組んでいます。

I always want to accomplish as much as possible.

私はいつも少しでも多くのことをやり遂げようとします。

I realized this could hurt the quality and I need to find the right balance between quantity and quality.

それにより、質が下がってしまうことに気づきました。そして、量と質の間で良いバランスを取ることが必要だと思っています。

I am sometimes too much a perfectionist.

私は完璧すぎることもあります。

As a result of this, I was occasionally behind the deadlines for my projects in the past.

その結果、過去にはプロジェクトの期日に遅れてしまうことがありました。

Now, I've learned to set early deadlines for myself, so that I will never miss the important due date.

現在は、自分自身に早めの期日を課し、重要な締切は決して逃さないようにしています。

I used to expect too much from subordinates.

私は部下に期待しすぎていました。

Now I understand how to delegate the workload effectively.

これで、仕事を効果的に委任する方法がわかりました。

I once expressed too much frustration with under-performing team members.

私はかつて、成績の悪いチームメンバーに不満を表しすぎていました。

I have improved my communication to have a better understanding of the problems other people have.

他の人たちが抱えている問題をよりよく理解できるよう、コミュニケーションを改善しました。

I am a perfectionist and was too critical of other people's work in the past.

私は完璧主義者であり、過去に他の人たちの仕事に批判的すぎました。

I was a bit too sensitive about claims from customers.

私は、顧客からのクレームに対して少し敏感すぎました。

Now I have sufficient experience to step back once and see the issue holistically.

今、私は一度戻って、問題を全体的に見るのに十分な経験があります。

4. 自分のキャリアの機会がどのようなものか前向きに 聞く（自分の夢を語る）　Track 74

I want to become a valued employee of a company.

私は会社にとって価値のある社員になりたいと考えています。

I want to make a difference and I'm willing to work hard to achieve this goal.

私は会社に変革をもたらし、この目標を達成できるよう一生懸命に働くつもりです。

I want to make a significant contribution to the growth of the company.

会社の成長に絶大な貢献をしたいと思っています。

I want to be an expert at my position and start training to be a department head.

担当分野の専門性に長け、部門長になるための教育を受け始めたいと考えています。

In two years or so, I hope to be working in increasingly responsible positions.

2年程度で、私はますます責任ある立場で働きたいと思っています。

My professional education has focused on, not only the technical aspects, but also on coaching people.

私の職業教育は、技術的側面だけでなく、人々を指導することにもフォーカスしてきました。

I am proud of being a great team player.

私は自分がすばらしいチームプレイヤーであることを誇りに思います。

I pride myself on my ability to quickly resolve conflicts among project members.

私はプロジェクトメンバー間の衝突を迅速に解決する能力に自信を持っています。

One of my greatest strengths is my intellectual curiosity.

私の最大の強みの1つは、私の知的好奇心です。

I enjoy researching the latest marketing trends and new business opportunities.

私は最新のマーケティング動向と新しいビジネスチャンスを研究するのを楽しんでいます。

I have developed my team player spirit through past projects working with a diversified group.

過去の多様な人材と働くプロジェクトを通じて、私自身のチームプレイヤーの精神を育成してきました。

I am fully prepared to take on any greater responsibilities as a manager.

私はマネージャーとして、より大きな責任を引き受ける準備が十分にできています。

In three years, I would like to become the best senior manager your company has.

3年間で、私は社内で最も優秀なシニアマネージャーになりたいと思います。

The management position in your company would be my dream job since your mission aligns perfectly with my goals.

御社のミッションは私の目標と完全に一致するので、御社のマネージメントのポジションは私の夢です。

My current and short-term goal is to develop my marketing and communications skills as a PR person for a global company like you.

現在および短期間の目標は、御社のようなグローバル企業の PR 担当者として、マーケティングとコミュニケーションスキルを伸ばすことです。

I would like to become a director or higher in the future. This might be a little ambitious.

将来、私はディレクターか、それ以上になりたいです。これは少し野心的すぎるかもしれません。

But I know I'll have a chance, and I'm willing to work hard.

しかしチャンスはあると思いますし、一生懸命に働く覚悟です。

I am so impressed with your open-minded culture.

私は御社のオープンマインドな文化にとても感銘を受けました。

I want my expertise to impact company performance in a positive way directly.

私は、私の専門知識が会社の業績に良い方向で直接影響を与えられるようにします。

I'm open to negotiate my working conditions.

労働条件については交渉したいと思います。

I appreciate your greater flexibility such as working from home.

御社の在宅勤務などの柔軟性を高く評価しています。

After learning about the work environment here, I felt this is exactly the type of place I want to work at.

御社の働く環境をお聞きし、こちらはまさに私が働きたいと思っていたタイプの職場だと感じています。

Chapter 4

5. 会社の環境やカルチャーが自分に合うか、適切な 言葉で聞き出す

What kind of training do you offer new managers?

新しいマネージャーにはどのような研修をしますか？

What are the people I'll be working with like?

私の同僚になる人たちはどんな感じの人たちですか？

Does this job usually move to other positions at the company?

この仕事は、通常、社内で別のポジションに異動することがあります か？

What type of management training do you provide here?

ここではどのようなマネージメントトレーニングがありますか？

How long is the training program?

トレーニングプログラムはどのくらいの期間ですか？

What opportunities for further advancement are available here?

ここでは、さらなる昇進の可能性はどのようなものがありますか？

How did this position become available?

このポジションはどのようにしてオープンになったのですか？

Is this a new position?

これは新しいポジションですか？

Which position has the previous employee transferred to?

前任者はどの役職に異動したのですか？

Is a written job description available?

文書にした職務記述書はありますか？

Please describe a typical day for this manager.

このマネージャーの典型的な1日を教えてください。

How does this position fit into the overall department structure?

このポジションは部門の全体の中でどのような位置づけですか？

Could you tell me more about the key day-to-day responsibilities of this management position?

この管理職の日々の重要な責務についてもっと教えてくださいますか？

Could you describe the culture of the company?

企業文化について教えてくださいますか？

How would you describe the culture of this organization?

この組織のカルチャーはどのようなものですか？

Where do you think the company is headed in the next five years?

今後5年間で、会社はどこに向かって行くと思いますか？

What are the biggest opportunities facing the department at this moment?

現時点で、この部門が直面している最大の機会は何ですか？

What do you like best about working in this organization?

この組織で働くことで、あなたは何が一番好きですか？

What will be the key factors which drive results in this job?

この仕事の結果を左右する主な要因は何ですか？

Would you describe the typical career path for someone in this role?

この仕事をした人の典型的なキャリアパスを教えてくださいますか？

How is this role expected to contribute to the company's highest priority?

この役割は会社の最優先事項にどのように貢献することが期待されていますか？

What do you expect me to accomplish in the first three months?

最初の３ヶ月に私が達成するように期待されることは何ですか？

What kind of career development plan does your company have?

御社ではどのようなキャリアの成長のプランをお持ちですか？

What are the best aspects of working in this company?

この会社で働くことの最も良い面は何ですか？

What do you see as unique about your company, compared with your major competitors?

主な競合他社に比べて、御社は何がユニークだと思いますか？

How are critical decisions made?

大事な決断はどのようになされますか？

How is this company financially doing in comparison with competitors?

この会社の業績は競合他社と比較して、どのような感じですか？

What is the company doing to maintain its market strength?

会社は市場優位性を維持するために、何をしていますか？

Do you know of any anticipated cutbacks in any departments in the near future?

近い将来、どこかの部門で人員削減を予定していますか？

What major problems has the company recently faced?

会社が最近直面した大きな問題は何ですか？

How many candidates have you interviewed for this position?

このポジションに対して、何名の志願者と面接をしていますか？

May I ask about the compensation for this position?

このポジションの報酬額について伺っていいですか？

When and how are employees evaluated?

社員はいつ、どのように評価されますか？

Could you explain your performance appraisal process?

業績評価プロセスについて説明してくださいますか？

How frequently do you evaluate your employees?

従業員をどのくらいの頻度で評価しますか？

Do you provide any bonuses directly linked to your performance?

パフォーマンスに直接関係するボーナスを提供していますか？

Who will be my direct report in this position?

このポジションで私の直属の上司は誰ですか？

Chapter 4

Is this position expected to work closely with a global team?

このポジションはグローバルチームと密接に働くことが期待されていますか？

Does this management position have a dotted line relationship with its headquarters?

このマネージメントポジションは本社にも報告する必要がありますか？

＊dotted line：仕事の関係で間接的に報告義務がある人を指す。
　solid（もしくは direct）line：直属の上司にあたる人を指す。

What are the most important criteria when you evaluate the daily performance of an employee?

社員の日々のパフォーマンスを評価する時、最も重要な基準は何ですか？

I prefer to keep a reasonable balance between work and life.

私は仕事と生活の適切なバランスを保ちたいと考えています。

It is my belief that I could be a more productive and valuable employee at work when I have sufficient time outside of work.

仕事以外で十分な時間があると、仕事でもより生産的で価値のある社員になると信念を持っています。

When I work, I have a full commitment to work to exceed expectations.

仕事する時は、私は期待を超えるために働くことに全力を尽くします。

Outside of work, I like to engage in my personal activities that I am passionate about.

仕事以外では、自分が情熱を傾けている個人的な活動に従事したいと考えています。

Could you describe the company's management style?

会社の経営スタイルについて教えてくださいますか？

Who does this manager report to?

このマネージャーの上司は誰ですか？

If I am offered this job, can I meet my team members before making my final decision?

この仕事のオファーをいただけた場合、最終の結論を出す前にチームメンバーにお会いすることはできますか？

What kind of fringe benefits are available?

どのような福利厚生が利用できますか？

How many employees do you have in the Tokyo office?

東京オフィスには何人の社員がいますか？

How many business trips per year does this position require?

このポジションは1年にどのくらい出張がありますか？

Is overseas relocation a possibility?

海外転勤は可能ですか？

What is the typical work week?

典型的な1週間はどのようなものですか？

What is the potential future for the advancement of this position?

このポジションの将来の昇進の可能性は何ですか？

How does this manager advance in the company?

このマネージャーは会社でどのように昇進していきますか？

Are there any examples of a career path beginning with this manager?

このマネージャーから始まるキャリアパスの例はありますか？

When can I expect to hear from you?

いつお返事をいただけますか？

Do you provide professional training opportunities?

専門的なトレーニングの機会を提供していますか？

What are the biggest challenges of this job?

この仕事の最大の課題は何ですか？

What's the most important skill I should have to be successful?

成功するための最も重要なスキルは何ですか？

How would you describe this company's values?

この会社の価値観をどのように説明しますか？

How has the company changed over the last decade?

過去 10 年間で、会社はどのように変化しましたか？

What are the company's plans for the development of employees?

社員を成長させるため、会社はどのような計画がありますか？

What are the biggest joys working for this company?

この会社で働いている最大の喜びは何ですか？

What's your least favorite part of working in this organization?

この組織で働くことで一番嫌いなことは何ですか？

What type of background do you think would be best suited for this position?

この役職にはどのようなタイプのバックグラウンドが最適だと思いますか？

How many references would you require?

レファレンスは何通必要ですか？

How soon would you like me to start if I get an offer?

オファーがあったら、どれくらい早くスタートする必要がありますか？

Could you tell me the characteristics that represent your company's values?

会社の価値を表す特性を教えてくださいますか？

What does success look like in this newly created position?

この新設されたポジションの成功とはどのようなものですか？

How are you planning to measure success?

成功をどのように測定する予定ですか？

Are there opportunities for cross-functional assignments?

部門を超えた配属の機会はありますか？

Who will I be working most closely with?

最も密接に仕事するのは誰ですか？

What will be the most challenging aspect for a new manager?

新しいマネージャーにとって、最も難しい側面は何ですか？

Is there anything about my experience that makes you question whether I am qualified for this position?

私の経験について、私はこのポジションの資格があるかどうか疑問に思うことはありますか？

What are some of the challenges this manager may face on a daily basis?

このマネージャーが日々直面する課題はどのようなものですか？

How long did the previous person hold the position?

前任者はどのくらいこのポジションにいましたか？

What is the personnel turnover in your organization?

御社の離職率はどのくらいですか？

What are you hoping people in this position will accomplish in the first year?

このポジションの人に最初の1年で成し遂げてほしいことは何ですか？

What type of people tend to really succeed in your company?

どのようなタイプの人が御社で本当に成功する傾向にありますか？

6. 転職の理由をポジティブに表現する　　　Track 76

I am interested in learning more about leading technology.

私は先端技術についてもっと学ぶことに興味を持っています。

This job provides an opportunity to leverage my current areas of expertise and further increase my skills as an engineer.

この仕事は私の現在の専門分野を活用し、エンジニアとしての私のスキルをさらに向上させる機会を与えてくれると期待しています。

I'm looking for a bigger challenge and to grow myself in a global environment.

私はもっと大きな挑戦を求め、そしてグローバルな環境の中で自分自身を成長させることを探しています。

I left my previous company so that I could give my full commitment to my job search.

就職活動に全力を尽くすことができるように、前の会社を辞めました。

I really enjoy developing junior employees.

若手社員の育成は、私にとって本当に楽しいものです。

Therefore, I am looking for an opportunity where I can focus more on this area.

従って、この分野にもっとフォーカスできる機会を探しています。

I have been relocated to this area due to family reasons and I left my previous position in order to make the move.

私は家族の都合でこの地域に引っ越して来ました。そのために以前の職を離れました。

I took two years of time-off to attend graduate school.

私は大学院に通うために２年間の仕事を休んでいました。

I would like to find a position with more opportunities.

私はもっといろいろな機会のあるポジションを見つけたいと考えています。

My current company was very small and didn't have opportunities for growth.

私の現在の会社はとても小さく、成長の機会がありませんでした。

The job with the current employer has a limited growth because the company is relatively small.

現在の会社での仕事は、会社が比較的小さいので、限られた成長しか望めません。

So, I have decided to look elsewhere to continue to grow.

ですから、私は成長し続けるために、どこか他に目を向けることにしました。

I had to leave my last position as our department was eliminated due to corporate restructuring upon merger.

合併による企業再編のため、私たちの部署は廃止されてしまい、前職を辞めなければなりませんでした。

I have learned a great deal in my current job, but now I am ready to assume a bigger responsibility as a manager.

私は現在の仕事で多くのことを学びましたが、今はマネージャーとして、より大きな責任を引き受ける準備ができています。

My current company is very large and it's difficult to do different tasks.

私の現在の会社はとても大きく、違うタスクをすることが難しいです。

I have routine work every day as a group leader.

私はグループリーダーとして、毎日決まった仕事をしています。

I would like to work in an environment where I can utilize more of my leadership skills.

私は自分のリーダーシップスキルをもっと活用できるような環境で仕事がしたいと考えています。

I am well prepared to move into a leadership position.

私は指導的立場になる準備ができています。

However, my current employer has very talented managers.

しかしながら、現在の雇用主は非常に有能な管理職を持っています。

I don't expect they will leave their positions anytime soon.

私は近いうちに空きが出るとは思っていません。

I would like to build on my people management skills by working in a diversified organization like you.

御社のような多様な人材が働く組織で働くことによって、人材管理の能力をより高めたいと考えています。

I am interested in learning more about global markets in this industry.

この業界のグローバル市場についてもっと知りたいと考えています。

This job provides an opportunity to leverage my current areas of expertise and increase my exposure to the global market.

この仕事は、私の現在の専門知識を活用し、グローバル市場により関わる機会を与えてくれると思います。

Your strength and focus in this technology are exactly matched with my expertise.

この技術における御社の強みとフォーカスは、まさに私の専門知識と一致しています。

I expect to increase my enjoyment and satisfaction with my work when I am able to work with you.

御社で働くことができたら、仕事の喜びと満足度が高まると考えています。

I have always enjoyed working with a great group of people on a challenging project.

私は常にチャレンジングなプロジェクトで大きなグループの人たちと働くことが好きです。

This opportunity in your company fits very well with my career desire to advance my project management skills.

御社のこの機会は、プロジェクトマネージメントのスキルを伸ばすという私のキャリアの夢とまさに合致します。

I was excited to see a job opening that's a perfect fit for my qualifications and expertise.

自分の資格と専門知識にぴったりの求人を見ることができて興奮しておりました。

This will be a great opportunity to utilize my technical skills in a new industry.

これは新しい業界で私の技術スキルを活用する絶好の機会と考えています。

Working in a start-up company, I wore many hats and had extensive experience.

スタートアップカンパニーで働いていたので、私は多くの役割を担い、幅広い経験をしてきました。

Now I'm looking for an opportunity to focus on this specialized area.

今度は、私はこの専門分野に集中する機会を探しています。

Chapter 4

I am confident that all the skills that I have developed from the current organization are transferable into this position.

現在の組織で培ったスキルは全て、このポジションに転用できると確信しています。

I have had wonderful opportunities to grow with my current employer for the last ten years.

過去10年間、現在の会社で成長するすばらしい機会を得てきました。

I have realized that this is the right timing to break my comfort area and take up new challenges in a different environment.

これは、私の快適な領域から離れ、異なる環境で新たな課題に取り組む良いタイミングだと考えています。

I would like to find a job closer to my new home.

私は新居のより近くでの仕事を探しています。

My current job is too far away to commute as a result of the office relocation.

私の現在の職場は移転した結果、通勤するのに遠くなってしまいました。

I am currently looking for a new opportunity that allows for scheduling flexibility when appropriate.

現在、必要に応じて柔軟にスケジュールを設定できる新しい機会を探しています。

7. 過剰にアグレッシブにならない程度に自分を売り込む
Track 77

One of my most important policies as a manager is to have open-door policies with their teams.

マネージャーとしての最も大事な方針の1つとして、チームメンバーがいつでも話に来られるようにしています。

I would like my members to feel comfortable to come to see me to discuss any issues.

メンバーには問題が起きた時に私に相談しやすいと感じてもらうようにしています。

I always respect my subordinates' opinions and collaborate with them to find the best solutions.

部下の意見を常に尊重し、最善の解決策を見つけるために彼らと協力しています。

I am highly motivated and willing to do difficult tasks.

私は大変やる気があり、難しい仕事を好みます。

I believe leadership skill is one of the must-have skills for everybody these days.

リーダーシップスキルは、最近では誰もが必要なスキルの1つと考えています。

I am sure that I would perfectly fit into this leadership position.

このリーダーのポジションに、私は完全に適していると確信しています。

I believe working as a project leader will prepare me to take on expanded management responsibilities in the future.

プロジェクトリーダーとして働くことで、将来的にマネージメントとしての責任を拡大できるようになると考えています。

I strongly feel that this position would be a good fit for me because of my excellent communication skills.

私の優れたコミュニケーションスキルから、このポジションに私が適任だという自信が大いにあります。

I am quite capable of dealing with pressure and stressful situations.

私はプレッシャーとストレスの多い状況に対処することが十分にできます。

My ultimate goal is to eventually become a department manager after I've proven my competencies in my analytical skills and team leadership.

私の最終的な目標は、分析スキルとチームでのリーダーシップの能力を証明した上で、部門長になることです。

When I have to handle stressful situations, I try to step back from the situation and examine all of the issues and viewpoints.

ストレスの多い状況に対処しなければならない時は、状況から一歩下がって、全ての問題と視点を検討するようにしています。

I find that the best way for me to control work stress is to do outdoor activities on weekends.

私が仕事のストレスを抑える最も良い方法は、週末にアウトドアの活動をすることです。

I like hiking and occasionally join local volunteer activities to take kids on a hike.

私はハイキングが好きで、時々子供たちをハイキングに連れて、地域のボランティア活動に参加しています。

As a result of having a broader perspective, I can reach win-win situations or reduce the overall stress of the situations.

より広い視野を持つことで、ウィン・ウィンの状況に到達し、また全体的なストレスを軽減することが可能となります。

I always stay focused on priorities and proceed one by one.

私は常に優先事項に集中し、1つずつ進めていきます。

I've had lots of experience working as a programmer.

プログラマーとして働いた経験が豊富です。

I am willing to work extra hours and will do what it takes to get the job done.

仕事を完了するには、残業することも厭いません。

I have also good ideas when and how to ask for help from my team members as well as from my supervisor.

いつ、どのようにして上司だけでなくチームメンバーから助けを求めればよいかもよく理解しています。

I am confident that I bring additional expertise that makes me the best person for this leadership position.

私はこのリーダーのポジションに最も適した、さらなる専門知識をもたらすと確信しています。

If I have a problem with subordinates, I believe it's very important to talk to them.

部下との間で問題が発生した場合、彼らと直接話すことがとても大事だと考えています。

It might be hard sometimes, but I try to communicate with them to solve the problems.

時には難しい場合もあると思いますが、彼らと直接話して問題を解決するようにします。

I've always been told that I'm a great supervisor to work with.

私はいつも一緒に働きやすい上司と言われています。

If I face any issue, I believe it is critical to listen well to others.

問題に直面した場合、他の人たちの話をよく聞くことが重要だと思います。

I am willing to do the task that is not on the job descriptions if needed.

必要であれば、職務記述書に記載されていないタスクを喜んで実行します。

One of my strengths is to provide clear directions to the team by clarifying priorities.

私の強みの１つは、優先順位を明確にしてチームに明確な指示を与えることです。

I am good at putting a plan into action and carry it out till the end.

私は計画を実行し、最後までそれを実行するのが得意です。

I am thinking about another offer I got, but I would like to keep my options open and learn about this opportunity.

別のオファーも考えていますが、選択肢を残して、この機会がどのようなものかも知りたいと思います。

One of my major accomplishments was to make a breakthrough product at my current company.

私の大きな成果の１つは、現在の会社で画期的な製品を出したことです。

I am confident to survive a tough environment with global players.

グローバル人材との厳しい環境でもうまくやって行く自信があります。

I will be able to leverage my expertise in sales and marketing to expand your overseas sales.

営業とマーケティングの専門知識を活用して、御社の海外での販売を拡大することができます。

With my managerial expertise, I am certain to successfully execute your organizational restructure.

私の経営上の専門知識により、御社の組織の再構築を成功裏に実行することを確信しています。

I have gained extensive knowledge of local regulations, which brings you a strong advantage.

私はローカルの規制に関する広範な知識を得ていて、それは御社の大きな強みになるでしょう。

I am always willing to take a challenging task and drive the results.

私は常にやりがいのある仕事を引き受け、結果を出したいと思っています。

I have led several cross-broader projects successfully.

複数のクロスブロードプロジェクトを成功裏に率いてきました。

I like taking time to learn new things to foster my personal growth.

時間をかけて新しいことを学び、自分の成長を促進するのが好きです。

Chapter 4

2 社内での昇進にチャレンジ

1. 自分が社内で達成してきたことを客観的に伝える
Track 78

I received the regional sales award for three years in a row.

私は3年間続けて地域販売賞を受賞しました。

I made a significant contribution to the increase of our branch sales by over 10% last year.

昨年、支店の売上が10%以上増加したことに大きな貢献をしました。

I found five new corporate customers and increased revenue by 20%.

5つの新しい法人顧客を見つけ、収益を20%増やしました。

I am always proactive in facing any client issue.

クライアントの問題に常に早急に取り組んでいます。

My team exceeded the monthly quota by 20% for twelve months in a row.

私のチームは、12ヶ月連続で月間クォータを20%超えました。

We have also successfully acquired three of the largest clients in our region.

また、私たちの地域で3つの最大のクライエントを獲得することに成功しました。

We have received no major complaints so far.

これまで大きな苦情はありません。

I have successfully negotiated with our supplier to reduce the cost by 5% this year.

今年、コストを 5 ％削減するために、サプライヤーとうまく交渉しました。

My team made a successful deal with company ABC and boosted our profit by 10%.

私のチームは ABC 社との取引を成功させ、利益を 10 ％押し上げました。

I am leading the company-wide project to reduce the operating cost by 3% every year.

会社全体のプロジェクトを率いて、毎年 3 ％の運用コストを削減しています。

The profitability analysis by our team has successfully identified the area for improvement.

私たちのチームによる収益性分析により、改善すべき領域が首尾よく特定されました。

I have successfully led the global team to introduce a standardized accounting system.

グローバルチームが標準化された会計システムを導入することに成功しました。

We have timely implemented a new communication tool to improve our company-wide communication.

全社的なコミュニケーションを改善するために、新しいコミュニケーションツールをタイムリーに導入しました。

We have simplified the client application procedures.

クライアントアプリケーションの手順を簡略化しました。

As a result of this, the satisfaction of our clients has significantly improved last year.

この結果、昨年のお客様の満足度は大幅に向上しました。

I led to reducing the back-office workload by eliminating redundant works.

余分な業務を排除することで、バックオフィスの作業負荷を削減しました。

Because of this effort, we achieved a 20% headcount reduction.

その努力の結果、20％の人員削減を達成しました。

I took a project which successfully reduced our paper usages by 20% this year.

今年は、紙の使用量を20％削減するプロジェクトを実施しました。

My idea of having once a month's department meeting has received extremely positive comments from my team.

毎月1回の部門会議を開催するという私の考えは、チームから非常に好評です。

My greatest accomplishment in the organization was the development of the company's new web site.

この組織での私の最大の成果は、会社の新しいウェブサイトの開発でした。

One of my accomplishments this year was recruiting five new excellent talents.

今年の私の成果の1つは、新しい5人の優秀な人材を採用したことです。

I have successfully trained my successor as a manager.

私はマネージャーとして、後継者を育てることに成功しています。

As a team manager, I learned the importance of setting clear goals for the team.

チームマネージャーとして、チームに明確な目標を設定することの重要性を学びました。

I have consistently encouraged the team to work toward those goals.

私は一貫して、チームがこれらの目標に向かって取り組むよう奨励しています。

I also learned a positive impact on employee satisfaction when the manager's direction is clear and timely communicated.

また、マネージャーの指示が明確でタイムリーに伝えられている場合、従業員の満足度にプラスの影響があることも学びました。

Since I took over this position, employee satisfaction has increased by over 15% in my department.

私がこの役職を引き継いでから、従業員の満足度は私の部門で15%以上、向上しました。

I also reduced the overall overtime work for my department by 20% last year.

また、昨年、部門の残業時間全体を20%削減しました。

Sales and profitability have both increased by over 8%.

売上と収益性の両方が8%以上、増加しました。

One of my strengths is project management skills.

私の強みの1つは、プロジェクト管理スキルです。

I have leveraged this skill to lead several company-wide projects for the last three years.

私はこのスキルを活用して、過去3年間に渡って、いくつかの会社全体のプロジェクトを率いてきました。

I have led the business development project which focused on improving our social media.

私はソーシャルメディアの改善に焦点を当てた事業開発プロジェクトを率いてきました。

We have updated our website design and developed a plan on how to utilize our social media.

ウェブサイトのデザインを更新し、ソーシャルメディアの活用方法に関する計画を策定しました。

We accomplished the dramatic increase in visitors to our site in less than six months.

当社のサイトへの訪問者の劇的な増加を6ヶ月未満で達成しました。

Consequently, sales have improved substantially.

その結果、売上は大幅に改善しました。

I have exceeded my KPIs every year for the last ten years.

過去10年間、KPIを毎年達成しています。

＊KPI（Key Performance Indicator）「重要業績評価指標」
　目標を達成する上で、その達成度合を計測するための定量的な指標。

I have been promoted three times in the last ten years.

私は過去10年間で、3回昇進しています。

Whenever we have a cross-functional global team, I could lead them successfully.

部門を超えたグローバルチームを持った時はいつも、彼らをうまく導くことができました。

One of my strengths is to get cross-functional project members on the same page.

私の長所の1つは、部門を超えたプロジェクトメンバーを、1つにまとめることです。

I've regularly brushed up my management skills through feedback from my team members.

チームメンバーからのフィードバックを通じて、管理スキルを定期的に磨いています。

I have taken any challenge as a chance to grow myself.

私はどんなチャレンジも自分自身を成長させるチャンスとして受けとめています。

I appreciate candid feedback from my supervisor as an opportunity for improvement.

上司からの率直なフィードバックを改善のための機会と思っています。

I have taken time to review my 360-degree feedback to identify my area for improvement.

私は自分の改善すべきエリアを特定するために、360度のフィードバックを時間をかけて確認しています。

Since I started managing my team, I have increased the employee retention by 30% over three years.

私のチームの管理を開始してから、3年間に渡って従業員の定着率が30％向上しました。

In my current role, my initiatives have streamlined the entire process and reduced the overtime work by 15%.

現職では、全体のプロセスを効率させ、残業時間を15％削減するイニシアチブをとりました。

2. 自分が昇進後のポジションにいかにふさわしいかを アピールする　　　　　　Track 79

After three years in my current position, I have learned about how to succeed in this competitive industry.

現在のポジションを3年間経験して、この競争の激しい業界でいかに成功するかを学びました。

I am ready to contribute more to increase our market share in the overseas market.

海外市場でのシェアの拡大に、より貢献する準備ができています。

I would like to use my leadership skills to lead a bigger group.

より大きなグループを率いるために、リーダーシップスキルを活用したいです。

I am confident to take the head of the Sales team to achieve the company's client acquisition goals.

会社の顧客獲得目標を達成するため、営業チームのトップになる自信があります。

I regard this opportunity will be a perfect fit for my career desires.

この機会は私のキャリアの要望に完全にフィットすると考えています。

I am passionate about supporting junior members.

若手メンバーをサポートすることに情熱を感じています。

I am good at providing mentoring to subordinates.

部下のメンターになるのが得意です。

Chapter 4

287

I am ready to make valuable contributions to the company by assuming a senior role.

よりシニアなポジションになり、会社に価値のある貢献をしたいと考えています。

My extensive experience with project management has significantly developed my problem-solving skills.

私のプロジェクトマネジメントの広範な経験は、私の問題解決能力を大きく向上させました。

I deeply understand the value of active listening.

アクティブリスニングが非常に大事だと考えています。

I am eager to listen to diversified ideas from different groups of people.

私は、様々なグループの人々からの多様なアイデアを聞きたいと思っています。

I like the collaborative atmosphere in this organization that further advances my career.

この組織の協力的な環境が好きで、さらにキャリアを伸ばして行きたいと考えています。

I find this organization reasonably competitive as well as very attractive.

この組織は、非常に魅力的であるだけでなく、かなり競争力があると考えています。

I worked as a manager at one of my retail stores and gained market insights.

私は小売店の1つでマネージャーとして働き、市場の洞察を得てきました。

After three years as a manager, I have learned that communication is critical.

マネージャーとしての3年間の後、コミュニケーションが重要だということを学びました。

By scheduling a weekly meeting, I have improved communication with other departments.

毎週のミーティングを予定することで、他部門とのコミュニケーションを改善してきました。

I am certain that better communications have contributed to realizing the department goal.

より良いコミュニケーションが部門の目標達成に貢献したと確信しています。

I have learned the importance of listening to the needs of my subordinates.

部下の要望に耳を傾けることの大事さを学んできました。

I always make sure to provide the necessary resources for my team to achieve their goals.

私のチームが目標を達成するために必要なリソースを提供するように常に心がけています。

I appreciate any candid feedback as I still have room for further improvement.

私にも改善の余地がありますので、率直なフィードバックに感謝しています。

I would like to create a collaborative and trusting team environment.

協力的で信頼できるチーム環境を作りたいと考えています。

My previous manager told me how to provide constructive criticism where needed.

先の上司は、必要な場合には建設的な批判をどのように提供するかを教えてくれました。

I understand the importance of providing timely feedback to the team members.

チームメンバーにはタイムリーなフィードバックをすることが大切だと理解しています。

Candid feedback is extremely valuable for personal development.

率直なフィードバックは、個人の成長に非常に価値があります。

I always make sure to communicate my feedback in a positive and constructive way.

私のフィードバックは前向きで建設的な形で伝えるように常に心がけています。

I highly value my current responsibility as a sales manager.

セールスマネージャーとしての現在の責任に高い価値を感じています。

On the other hand, the position does not provide opportunities for growth that align with my career goals.

一方、このポジションは私のキャリアの目標に合致する成長の機会を与えてくれません。

I am ready to advance my career by taking this position to fulfill my career goals.

キャリアの目標を達成するためにこのポジションを得て前進したいと思います。

When I began looking for a new position, I purposefully sought out the position that increases global exposure.

新しいポジションを探し始めた時、私は敢えてグローバルな露出を増やすポジションを探しました。

I would like to use my overseas experience and be a part of the new business development team.

海外での経験を生かして、新しいビジネス開発チームの一員になりたいと考えています。

I am perfectly fit for the position as proven by my ability to lead a diversified group.

私は多様なグループをリードする能力を実証済みで、このポジションにまさに適任です。

I have a strong belief in our products and know exactly how I could drive even greater results.

私は私たちの製品を強く信じており、さらに大きな成果を上げる方法をまさに知っています。

In my previous role as an office manager, I came up with several ideas for cost reduction.

以前のオフィスマネージャーとしての役割で、コスト削減のためのいくつかのアイデアを思いつきました。

I always look for an opportunity to further use my personal skills to lead a bigger team.

私は自分のスキルをさらに活用して、より大きなチームをリードする機会を常に探しています。

Chapter 4

I learned people management skills in my previous career that helped me become a good manager.

私は、以前のキャリアで人事管理スキルを学びました。これは優れたマネージャーになるのに役立ちました。

The technical skills that I have developed are well transferable to this position.

私が開発した技術的スキルは、このポジションに十分に転用できます。

Currently, I feel that I'm ready for another stage in my career that brings a new challenge.

現在、私は自分のキャリアの中で新たな挑戦をもたらす別の段階の準備ができていると感じています。

I would like to use my sales experience to become an effective marketer for the company.

営業経験を活かして、会社の効果的なマーケティング担当者になりたいです。

The negotiation skills that I have developed over the past few years can add value to the team to survive the competition.

過去数年に渡って私が開発した交渉スキルは、競争に勝つためにチームに価値を加えることができます。

The company is now facing tougher competition.

同社は現在、より厳しい競争に直面しています。

I have several ideas on how to recover our market share.

市場シェアを回復する方法について、いくつかのアイデアがあります。

I have organized brainstorming sessions with my team to identify several process improvements.

チームとのブレインストーミングセッションを開催して、プロセスの改善点をいくつか特定しました。

I always make sure to execute and implement the new processes.

私は常に新しいプロセスを導入するために実行するようにします。

Our process has become the best practice for the entire company.

我々のプロセスは、会社全体のベストプラクティスとなっています。

I feel I have done a lot with my current role and would like to be transferred to a new department.

私は自分の現在の役割で多くを成し遂げたと感じており、新しい部署に異動したいと思っています。

With my extensive knowledge about the company and our products, I should stand out from other candidates.

会社と製品についての広範な知識があるので、私は他の候補者よりも際立つはずです。

I regard customer understanding as the most important quality for this position to be successful.

このポジションを成功させるには、顧客の理解が最も重要な品質だと思います。

I am confident to have this knowledge more than anyone else.

私は他の誰よりもこの知識を持っていると確信しています。

I have seen the change in the market trend for the last several years and ready to meet the new trend.

過去数年間、市場のトレンドに変化を見てきて、新しいトレンドに対応する準備ができています。

I would like to be senior management in ten years and this position will be a perfect step for this.

私は10年後に上級管理職になりたいと思います。このポジションはこのための完璧なステップになります。

I have a collaborative relationship with everyone in the organization.

組織内の全員と協力関係を結んでいます。

This will help me lead this cross-function project.

これは、この部門を超えたプロジェクトをリードするのに役立ちます。

How can I make the position better than the past?

この役割をこれまでより改善するにはどうすればよいですか？

Do you have any reservations about my capability for this role?

この役割に対する私の能力について、何か保留することはありますか？

I have a collaborative leadership style, which has been highly regarded by others.

私は、他の人たちから高く評価されている協調的なリーダーシップスタイルを持っています。

What type of profile do you expect the perfect candidate to have?

完璧な候補者にはどのようなタイプのプロフィールを期待していますか？

What are the potential concerns that might stop you from the selection?

選定を妨げる可能性のある懸念は何ですか？

I would like to make this move to be a big step forward for me in terms of both responsibility and compensation.

責任と報酬の両面で、この異動を私にとって大きな前進にしたいと思っています。

As I mentioned during my interview process, I am ready to take up a bigger management responsibility.

面接プロセスで述べたように、私はより大きな管理責任を引き受ける準備ができています。

I will be speaking with a couple of other companies if I don't get this opportunity.

この機会を得られない場合は、他のいくつかの企業と話すつもりです。

Chapter 4

If I don't get this position, I am happy to continue in the current role.

この役職に就けない場合は、現在の役割を継続させていただきます。

I am willing to apply for a similar position again in the future by further developing myself.

私は自分自身をさらに成長させ、将来同様の職に再び応募したいと思っています。

I am eager to get this promotion.

ぜひこの昇進を得たいと思っています。

If not, I would think about my career opportunities once again.

得られない場合、自分のキャリアの機会についてもう一度考えたいと思います。

I would like to follow up regarding our conversation about the potential job transfer.

配置転換の可能性についてお話ししたことをフォローアップしたいと思います。

Would you please update the selection process?

選定過程がどうなっているか教えていただけますか？

I recall you mentioned the management will make a decision by the end of last month.

先月の終わりまでに経営陣が決定を下すとおっしゃっていたと思います。

I just wanted to check to see where you are in that process.

どのような状況か、ちょっと確認したかったのです。

Thank you in advance. I look forward to hearing from you.

よろしくお願いいたします。ご連絡いただけるのをお待ちしています。

＊Thank you in advance.「よろしくお願いいたします」（依頼する時など）

I must say I am deeply disappointed to hear the decision.

決定を聞いて、非常にがっかりしていますと言わざるを得ません。

I wish I could have assumed this role.

この役割を引き受けられたら良かったと思います。

Are there valid reasons for declining my application?

私の応募が通らなかった特定の理由がありますか？

Thank you very much for taking the time to consider my application.

私の要望を検討するお時間をとっていただき、どうもありがとうございます。

Could I have some feedback behind this selection?

今回の選定についてのフィードバックをいただけますか？

Could you explain how the decision was made?

どのように決断がなされたのか教えていただけますか？

Could you give me some examples of where I should improve further?

どの辺をさらに改善すれば良いのか、具体的な例をいただけますか？

I would like to have the opportunity to discuss my development plan separately.

私の成長の計画については別途お話しする機会をいただきたいと思います。

Please note that I would like to consider another opportunity as they arise.

別の機会があれば、また検討したいと考えています。

I am truly excited by this opportunity to work together in the future.

これからも一緒に働くことに本当に興奮しています。

I am sure to keep working hard toward company goals and grow my personal responsibilities.

私は、会社の目標に向けて一生懸命に努力し続け、自分の責任を果たすことを確信しています。

I would be grateful if you consider the salary adjustment at this opportunity.

この機会に、給与調整をご検討していただければ幸いです。

I would prefer not to leave the company, even if I don't get this promotion this time.

今回はこのプロモーションを得られなくても、会社を辞めたくはないと考えています。

I would appreciate it if we spent some time to discuss my compensation at the next performance review meeting.

次回のパフォーマンスレビュー会議で報酬を議論するためにお時間を割いていただければ幸いです。

I would like to set a short meeting to discuss my salary increase.

昇給について話し合うための短い会議を設定したいと思います。

I'm excited to talk about some of my recent accomplishments with you.

最近の成果について、あなたとお話しできることを楽しみにしています。

Thank you for your time to discuss my recent contribution and salary.

私の最近の貢献と給与についてお話しする時間をありがとうございます。

Based on my research, the average salary of this position is quite competitive in this industry.

私が調べたところ、この業界のこのポジションの平均給与は非常に競争力の高いものです。

I found that the current market offers significantly higher salaries to a similar position.

私は、現在のマーケットは同様のポジションにかなり高い給与を提供していると思います。

I have researched salaries for a similar position in the industry.

私は業界で同様のポジションの給与について調べてみました。

It looks like my current salary is below the mid-point.

私の現在の給与は中間点を下回っているようです。

It has been three years since I joined this team as a manager.

私がマネージャーとしてこのチームに加わってから3年が経ちました。

I would like to revisit my salary now that I'm assuming significantly broader responsibilities.

大幅に幅広い責任を負うようになっているので、給与についてお話ししたいと思います。

As you know, I brought significant value to the company by leading the successful new product launch.

ご存知のように、私は新製品の発売を成功させることで会社に大きな価値をもたらしました。

As you know, I have consistently exceeded my sales objectives.

ご存知のように、私は一貫して販売目標を超えています。

Considering my performance results and years of experience, I believe a salary increase of 5% is appropriate.

私の業績と長年の経験を考慮して、5％の昇給が適切であると考えています。

Since my last salary adjustment, I have successfully led several projects that have added significant value to the company.

前回の給与調整以来、私は会社に大きな価値をもたらした、いくつかのプロジェクトを成功裏に率いてきました。

I would highly appreciate it if you could reflect this contribution for the next pay increase.

この貢献を次回の昇給に反映できれば幸いです。

I would be more comfortable if you could give a one-time bonus reflecting my contribution this year.

今年の私の貢献を反映した1回限りのボーナスをいただければ、さらにうれしいです。

I would like to find out whether I am being fairly compensated.

私はフェアな報酬を受けているかどうか確認したいと思います。

I would like to request compensation adjustments to match the compensation for similar positions.

同様のポジションの報酬と一致するように、報酬の調整をお願いしたいと思います。

I have more than ten years of experience in retail sales.

私は小売販売で10年以上の経験があります。

In addition, I have worked in leadership positions for the past six years.

そして、過去6年に渡ってリーダーのポジションにいます。

In my last role, I increased the branch sales by nearly 40% year over year.

前の役職では、支店の売上を前年比でほぼ40％増やしました。

Given my experience and expertise, I would like to request slightly higher salaries than your proposal.

私の経験と能力を考慮して、現在ご提案いただいているよりも少し高い給与をお願いしたいと思います。

I know I can bring a great deal of value to you.

私は御社に多大な価値をもたらすことができます。

I am confident to help you exceed your revenue targets every year.

毎年、収益目標を超えることに貢献できると確信しています。

I understand that the market for people with my skill set is slightly higher than what you offer this time.

私のスキルセットを持つ人材の市場は、今回ご提示いただいているものより少し高いと思います。

I was a little surprised at the base salary.

基本給のレベルに少し驚きました。

I must say it came lower than what I've seen in the job market.

ジョブマーケットで見るよりも低いと言わざるを得ません。

Do you provide any incentive bonuses?

インセンティブボーナスがあるのですか？

As for the compensation, is the current offer flexible at all?

報酬についてですが、現在の条件は変更の余地はありますか？

Before I can accept your offer, I want to talk about the proposed compensation.

お申し出を受ける前に、ご提案いただいた報酬について話したいと思います。

It would be great if you provide an additional one-week paid vacation.

追加の1週間の有給休暇をいただけたらうれしいです。

I would like to take a couple of days to consider your offer if you don't mind.

可能であれば、数日かけてオファーを検討したいと思います。

This is a major life decision, and I would like to discuss it with my family.

これは人生の大きな決断ですので、家族と話し合いたいと思います。

I would like to request one week to consider it.

検討のために1週間いただけたらと思います。

I would be eager to accept this offer if you are able to allow me to work from home when feasible.

可能な限り自宅から仕事をすることを許していただけるなら、このオファーを受けます。

Would it be possible for you to consider a signing bonus for me?

契約時のボーナスを考慮することは可能でしょうか？

I am open to discussing alternative compensation, if possible.

可能であれば、別の形での報酬について話したいと思います。

Are there any opportunities for stock options or additional performance-based bonuses?

ストックオプションや、パフォーマンスベースのボーナスを追加する機会はありますか？

Are there any specific skills I should develop before requesting a promotion?

昇進をリクエストする前に、伸ばす必要がある特定のスキルはありますか？

Could I assume that you have been satisfied with my overall performance?

私の全体的なパフォーマンスに満足していると思いますか？

Could I have a better time to discuss this topic again in the near future?

近い将来、このトピックについて再度議論する、より良い時間があるでしょうか？

I would like to schedule a time for us to discuss how I can move ahead at this company.

この会社で私がどのように前進できるかを議論する時間をスケジュールしたいと思います。

I would like to sit down with you to talk about my career path in this company.

この会社での私のキャリアパスについて、あなたとお話ししたいと思います。

I'm eager to hear your thoughts on how management sees my recent performance.

経営陣が私の最近の業績をどのように見ているかについて、あなたの考えを聞きたいと思います。

What would be the best way to get promoted?

昇進する最善の方法は何でしょうか？

Could you give me some advice on how I can get a broader responsibility here?

ここでより広い責任を果たす方法についてアドバイスをいただけますか？

What do you think we should do?

私たちは何をすべきだと思いますか？

I understand that the budget is tight this year.

今年は予算が厳しいことを理解しています。

What can we do to find a solution that works for both of us?

私たち両方に有効なソリューションを見つけるために何ができますか？

I understand you don't have a budget this year to accept my salary increase.

今年、私の給与の増加を受け入れる予算がないことを理解しています。

Are you generally in agreement to raise my compensation?

一般的に私の報酬を上げることに同意していますか？

Would you be able to make it happen next year?

来年、それを実現できますか？

I am pleased to hear that you agree that my request for a pay increase is appropriate.

私の昇給要求が適切であることに同意していただいたことを聞いてうれしく思います。

Chapter 4

ビジネスシーンの英会話は
大げさなくらいがちょうどいい

　「はじめに」でも少し触れましたが、ビジネスシーンで使う英語は、多少大げさなくらいがちょうどいいことが多いものです。

　一般的に、欧米人は健全な議論を好みます。子供の頃から、自分の意見を持って、人と反対の意見を言うことが普通のことです。
　議論をすることが、より良い結果に導くプロセスの一つという考え方が、ビジネスシーンにも浸透しています。彼らを相手にしていると、遠慮した表現で反対意見を述べても、簡単に論破されてしまいます。
　この案件は正確に理解してもらいたい、この問題は真剣に考えてほしいという場合は、**思い切って大げさに、アサーティブに**（自信を持って断言するように）伝えてみましょう。
　「この件は、ちょっと心配です。」というような場合の"ちょっと"はなし、「あなたがこの問題を過少評価するのは問題かもしれない。」よりも、「あなたはこの問題を過小評価すべきではない。」と言い切るようなイメージです。
　私自身、自分が英語で話したことを、後から日本語にして反芻してみると、すごく強いことを言っていると驚くことがあります。

　一方、**どんな時でも相手の立場を尊重し、失礼な言い方はしない**、そして前向きな姿勢を崩さない限り、後に引きずるような関係悪化に至ったことは一度もありません。
　どんなに議論が白熱しても、その話題が終われば、あっけらかんとしているのが普通です。そのようなものだと割り切って、リーダーはメンタルを強く持って、日々議論に臨んでください。

Chapter 5

ビジネスを急成長させるための
最強フレーズ

　欧米社会では初対面の時、自分の言葉で相手の印象に残る自己紹介をすることが
重要視されています。欧米人との商談・交渉に臨む際には、提案事項や論点を、ロ
ジカルにまとめて話すように心がけることが成功の秘訣です。一方、ストレートす
ぎる表現は反感を買うことがあるので要注意です。

1 効果的な自己紹介

1. 初対面の挨拶、社名やポジションを伝える　Track 81

Hello, Mr. Smith.
スミスさん、こんにちは。

I'm Ken Saito.
サイトウ・ケンと申します。

I'm Masataka Tanaka, but please call me Masa.
タナカ・マサタカです。マサと呼んでください。

It's very nice to meet you.
お会いできてとてもうれしいです。

It's a pleasure to meet you.
お会いできてうれしいです。

I'm pleased to finally meet you.
やっとお会いできてうれしいです。

It is great to meet you at last after all those emails.
メールのやり取りだけでしたが、遂に初めてお会いできてうれしいです。

I just wanted to introduce myself. I'm Ken Sato.
自己紹介をさせていただきます。サトウ・ケンです。

I don't think we have formally met yet, my name is Ken Sato.
まだ正式にご挨拶する機会がありませんでした。私はサトウ・ケンです。

I would like you to meet Mr. Kato from my company.

我社のカトウさんをご紹介します。

He is our Marketing Manager.

彼はマーケティングマネージャーです。

Let me introduce you to my supervisor.

上司をご紹介させていただきます。

He is in charge of the entire East Asia operation.

彼は東アジア全体のオペレーションの責任者です。

Who do you work for?

お仕事は何ですか？

I work for ABC company.

ABC 社に勤めています。

I work as an accountant at the ABC company.

ABC 社で経理をしています。

I'm in charge of marketing at the ABC company, just outside Tokyo.

東京の郊外にある ABC 社でマーケティングを担当しています。

I'm in charge of the sales department.

セールス部門の責任者です。

I am responsible for R&D.

R&D の責任者です。

I am responsible for this global project.

私がこのグローバルプロジェクトの責任者です。

I head the HR Department at the ABC company.

ABC 社の人事部門の責任者です。

I manage the project team in the sales department.

営業部でプロジェクトチームを取りまとめています。

I am a chief accountant, leading 3 team members.

チーフアカウンタントで、3名のチームメンバーを率いています。

I report to the Head of Finance.

財務部長が上司です。

I joined this company 10 years ago.

この会社には 10 年前に入りました。

I have worked for this company all my life.

私はずっとこの会社で働いています。

I have spent more than 10 years in this industry.

この業界に 10 年以上います。

I speak English and Spanish fluently.

英語とスペイン語を流暢に話します。

I am self-employed and manage a consulting firm.

私は自営業でコンサルティング会社を経営しています。

I have just launched a start-up company.

ちょうどスタートアップの会社を立ち上げました。

I run my own business.

自営業です。

My family runs a retail store.

家族で小売業を経営しています。

I am now with an insurance company.

私は今、保険会社で働いています。

We are based in Tokyo.

私たちの拠点は東京です。

My company is based in Tokyo, but I myself travel a lot to help clients all over Japan.

私の会社は東京にありますが、私自身は各地のクライエントを助けるために、日本中をまわっています。

2. 自分の経験やスキルをアピールする   Track 82

We specialize in Consumer Marketing.

私たちは消費者マーケティングの専門です。

I specialize in digital marketing.

私はデジタルマーケティングを専門としています。

I've got 15 years' worth of experience in Marketing.

私は 15 年間のマーケティングの経験があります。

I am about to complete my part-time MBA.

パートタイム MBA を修了しようとしています。

I previously worked in a similar industry overseas.

以前は海外の同様の業界で働いていました。

What I'm good at is making an effective web advertisement.

私が得意なことは、効果的なウェブ広告を作成することです。

My professional expertise is to develop a cost-cutting strategy.

私の専門知識はコスト削減戦略を立てることです。

I'm passionate about developing talents.

私は人材開発に情熱をもって取り組んでいます。

I'm the project manager for the Japan team and coordinate our teams in the Tokyo, Osaka, and Nagoya sites.

私は日本チームのプロジェクトマネージャーで、東京、大阪、名古屋支店のチームをまとめています。

I have a lot of talent on my team.

私のチームには有能な人材がたくさんいます。

Outside of my work, I am really into yoga.

仕事以外では、ヨガにはまっています。

I like golf quite a lot.

私はゴルフがとても好きです。

I play myself and enjoy watching professional tournaments as well.

自分でプレイしますし、プロのトーナメント戦の観戦も好きです。

3. 印象づける自社紹介のフレーズ　　Track 83

We're the number one private company in Tokyo.

当社は東京で一番のプライベートカンパニーです。

We're a small consulting company, specializing in retail business.

当社はリテールビジネスに特化した、小規模なコンサルティング会社です。

We're in manufacturing.

我々は製造業です。

Our main business is sales consulting.

当社のメインビジネスはセールスコンサルティングです。

He is an expert in consulting small business.

彼は中小企業のコンサルティングの専門家です。

We're in the marketing business.

我々はマーケティング業界にいます。

We've been in business for 10 years.

当社が創業して 10 年です。

We've been in business since 2010.

当社は 2010 年からビジネスしています。

Our sales are expanding rapidly in the Chinese market.

当社の売上は中国市場で急激に拡大しています。

Our sales are expanding by more than 10% every year.

当社の売上は毎年10%以上、拡大しています。

We have offices in both Tokyo and Osaka.

当社は東京と大阪の両方にオフィスがあります。

We have a long-term business relationship with Sony.

我社はソニーと長期に渡って取引しています。

Our competitors are Panasonic and Hitachi.

我社の競合社はパナソニックや日立です。

We can help your organization improve productivity through our consulting.

当社のコンサルティングで、御社の生産性を改善することができます。

4. スマートに連絡先を交換して会話を終える　Track 84

Let me give you one of my business cards.

こちらが私の名刺です。

My contact information is on my business card.

私の連絡先は名刺にあります。

May I have your business card?

お名刺をいただけますか？

What is the best way to contact you?

どのようなご連絡方法が一番良いですか？

How can I reach you?

どのようにご連絡できますか？

It was a pleasure to talk with you.

あなたとお話しできて楽しかったです。

It's a pleasure talking to you.

あなたとお話しできて楽しかったです。

It was very nice to meet you.

お会いできて良かったです。

I hope we meet again soon.

近いうちにまたお会いできますように。

I would like to schedule a meeting with you.

あなたとミーティングを予定したいです。

I look forward to working with you.

これからどうぞよろしくお願いいたします。

I look forward to hearing from you.

あなたからのご連絡をお待ちしています。

I look forward to seeing you next Friday.

次の金曜日にお会いするのを楽しみにしています。

This has been a great opportunity to get to know you better.

今回はあなたを良く知ることができたすばらしい機会でした。

2 商談・交渉

We appreciate you taking time out of your busy schedules to meet us today.

本日は、お忙しいスケジュールの中からお会いするお時間をいただき、ありがとうございます。

We are excited to have this opportunity to meet with you today.

本日お話する機会を持つことができ、うれしく思います。

It's a great pleasure to have a face-to-face meeting finally after the series of emails.

一連のメールを経てようやく対面でのミーティングをすることができ、とてもうれしいです。

Today we are going to talk about new business opportunities.

今日は新規ビジネスの機会について話します。

We are glad that you could come.

来ていただいてありがとうございます。

It's our great pleasure to welcome you to our head office in Tokyo.

東京の本社に来ていただいて、大変うれしく思います。

We hope we will have a great discussion.

良いディスカッションにしましょう。

Let's begin the discussion with the most important topic.

一番大事な話題から話しましょう。

Let's tackle the most important topics first.

最初に最重要項目から取り組みましょう。

I would like to outline our aims and objectives first.

最初に目標と目的の概要を説明します。

I would like to begin by suggesting the following agenda.

まず以下のアジェンダを提案します。

Does that sound OK to you?

大丈夫そうですか？

I think we should establish the overall schedule.

まずは全体的なスケジュールを立てたほうがいいですね。

This meeting will be a valuable opportunity to talk about pending issues.

この会議は、懸案事項について話す貴重な機会となります。

We would like to follow up on our previous conference call discussion.

以前の電話会議の議論をフォローアップしたいと思います。

We would like to use this opportunity to have a better understanding of what's on your mind.

この機会を利用して、あなた方のお考えをよりよく理解したいと思います。

I would appreciate your candid opinions as they will help us to serve you better in the future.

将来のより良いサービスを提供させていただくために、率直なご意見をお願いします。

As we go forward, we would like your comments and questions.

話している最中、コメントや質問などをお願いします。

Well, let's get down to business.

それでは、始めましょう。

With your inputs, we know for sure that we're on track to help your business.

インプットをいただく中で、お役に立つ話が出ているか確認したいと思います。

We are here today to do everything we can to help to be more profitable.

今日は御社の利益をより改善するためにできることをここでお話しします。

As this is our first meeting, let me begin with our brief company history.

今回が初めてのミーティングなので、弊社の簡単な歴史から始めさせていただきます。

As you know, our company has been expanding our market share in North America.

ご存知のように、当社は北米での市場シェアを拡大しています。

We are looking for a global partnership to expand our business.

私たちはビジネスを拡大するためのグローバルなパートナーシップを探しています。

As explained in our previous correspondence, we are looking for a business partner to drive our growth in this market.

先にお知らせしました通り、当社はこの市場における当社の成長を促進するためにビジネスパートナーを探しています。

Here are what we see as the biggest challenges.

当社が最も大きなチャレンジと考えているのは以下です。

We have prepared a list of the discussion points for today's discussion.

今日のディスカッションの議論のポイントをリストで準備しました。

Our aim today is to agree on a fair condition that suits both parties.

私たちの今日の目的は、両者に適した公正な条件に同意することです。

2. 自社の商品やサービスを紹介・提案する　　Track 86

We would like to introduce our new product.

当社の新製品を紹介します。

We have just launched a variety of new products.

当社はいろいろな新商品を発売したところです。

We will need about 30 minutes to introduce our new product.

新製品を紹介するのに 30 分程度必要です。

Our product has many advantages over those of our competitors.

我々の製品は、他社の製品より多くの良い点があります。

I would like to give you an outline of our new features.

新しい特徴の概要を説明させていただきたいと思います。

Let us explain our proposal today.

本日は我々の提案をご説明させてください。

It is excellent in durability.

耐久性に優れています。

You can reduce your production costs by 8 percent.

生産コストを8％下げることができます。

How does this sound to you?

いかがでしょうか？

3. 具体的なリクエスト、提案や質問をする　　Track 87

We would like to understand your needs in detail.

御社のニーズの詳細を詳しく伺いたいと思います。

Please share your current situation to the extent that you are comfortable with it.

差し支えない範囲で現状を教えてください。

Your company has not yet introduced the XX system, right?

御社ではXXシステムをまだ導入されていませんね？

We are interested in your products.

私たちは御社の製品に興味を持っています。

We want to buy your products and sell them.

御社の製品を買い付け、そして販売をしたいと思っています。

We would like to sell your products in Japan.

日本で御社の製品を販売したいのです。

I would like to ask some questions about your proposal.

ご提案について、いくつか質問させていただきます。

We are seeking to understand your proposal more fully.

御社のご提案を十分に理解したいと思います。

If I understand you correctly, you have asked for the exclusive distribution rights?

私の理解が正しければ、あなたは独占販売権を要求していますか。

You mentioned that you can reduce your production costs by 8 percent.

あなたは、生産コストを8%削減できると述べました。

Is that right?

これは正しいですか？

Could you be more specific?

もう少し具体的にご説明いただけますか？

Could you give us some more details about this point?

この点について、もっと詳しく教えていただけますか？

How confident are you of this proposal?

このご提案について、どの程度自信がありますか？

I apologize if you have covered this before, but I have one more important question.

既に説明されていたら申し訳ないのですが、もう一つ重要な質問があります。

Could you show us the specifications of your products?

製品の仕様書を見せていただけますか？

What is the selling point of your new product?

新製品のセールスポイントは何ですか？

There are many significant benefits.

たくさんの優れた点があります。

The product is easy to operate.

その製品は操作が簡単です。

Our proposed new service is available 24/7.

我々が提案する新サービスはいつでも利用できます。

＊24/7「1日24時間／週7日営業」（無休）の意。

Do you offer warranties on your products?

御社の製品に保証は付いていますか？

These products have a five-year warranty.

これらの製品は、5年間の保証付きです。

As long as maintenance is required, we provide technical support flexibly.

メンテナンスが必要である限り、私たちは柔軟にテクニカルサポートを提供します。

Within the warranty period, repairs are free.

保証期間内は、修理は無料です。

What do you mean by free?

無料とはどう意味ですか？

I don't follow you completely.

おっしゃることが完全に理解できません。

Could you clarify your service once again?

サービスについて再度、明確に説明していただけますか？

Could you expand on your last point?

最後の点をもっと詳しく説明していただけますか？

4. 質問に対して即答できない時   Track 88

That's an excellent point.

すばらしいご指摘です。

Please allow me to gather my thoughts for a moment.

ちょっと考えるのにお時間ください。

Thank you for raising an interesting question.

おもしろい質問をいただきありがとうございます。

Could you clarify your point once again?

もう一度、要点をお話しいただけますか？

We need to do more research to give you a clear answer.

明快なお答えをする前に、もう少し調べる必要があります。

I understand that a lot of people share that concern these days.

最近は多くの人がそのような懸念をもっているようです。

Let me give you the short answer now and I will come back to you with more detailed information.

ここでは手短にお答えし、後ほど詳しくご説明します。

What do you think?

あなたはどうお考えですか？

We have not got that information yet.

その情報についてはまだ入手できていません。

I will let you know as soon as I have gathered enough information.

十分な情報を入手したら、すぐにご連絡します。

Unfortunately, we are not ready to share that information with you.

あいにく、その情報をシェアする段階ではないと考えています。

5. 相手の考えや懸念点を確認する時　　Track 89

What are your thoughts about our proposal?

私たちの提案についてのあなたの考えはどうですか？

Could you explain to us a bit more about your concern?

あなたの懸念事項について、もう少し詳しくお聞かせください。

Could you help me understand why that is important for you?

その点がなぜ御社にとって大事なのか、もう少し教えてくださいますか？

Why do you think this will be problematic for you?

これがなぜ御社にとって問題になると思われますか？

How about that part?

その点については、どうですか？

What do you think about that?

それについて、どうお考えですか？

Could I have your input on how we can work together more effectively?

私たちがより効果的に協力する方法について、あなたの意見を聞かせていただけますか？

What do you think of this matter?

この問題については、どうお考えですか？

May we offer an alternative?

代替案を提供してもいいですか？

What's stopping you from pulling the trigger today?

今日最終決断することを止める理由は何ですか？

How would this help your business if you had this service now?

このサービスを今購入したら、ビジネスはどうなると思いますか？

What other options are available for you?

他にどのような選択肢をお持ちですか？

6. 反論・説得・反対意見を言う時　　　　Track 90

I can understand the arguments against my proposal.

私の提案に対する論点はごもっともです。

Now, let's go through them one by one so that I can address them.

それでは、それらの一つひとつをご説明したいと思います。

I understand your point of view completely, but we shouldn't underestimate the competition.

あなたの見解はまったくごもっともですが、競合を過小評価すべきではありません。

Obviously, our service has several competitive advantages.

明らかに、我々のサービスはいくつかの競争上の優位性があります。

Clearly, our product will work to improve your productivity.

明らかに、我々の製品は御社の生産性を向上させます。

I am sure that you will see the benefits of this.

このベネフィットを感じていただけると確信しています。

If we don't act now, it will be too late.

今行動しなければ、遅すぎることになります。

It is an interesting idea, but it may not be feasible.

興味深い考えですが、実現可能ではないかもしれません。

I understand that we can't do that, but can we discuss some other alternatives?

それは難しいのはわかりましたが、他の選択肢について話し合うことはできますか？

I hear what you're saying, but our bottom line is very clear on this one.

あなたがおっしゃることはわかりますが、結論はこれでとてもはっきりしています。

We have heard your point of view.

そちらの考えは伺いました。

Now let us tell you how we see it.

では、我々がどう考えるかお話しします。

Could we just take a moment to confirm the details in Japanese?

詳細を日本語で確認する時間を少々いただいてよろしいでしょうか？

I see things differently.

私は違った見方をしています。

I take your point, but I still have some concerns about your new service.

おっしゃる意味はわかりますが、御社の新サービスについてまだ懸念があります。

I respect your opinion, but I think we should take the competition into consideration.

ご意見は尊重しますが、競合を考慮すべきだと考えています。

I'm afraid we have some reservations on that point.

申し訳ありませんが、その点については保留したいと思います。

We must say this is beyond the scope of today's discussion.

これは今日の議論の範囲を超えていると言わなければなりません。

We agree on some basic points, but not everything at this moment.

いくつかの基本的な部分では合意していますが、現時点では全てではありません。

7. 誤解を解く時　　　　　　　　　　　　　Track 91

I am afraid there seems to be a slight misunderstanding.

申し訳ありませんが、少し誤解があるようです。

Perhaps, I haven't made myself clear.

おそらく、私が明確にしていなかったようです。

I'm not sure I fully understand your point.

あなたのおっしゃることを完全に理解しているかどうかはわかりません。

I'm afraid you don't seem to understand.

ご理解いただいていないようです。

8. 妥協案を話し会う時　　　　Track 92

How far are you willing to compromise?

どこまで妥協することができますか？

How can we deal with the concerns that have been raised?

これまでに上がった懸念に対して、私たちはどのように対処できますか？

What can we do to persuade you?

どうすればご納得いただけますか？

Do you have any suggestions about the next step?

次にどうするか、何かご提案はありますか？

We are ready to accept your offer.

私たちはあなたの申し出を受け入れる準備ができています。

However, there would be one condition.

ただし、1つの条件があります。

How about if we offer free samples?

無料のサンプルを提供させていただいたらどうですか？

What about if we extend the trial period?

試用期間を延長したらどうでしょうか？

How would it work if we reconsider the terms and conditions?

私たちが取引条件を再考したとすると、どのようにお考えですか？

As an alternative, would it be possible to consider a different service?

代替案として、違うサービスをご検討いただくことは可能ですか？

9. 時間を稼ぐ時   Track 93

Regarding your proposal, we would like to have a few days to consider.

あなたのご提案について、私たちは数日間検討したいと思います。

I need to consult with our legal department before I can answer.

お答えする前に、法務部に相談する必要があります。

I need to check on that once I go back to the office.

その点については、会社に戻って確認しなければなりません。

I would like to consult with my supervisor, and I'll get back to you.

上司と相談の上、ご連絡いたします。

Please give me a few days.

2～3日、お時間ください。

10. 解決策を話し合う時 Track 94

Can we summarize your position up to this point?

ここまでのあなたの意見をまとめていただけますか？

Let's talk about what we can do to resolve the issue.

その問題の解決のために何ができるか話し合いましょう。

Let's figure this out right now.

これを今、解決しましょう。

Let's see what we can do about this.

この点について、何ができるか考えてみましょう。

Let's just step back from the problem and think about what the most important part of this argument is.

問題から離れて、この議論の最も重要な部分が何であるかを考えてみましょう。

Can you do any better on the terms?

条件をもっと良くできませんか？

If you don't agree to our terms, then I don't think this is going to work out.

御社が我々の条件に同意できなければ、この件はうまく行かないでしょう。

I am not sure where we should go from here.

ここからどう抜け出しましょうか。

This is our final offer.

これが最終的なオファーです。

Unfortunately, we would be unable to accept your request.

残念ながら、御社のリクエストにお応えすることができません。

Let us think it over.

少し考えさせてください。

I'm afraid that those conditions are unacceptable.

残念ながら、これらの条件を受け入れることはできません。

Unless we agree on this critical point, we are unable to proceed.

この重要な点に同意しない限り、先に進むことはできません。

I'll be in touch again soon with more details.

詳細を準備の上、再度ご連絡します。

Let's talk next week and see how things are going.

来週、再度話し合って、状況を見てみましょう。

That's not exactly how I look at it.

それは私の見方とは異なります。

We would find this somewhat difficult to agree to.

どうやら合意するのは難しいようです。

It seems we are not going to reach an agreement today.

今日のところは合意に達するのが難しいようです。

Unfortunately, we are in a deadlock.

残念ながら、暗礁に乗り上げたようです。

I think it is best to end our meeting for now.

一度ここで話を切り上げましょうか。

We were rather hoping to finalize the deal today.

我々はむしろ今日最終判断することを望んでいました。

I'm sorry but we're not very happy with this offer.

申し訳ありませんが、この提案は快く受け入れられません。

I'm afraid that those conditions are unacceptable.

申し訳ありませんが、これらの条件は受け入れられません。

I'm afraid we couldn't agree to that point.

申し訳ありませんが、その点については合意できません。

I don't think your solution is going to work.

あなたの提案がうまく行くとは思えません。

The most important issue for us is the delivery date.

我々にとって、最も大事な問題は納期です。

We would like to get your perspective on this matter.

この問題についてのあなたの見解を得たいと思います。

We have a broader perspective on this issue.

この問題については、より広い視野があります。

Our main priority is the quality control.

私たちの優先事項は品質管理です。

It seems that there are some gaps to reaching an agreement.

合意に達するまでにはギャップがあるようです。

Based on the available information, it would be difficult for us to enter this contract today.

入手可能な情報に基づいて、今日この契約を締結することは困難です。

This is our comprehensive proposal, which we are unable to further compromise.

これは私たちの包括的な提案であり、これ以上妥協することはできません。

I wish we can work something out.

何か解決策を出せれば良いのですが。

We need to postpone our decision to the next meeting.

決定を次の会議に延期する必要があります。

Unfortunately, we are unable to accept your offer at this time.

残念ながら、今回はご提案をお受けできません。

It seems like we are unable to draw any conclusion today.

今日は合意に達することはできないようです。

I must say that the final decision is out of my control.

申し訳ありませんが、最終決定権は私にありません。

We would highly appreciate it if you keep the door open.

今後また機会をいただければ幸いです。

We are sorry, but we have decided to do business with another company.

申し訳ありませんが、他社と取引することを決定しました。

Thank you for your efforts to work on this situation.

この状況に努力いただきありがとうございます。

Shall we reopen the negotiation two weeks from now?

２週間後にまた交渉を再開しませんか？

12. 後ほど返事を聞く場合　　　　Track 96

When do you think you will be able to get back to us about this deal?

この取引について、いつ頃お返事をいただけますでしょうか？

We are looking forward to your response.

お返事をお待ちしています。

Would it be possible to hear from you by the end of this week?

今週末までにお返事をいただくことは可能でしょうか？

Could you finalize your proposal by next week?

来週までにご提案を確定していただけますか？

13. 合意した時　　　　Track 97

We are gratified to accept your proposal.

喜んで提案を受け入れます。

Let's shake hands on it.

同意の握手をしましょう。

Is there anything else we need to discuss now?

他に何か議論しなければならないことはありますか？

I think we have reached a mutual understanding.

合意に達したと思います。

I am sure that the agreement will bring mutual benefits to both of us.

この合意は、私たち双方に相互利益をもたらすと確信しています。

This agreement is acceptable to us.

この合意は了承できます。

I think we have reached an agreement finally.

やっと合意に達しましたね。

That sounds reasonable.

妥当だと思います。

All things considered, we are happy with the agreement.

いろいろ考え合わせてみても、合意には満足です。

I think we have covered everything.

全てカバーしましたね。

Could you formalize what we talked about today?

今日話したことを正式なものにしてもらえますか？

I'll draw up a draft of the contract and send one.

では、契約案文を作成してお送りします。

We would like you to e-mail it to us by the end of this week.

今週末までに私たちにメールで送ってください。

Would that be acceptable to you?

これで良いでしょうか？

Shall we have another meeting sometime soon?

近いうちにまた会合を持ちませんか？

To summarize what we have discussed today, we have agreed on the terms and conditions.

本日話し合ったことをまとめますと、我々は支払い条件に合意しました。

We are very pleased to enter into a contract with you finally.

ようやく契約することができ、大変うれしいです。

We are looking forward to continuing our relationship in the future.

今度ともよろしくお願いいたします。

Thank you for your cooperation.

ご協力に感謝いたします。

We do really appreciate your business and we're determined to keep providing best-in-class service.

ビジネスの機会を本当にありがとうございます。これからも最高のサービスを提供し続けます。

14. 価格について交渉する時　　　　　Track 98

I will send you the revised price list by the end of this week.

今週末までに改定した価格表をお送りします。

What are your conditions of the sale?

販売について、何か条件がございますか？

Would that be satisfactory to you?

これで、よろしいでしょうか？

Would that be acceptable to you?

これで、良いでしょうか？

Could you offer us a better deal?

値引きしていただけますか？

Could we have a volume discount?

数量の値引きはできますか？

If you give us a 10% discount, we will double the order.

10% 値引きしていただけたら、注文を 2 倍にします。

We can consider the terms and conditions that you want.

ご希望の取引条件も検討いたします。

This is over our budget.

これは当社の予算を超えています。

The price you quoted is higher than we expected.

お見積もり金額は思っていたより高いですね。

I'm afraid this is the best price we can offer.

残念ながら、これは私たちが提供できる中で最も良い価格です。

How much have you budgeted for this project?

このプロジェクトへいくら予算をとっていましたか？

My expectation is in the range of $100 and 102 per each.

私の想定は単価 100 ドルから 102 ドルの範囲です。

Could you make it $900?

900 ドルになりませんか？

Let's each go halfway and make it happen.

それぞれ半分譲歩して、合意しましょう。

It's difficult to give you any further discount.

これ以上のディスカウントは難しいです。

This is a very competitive price for the quality of the brand-new product.

この新ブランドの品質にしては、とても競争力のある価格です。

Please note the current special price is only good until March 31st.

現在の特別価格は 3 月 31 日まで有効です。

We can give you a discount, but we need you to give us something in return.

何か見返りがあればですが、値引きすることは可能です。

I have made concessions, now it's your turn.

私は譲歩しましたので、あなたもお願いします。

I am sorry we will not be placing an order this time, as the price is higher than we expected.

価格が予想を上回りましたので、申し訳ありませんが今回は注文を見合わせます。

15. 発注する時 Track 99

What is your minimum order quantity?

最低何個から注文できますか？

We accept an order with a minimum of 50 units.

ご注文は最低 50 個から承ります。

Is there a discount for a bulk order?

大量注文の場合、割引がありますか？

There is a discount depending on the quantity.

数量によっては値引きがあります。

When can you ship the product?

製品をいつ出荷してもらえますか？

Can you deliver the full quantity on June 1?

全数量を 6 月 1 日に納品していただくことはできますか？

Could you send them to us by airmail?

航空便で送っていただけますか？

Could you send them to us by cash on delivery?

代金引換で送っていただけますか？

We would like to send them by sea.

船便で送りたいと思います。

Could you also take care of insurance?

保険のほうもご手配をお願いできますか？

We won't be able to meet the deadline.

納期に間に合いません。

What are the terms of payment?

支払条件はどのようになっていますか？

We would like you to pay within 30 days upon receipt of the order.

注文受領後 30 日以内にお支払いいただきますようお願いいたします。

We would like to make payment in three installments.

支払いは 3 回の分割払いにしたいと思います。

The terms of payment are 30 days upon receipt of the order.

支払条件は注文受取後 30 日です。

Is it possible to extend the deadline for payment?

支払期限を延ばすことは可能ですか？

3 海外企業とのM&A・事業再編・ジョイントベンチャー

I think the alliance will give us the opportunity for diversification.

アライアンスを組むことで多様性の機会を得ると思います。

The acquisition will be the best way to achieve greater efficiencies of scale and productivity in this market.

買収は、この市場で規模と生産性の効率を高める最良の方法です。

Now is the right timing for us to acquire another company to attract more customers.

今こそ、より多くの顧客を引き付けるために別の会社を買収する適切なタイミングです。

We set certain criteria to search target companies.

対象企業を検索するために一定の基準を設定しよう。

The criteria include geographic expansion, diversified customer base, and higher profit margin.

この基準には、地理的拡大、多様な顧客基盤、および高い利益率を含みます。

We have listed the potential acquisition targets which help us to gain access to new markets.

新しい市場へのアクセスの助けになる買収候補（会社）をリストアップしてみました。

We need to understand the different tax and legal environments before expanding our business overseas.

海外で事業を展開する前に、様々な税法と法的環境を理解する必要があります。

The acquisition of this company will help us to expand product lines.

この会社の買収は製品ラインの拡大に役立つでしょう。

We need someone with expertise to develop a competitive compensation package in this market.

この市場で競争力のある報酬体系を作るには、専門知識を持つ人が必要です。

The merger is expected to increase the efficiency of product manufacturing by creating economies of scale.

この合併には規模の経済を生み出すこと、製品製造の効率性を高めることを期待している。

Chapter 5

The purpose of this strategic alliance is to get the fastest distribution in the foreign market.

この戦略的提携の目的は、海外市場で最速の流通網を得ることです。

We expect synergies in increased revenues and lower expenses by merging this company.

この会社を合併することで、増収と経費削減の相乗効果を期待している。

Two companies could bring complementary strengths to the advanced technology field once combined.

２社がいったん統合すれば、先端技術分野に補完的な強みをもたらすことができるはずだ。

We need to consider the alternatives before deciding on the acquisition target.

買収対象を決定する前に、代替案を検討する必要があります。

The company's sales are growing at an average annual rate of 8 percent.

この会社の売上は年平均 8% の割合で増加しています。

Merging this company which has built a strong reputation in this market will enhance our sustainable strategy.

この市場で高い評価を得ているこの会社を合併することは、私たちの持続可能な戦略を強化するであろう。

Aside from having advanced technology, they have a good management team.

先端技術を持つ他に、優秀な経営陣がいます。

One of the significant benefits from this M&A is to acquire some exclusive products.

この M&A から得られる大きな利点の 1 つは、独占的な製品を入手することです。

On top of expanding our product portfolio, we can expect to boost our profitability.

製品ポートフォリオの拡大に加えて、収益性の向上が期待できます。

With this merger, we can enhance our diversification strategy into the new markets.

この合併により、私たちは新しい市場への多様化戦略を強化することができます。

The overseas expansion will request us to further invest in corporate language training.

海外への進出は、企業語学研修へのさらなる投資を必要とします。

The bottom line is that we cannot compromise the cultural fit of the two companies.

結論として、2社の文化的適合性に妥協することはできません。

---

2. 交渉相手のビジネスを分析する　　Track 101

We are expected to examine the wide range of the target company's business using the checklist.

このチェックリストを用いて、対象企業の事業を幅広く調査します。

The small issue could turn out to be a bigger problem if underestimated.

過小評価していると、小さな問題が後により大きな問題になる可能性がある。

We have drafted the confidentiality agreement to protect our respective trade secrets.

それぞれの企業秘密を守るための機密保持契約を起草しました。

We make sure to exchange a non-disclosure agreement before kicking off the due diligence process.

デューデリジェンスのプロセスを開始する前に、秘密保持契約を確実に交換する。

＊due diligence：企業買収などで行われる、財務情報やその他、会社をとりまく情報を詳細に調査して評価すること

The finance team will start by analyzing the tax returns to understand their past financial performance.

財務チームは、納税申告書を分析して過去の財務実績を把握することから始めます。

The company generates the most sales from their core product, while peripheral items generate most profits.

この会社はコア製品から最も多くの売上を生み出していますが、周辺品目は最も多くの利益を生み出しています。

We should find out whether their product portfolios complement ours.

私たちは彼らの製品ポートフォリオが私たちのものを補完するかどうかを調べるべきです。

We have identified some issues in their North American sales for the past three years.

彼らの過去3年間の北米の売上高には、いくつかの問題があるようだ。

We need to make sure to have upfront discussions to get the whole picture of the situation.

状況の全体像を把握するためには、事前に話し合っておく必要があります。

We need to request them to provide additional information to help us identify any risks involved in the transaction.

この取引に関連するリスクを特定するため、追加情報を提供するように彼らに要求する必要がある。

We need to be prepared to decide based on the materials available at the end of the process.

私たちは入手可能な資料に基づいて最終的には決定を下す準備をしなければならない。

3. 交渉相手と条件をつめる　　　　　Track 102

Could you explain these unusual patterns in sales last year?

昨年の売上高における、これらの異常なパターンを説明していただけますか？

We would like you to explain the non-recurring big expenditures listed here.

ここにリストアップしてある臨時的な大きな支出について説明してください。

There seems to have been a slight misunderstanding with our side.

私たちの側に少々誤解があったようです。

We would like to get this issue straight.

この問題を明確にしたいと思います。

Please provide the information whether any of your product features have been protected by patents.

製品機能のいずれかが特許によって保護されているかどうかについての情報を提供してください。

Could you explain how you have performed compared with the budget for the last two years?

過去２年間の予算と比較して、御社の業績はどうだったかを説明していただけますか？

Please provide your financial performance projections for the next three years.

今後３年間の財務業績予測を教えてください。

We would request additional information in your cost structure to identify any opportunities for operational efficiency.

運用効率化の機会を特定するために、コスト構造の追加情報を要求します。

Could you provide the detail conditions of IT infrastructure of your company?

あなたの会社のITインフラの詳細な条件を教えてくださいますか？

We regard the alliance as the only way to enter this market.

アライアンスはこの市場に参入する唯一の方法であると考えています。

What are the most important criteria for this acquisition?

この買収の最も重要な基準は何ですか？

What do you know about what has happened among the competitors?

競合他社の間で何が起こったかについて、あなたは何を知っていますか？

Could you provide the detail of retirement plans and all other benefits for the employees?

退職金制度の詳細およびその他すべての従業員への給付を提供していただけますか？

Do you expect any synergies in revenue upon this merger?

この合併による収益の相乗効果は期待できますか？

Could you walk me through the cost synergies if we merged?

合併した場合のコストの相乗効果について教えてください。

How do you determine the purchase price for the company abroad?

海外の会社の購入価格をどのように決定しますか？

Are there any tax benefits upon this merger?

この合併に税制上の優遇措置はありますか？

We believe diversification is one of the most important reasons for the merger.

多様化が合併の最も重要な理由の１つであると考えています。

Is there any intangible asset that could impact the value of your company?

御社の価値に影響を与える可能性のある無形資産はありますか？

Would it be possible to get your response by the end of this week?

今週末までに回答を得ることは可能でしょうか？

Chapter 5

As you may recall, we are willing to cover extra costs for the consolidation.

ご承知いただいている通り、統合の追加費用は喜んで負担します。

If we don't work together to boost our business today, we will miss the opportunities in this market.

今お互いのビジネスを伸ばすための協力をしなければ、この市場での機会を逃してしまいます。

Keeping this in mind, we propose to move quickly to close the deal.

この点を念頭に置いて、取引を完了するために迅速に動きましょう。

It has come to my attention that we should be able to get synergies from this alliance.

私たちはこの連携から相乗効果を得ることができるはずですよね。

We are eager to reach consensus on the remaining issues before the end of this month.

私たちは、今月末までに残りの問題について合意に達することを切望しています。

Unfortunately, those terms are unacceptable to us.

あいにく、これらの条件を受け入れることはできません。

4. 感想・考えを述べる　　　　　　　　　　Track 103

That's a fair suggestion.

それは公正な提案です。

Your argument is quite compelling.

あなたの議論は非常に説得力があります。

I'm afraid that does not work for us.

うまく行かないのではないかと思います。

I don't see any problem with your request.

リクエストに問題はありません。

We need to make sure we are on the same page on the next steps.

次のステップについて同じ理解でいるか確認が必要です。

We may accept your offer on one condition.

１つの条件次第でオファーを受け入れます。

As far as your proposal on the price is concerned, we are ready to accept it.

価格に関するあなたの提案に関しては、我々はそれを受け入れる準備ができています。

How flexible are you on the acquisition price?

買収価格にはどの程度柔軟ですか？

That's not exactly how we see this issue.

それは、この問題の正確な見方ではありません。

Obviously, this issue could be solved immediately.

明らかに、この問題はすぐに解決できます。

This can be fixed by further discussion.

これはさらに議論することで修正できます。

Although it may seem complicated, it will be a simple process in reality.

複雑に見えるかもしれませんが、実際には単純なプロセスになります。

The consolidation will be a remarkable opportunity for our future.

この統合は、私たちの将来にとって大きなチャンスです。

Would you be willing to take the lower price if we accept this request?

このリクエストを受け入れた場合、より安い価格を受け入れてもらえますか？

How could we ensure that our employees are taken care of after the acquisition?

買収後、我々の従業員が面倒を見てもらえると確認できる方法はありますか？

How long will we need to anticipate for the successful merger?

合併が成功するまでどのくらいの期間を予測する必要がありますか？

How long will it take to merge your business?

ビジネスを統合するにはどれくらい時間がかかりますか？

How did you arrive at this valuation?

どうしたらこの評価になりましたか？

What do you think of this approach as an alternative solution?

このアプローチを代替案としてどう思いますか？

With all these benefits we discussed, don't you agree with this proposal?

私たちが議論したこれらの全ての利点を考慮して、この提案に同意しませんか？

How much more will this cost if we delay this negotiation?

この交渉を遅らせた場合、これにはさらにどれくらいの費用がかかりますか？

Could you provide us with more detail on how you developed your strategy in this market?

この市場でどのように戦略を開発したかについて、詳細を教えていただけますか？

How do you feel about the impact of diversification?

多様化の影響についてどう思いますか？

We have a slightly different view on that.

その点については、少々異なる見方をしています。

Unfortunately, that is out of the question for us.

残念ながら、それは私たちにとっては問題外です。

We are afraid we find those terms unfavorable.

それらの条件は好ましくないと思われます。

We are afraid we have to respectfully decline this deal.

残念ながら、この契約は辞退させていただきます。

I'll be in touch again next week with more details.

詳細については、来週また連絡します。

Let's talk later this week once again and see how things are going.

今週後半にもう一度話して様子を見ましょう。

Your suggestion will make this deal less attractive because of the complexity.

あなたの提案によって複雑になり、この取引の魅力が減ります。

Maybe it would be better to look at the synergies once again.

シナジーをもう一度見てみるほうが良いでしょう。

Perhaps a better idea would be pursuing a partnership.

パートナーシップを追求したほうがより良いかもしれません。

We think it's important to accelerate the progress to close the deal as planned.

計画通りに取引を成立させるには、進捗を早めることが重要です。

I think we have a deal.

契約ですね。

These conditions are acceptable to us.

これらの条件は受け入れることが可能です。

Let's make it happen.

実現させましょう。

Shall we go over what we decided to do?

決めたことを確認しましょうか？

I am afraid that we can't match the competitor's offer.

あいにく、競合他社のオファーと一致することはできません。

5. 弁護士などの専門家を交渉に使う　　Track 104

We will get an outside investment adviser to perform the financial valuation of this acquisition.

この買収額の財務評価を外部の投資顧問に依頼します。

Our legal advisers will confirm whether there are no pending legal litigations.

当社の顧問弁護士が、係属中の訴訟がないかどうかを確認します。

We will make a final offer price based on the valuation of the target company and the strategic fit to our business.

ターゲット企業の評価と当社の事業に対する戦略的な適合性に基づいて、最終的なオファー価格を決定します。

We are willing to pay a premium price if we identify a greater strategic rationale for the merger.

合併により大きな戦略的根拠がある場合、当社は割増価格を支払う意思があります。

Chapter 5

1. クライアントを接待に誘う　　　　Track 105

We would like to take you out to dinner.

ディナーにお連れしたいと思います。

Since you will be in town Wednesday night, I was hoping you would join me for dinner.

あなたが水曜の夜にこちらにいらっしゃるので、ディナーをご一緒できないかと思っています。

I would be delighted if you could join us for lunch on Friday after our meeting.

金曜の会議の後に、ランチをご一緒できたらうれしいです。

Would you like to go out for a drink after work?

仕事の後に一杯飲みに行くのはいかがですか？

We will pick you up at 7 o'clock at your hotel.

7 時にあなたのホテルでピックアップします。

Sounds great. That's very kind.

いいですね。ご親切にありがとうございます。

I'm afraid I have another appointment.

あいにく、別の約束があります。

When will it be convenient for you?

いつがご都合よろしいですか？

I'll adjust my schedule accordingly.

そちらのご都合に合わせます。

Why don't you come along with us to the party this evening?

今夜、一緒にパーティーにいらっしゃいませんか？

Yes. I'd love to. Thank you.

ええ。喜んで。ありがとうございます。

Unfortunately, I have plans this evening.

残念ながら、今夜は予定があります。

I'm afraid my schedule is a little tight that day.

あいにく、その日のスケジュールは少しきついです。

Could you reschedule my appointment for next Wednesday?

約束を来週の水曜日に変更していただけますか？

2. 相手の好みを確認する　　　　　　Track 106

Do you have any preference on the type of restaurant?

どのようなタイプのレストランがいいか、何かご希望はありますか？

Is there anything specific you would like to try while you are here?

こちらにいらっしゃる間に、特に試してみたい（食べ）物はありますか？

Is there a particular restaurant you would like to go to?

特に行ってみたいレストランはありますか？

Could I pick the place?

場所をおまかせいただけますか？

Would you like to try the new Italian restaurant that opened up near your office?

あなたのオフィスの近くにオープンした新しいイタリアンレストランを試してみませんか？

What kind of Japanese food would you like to try?

どんな日本料理を試してみたいですか？

Do you have any allergies or dietary restrictions?

あなたは何かアレルギーや食事制限などはありますか？

Are there any types of food you would like to avoid?

避けたほうがよい食べ物はありますか？

Would you like Japanese, Chinese, Italian, French or American?

日本食、中華、イタリアン、フレンチ、またはアメリカン、どれがいいですか？

Is there any kind of food that you dislike?

苦手な食べ物はありますか？

Are there any vegetarians in your team?

チームにベジタリアンの方はいらっしゃいますか？

Is there anything you prefer not to have?

あまりお好きでないものはありますか？

Are there any types of food that you don't eat?

召し上がらない食べ物はありますか？

I'm thinking of either sukiyaki or a traditional Japanese restaurant. Do you have any preference?

すき焼きか伝統的な和食のレストランを考えています。何かお好みはありますか？

3. 会食を楽しい会話で盛り上げる　　Track 107

We appreciate your coming all this way.

遠路をお越しいただき、ありがとうございます。

Thank you for coming here today.

本日は来てくださってありがとうございます。

Let's go into the lounge.

ではラウンジに入りましょう。

So, what do you think about Japan so far?

今のところ、日本はいかがですか？

What's your favorite cocktail?

どのようなカクテルが好きですか？

Would you like to have a drink?

何かお飲みになりますか？〔アルコールをすすめる〕

I assume you are not driving tonight.

今夜は運転なさらないですよね。

Are you ready to eat now?

そろそろ食事にいたしますか？

We have taken you to this place as your preference is the casual and real local place.

カジュアルで本物の地元の場所をご希望とのことでしたので、この場所にお連れしました。

I picked this place as you asked me to take you to the place where you cannot go alone.

ご自身で行けない場所をお望みでしたので、この場所を選びました。

Hope you enjoy this experience.

この経験をお楽しみください。

This is my favorite Izakaya.

これは私の好きな居酒屋です。

Izakayas normally serve small dishes, called Otoshi.

居酒屋は通常お通しという、小さな食べ物を出します。

Otoshi is a kind of appetizer.

お通しは前菜のようなものです。

They serve it in exchange for a table charge.

テーブルチャージの代わりに提供されます。

They serve the best shrimp tempura here.

この店は最高のエビの天ぷらを出します。

This is the steak I was telling you about earlier.

これが、私が前にお話ししたステーキです。

Is there a house specialty?

このお店のおすすめはありますか？

Please enjoy the food while it's still warm.

温かいうちにお召し上がりください。

Let's make a toast to Mr. Smith.

スミスさんに乾杯しましょう。

Cheers!

乾杯！

4. 会食中の気配りフレーズ　　Track 108

Please pass me the salt.

塩を取ってください。

What would you like to drink next?

次は何を飲まれますか？

Would you need a refill?

飲み物のおかわりは必要ありませんか？

Did you have any problems finding this place?

こちらへ来るのに何か問題はありませんでしたか？

How was your flight?

フライトはどうでしたか？

Are you jet lagged?

時差ボケはありますか？

Where is the restroom?

トイレはどこですか？

It's the third door on your left down this hall.

この廊下をちょっと行って、左側３番目のドアです。

Do you drink?

お酒は飲みますか？

I'm a social drinker.

たしなむ程度です。

How much do you drink?

お酒をどのくらい飲みますか？

I enjoy a drink occasionally.

たまにお酒を楽しみます。

I don't drink very much. I just drink socially.

お酒はあまり飲みません。たしなむ程度です。

I am just a little tipsy.

少し酔いました。

5. スマートに支払いを済ませる　Track 109

We'll get this.

ここは私たちがお支払いします。

Let us pay this time.

今回はこちらで払わせてください。

You treated us last time.

前回ごちそうになったので。

We insist.

本当に支払わせてください。

6. その他の接待・さわやかなお見送りのフレーズ　Track 110

Before we leave, this is a small gift from us.

お開きの前に、これは私たちからのささやかなプレゼントです。

I hope you'll like it.

気に入っていただけると良いのですが。

May I present you with a small gift?

ささやかなプレゼントを差し上げさせていただけますか？

Here you are.

はい、どうぞ。

Please take this.

どうぞ受け取ってください。

I'm glad you liked it.

気に入っていただいて良かったです。

Please give my regards to the staff back in New York.

ニューヨークのスタッフの方によろしくお伝えください。

Are you ready to go back to your hotel?

ホテルにお帰りになるご用意はできましたか？

7. 誘う Track 111

Would you like to come to my house next Sunday?

来週の日曜日に家にいらっしゃいませんか？

Would you be interested in watching sumo wrestling?

相撲見物にご興味はおありでしょうか？

I wonder if you would be interested in watching a baseball game.

野球観戦に興味がおありでしょうか。

Let's go to the airport early enough so as not to be caught in a traffic jam.

交通渋滞が心配ですので、早めに空港へ行きましょう。

Thank you very much for taking care of us.

いろいろとお世話になり、どうもありがとうございました。

Thank you for your kind hospitality.

親切なおもてなしをありがとうございました。

Thank you very much for coming to the airport.

空港までお見送りいただき、どうもありがとうございます。

Well, we will communicate with you by E-mail.

では、今度はＥメールで連絡します。

Have a good trip.

良いご旅行を。

8. 接待を受けた後のお礼　　　　　　Track 112

Thank you very much for the wonderful dinner last night.

昨夜は、すばらしいディナーへご招待いただき、どうもありがとうございます。

We enjoyed very tasty Japanese foods.

とてもおいしい日本食を堪能しました。

Next time when you are in New York, we would like to take you out for dinner.

次にニューヨークにいらっしゃる時は、我々がディナーにお連れします。

I am glad that you had a chance to try Japanese sake.

日本酒を試していただいて良かったです。

We hope to see you again soon in Tokyo.

近いうちに東京で再びお会いしたいと思います。

Chapter 5

9. バーなどでのカジュアルな会話 Track 113

Let me buy you a drink.

一杯おごります。

The next round is on me.

次は私が払います。

It's my turn to get the drinks.

今度は私が払う番です。

What will you have?

何にしますか？

---

10. 日本食・日本酒の説明をする Track 114

Sashimi is thinly sliced raw fish.

刺身は薄くスライスされた生魚です。

Sashimi is made from several kinds of raw fish and shellfish.

刺身はいろいろな種類の生魚や貝で作られます。

We eat sashimi with wasabi, Japanese horseradish and dip it in soy sauce.

刺身をワサビ、つまり日本のホースラディッシュと一緒に醤油につけて食べます。

Wasabi has the hot flavor to stimulate the nose.

ワサビは鼻を刺激する辛みがあります。

There are many kinds of sushi, such as Nigiri-zushi and Maki-zushi.

握り寿司、巻き寿司など、たくさんの種類の寿司があります。

Nigiri-zushi is what people call "Sushi" generally.

握り寿司が一般的に「寿司」と呼ばれているものです。

Nigiri-zushi is oval-shaped vinegared rice topped with raw fish.

握り寿司は楕円形の酢飯で、トップに刺身（生の魚）があります。

「マグロ」Tuna	「サーモン」Salmon	「タイ」Snapper
「うなぎ」Eel	「ブリ」Yellowtail	「サバ」Mackerel
「タコ」Octopus	「カンパチ」Amberjack	

Maki-zushi is sushi rolled with seaweed.

巻き寿司は海苔で巻かれた寿司ロールです。

Tempura is deep-fried seafood and vegetables. It is coated with a batter.

天ぷらはよく揚げたシーフードや野菜のフライです。衣に包まれています。

The batter is made from flour and egg.

衣は、小麦粉と卵から作られています。

We eat tempura with a dipping source called Tentsuyu.

天ぷらを天つゆと呼ばれる付けダレと一緒に食べます。

Okonomiyaki is like a Japanese pancake. It is made from dough, a mixture of flour and water.

お好み焼きは日本のパンケーキのようなものです。小麦粉と水を混ぜ合わせた生地でできています。

It contains lots of ingredients such as cabbage, pork, eggs, seafood and so on.

多くの材料、キャベツ、豚肉、卵、海産物などが入っています。

We normally eat it with mayonnaise and special sauce.

私たちは通常、マヨネーズと特別なソースでそれを食べます。

Takoyaki is known as octopus dumplings.

たこ焼きは、たこの餃子として知られています。

It is round and made from dough, a mixture of flour and water.

丸い形をしていて、小麦粉と水を混ぜ合わせた生地でできています。

It contains pieces of octopus and some vegetables such as cabbage, green onion and so on.

ぶつ切りのタコ、そしてキャベツ、ネギなどの野菜が入っています。

Japanese sake is an alcoholic drink made from fermented rice.

日本酒は発酵米から作られたアルコール飲料です。

There are many kinds of Japanese sake such as "Junmai-shu", "Honjouzou-shu", and "Ginjou-shu."

日本酒には、「純米酒」「本醸造酒」そして「吟醸酒」などの多くの種類があります。

They have different brewing processes and different levels of rice polish.

日本酒はその製法や精白の違い等で区別されます。

"Hiya" means Japanese sake served at normal temperature.

「冷や」は常温で飲む日本酒を意味します。

"Atsukan" means Japanese sake warmed to around 50 degree celsius.

「熱燗」は50度程度に温めた日本酒を意味します。

Once Japanese sake becomes "Atsukan", its aroma grows stronger.

日本酒を「熱燗」にすると、香りが強まります。

5 海外出張

1. 訪問先とアポをとる　　　　　Track 115

I would like to set up an appointment to meet with you.

お会いする機会をお願いしたいと思います。

If it's possible, we would like to meet and introduce our services.

可能であれば、お会いして当社のサービスを紹介させていただきたいと思います。

I would like to drop in and say hello when I go to the US next month.

来月に渡米した際、ごあいさつに伺いたいと思います。

Do you think we could get together sometime next week?

来週のどこかでお会いすることは可能ですか？

I will be in New York on business next month.

来月に仕事でニューヨークに行きます。

I am planning to make a day trip from New York to Boston.

ニューヨークからボストンへの日帰り旅行を計画しています。

I am going to London on business next week.

来週に仕事でロンドンに行きます。

It will be great if I could sit down with you and show you samples of our products.

あなたに当社の製品サンプルをお見せできたらと思います。

When will be convenient for you?

いつがご都合よろしいでしょうか？

I would like to go to your office at 10 am on May 10.

御社へ 5 月 10 日の午前 10 時に伺いたいと思います。

I would like to meet with you and discuss some details before finalizing the contract.

契約を締結する前に、あなたと詳細の話し合いに伺いたいと思います。

We would like to take a tour of your factory, if possible.

可能であれば、工場を見学させていただきたいと思います。

Would you let me know your availability on that day?

その日のご都合をお知らせくださいますか？

I'm afraid I won't be able to make it next week.

申し訳ないですが、来週は都合がつきません。

How about the following week?

翌週はどうですか？

Could you let me know when would be a good time?

ご都合が良いのはいつでしょうか？

Do you have time from 10 am on June 6?

6 月 6 日の午前 10 時からお時間ありますか？

Could you reschedule my appointment for Tuesday after next?

再来週の火曜日に約束を変更していただけないでしょうか？

＊「再来週の～」～ after next

Is it possible to postpone the meeting?

ミーティングを延期することは可能でしょうか？

I'll be flying in on Monday and return on Friday.

私は月曜に飛行機で行き、金曜に帰る予定です。

I am planning to arrive on June 1 and return on June 6.

私は６月１日に到着して、６月６日に帰る予定です。

Would you have time to meet with me during that week?

その週にお会いする時間はありますか？

It would be great if you would keep that afternoon free.

その日の午後、予定を入れないでいただけると幸いです。

Can we meet first thing in the morning on Friday?

金曜の朝一番にお会いできますか？

Is there anyone else I should meet this time?

今回どなたか他にお会いすべき人はいますか？

Could you introduce someone from the local bank?

地元の銀行の人をどなたかご紹介いただけますか？

Unfortunately, I will be away from the office and will be back on June 10.

あいにく、不在にしておりまして６月１０日に戻ります。

I will be available. Let 's meet at 10 am on June 5.
大丈夫です。6月5日の午前10時に会いましょう。

I will go directly to your office from the airport.
空港から直接そちらのオフィスに向かいます。

I will confirm our plan before I leave Japan.
日本を出発する前に、予定を確認します。

I will send my travel itinerary by email.
私の旅程表をメールで送信します。

I will check in my hotel first then go to your office.
ホテルにまずチェックインし、そしてオフィスに伺います。

Unfortunately, I need to delay my trip for a few months.
あいにく、出張を数ヶ月延期しなければならなくなりました。

I am very sorry but something urgent has come up.
大変申し訳ありませんが、急用ができてしまいました。

I am afraid I have to cancel my trip next month.
申し訳ありません、来月の出張をキャンセルしなければなりません。

We will let you know when we reschedule our trip.
出張の日程を変更したら、またご連絡します。

I am very pleased that you have taken the time to meet with me.
お会いするお時間を割いていただき、非常にうれしく思います。

We would like to recap what I told you over the phone the other day.

先日あなたに電話でお伝えしたことをまとめたいと思います。

2. 旅行手配と旅行中の会話 Track 116

I would like to reserve a ticket to New York.

ニューヨーク行きのチケットを予約したいです。

Can I get a late flight?

遅い時間のフライトをとれますか？

I would like to book a seat on the next available flight to Seoul.

ソウルに行く次のフライトの座席の予約をお願いします。

I would like to have an aisle seat.

通路側の席をお願いします。

I would prefer a window seat if possible.

可能であれば、窓側の席をお願いします。

Is business class available?

ビジネスクラスは利用できますか？

Could you let me know if the plane is equipped with Wi-Fi?

飛行機に Wi-Fi が装備されているかどうかを教えてくださいますか？

Is there any single room available next Monday?

来週の月曜、シングルルームの空きはありますか？

I would like to reserve a room from April 23 to April 27.

4月23日から4月27日までの部屋の予約をお願いします。

I have a reservation for 5 nights from June 1, but I would like to extend my stay to 6 nights.

6月1日から5泊予約をしていますが、6泊に延長をお願いします。

I missed my flight because of the bad weather.

悪天候で飛行機に乗り遅れました。

I would like to take the next flight from LA to NY.

ロサンゼルスからニューヨークへの次の便に乗りたいのですが。

3. たずねる、依頼する   Track 117

Do you have Wi-Fi?

Wi-Fi はありますか？

We need help connecting to the internet. Could you send someone to help?

インターネットの設定をしなければなりません。誰かに助けてもらえ ますか？

Could you reserve a meeting room at headquarters for three hours tomorrow morning?

本社の会議室を明日午前に3時間予約しておいていただけますか？

Will any of your conference rooms be available for a meeting tomorrow?

明日の会議のために会議室はどこか空いていますか？

Will it be possible to set up a projector?

プロジェクターを設置することは可能でしょうか？

Could you arrange for a taxi to take me to the airport on Monday at 5 pm?

月曜の午後５時に空港まで行くタクシーの手配をお願いできますか？

I'll only be here for three days. What do you recommend I see in New York?

こちらには３日しかいません。ニューヨークで何を見るのがおすすめですか？

May I have a receipt for that please?

領収書をお願いできますか？

Could you help me to reserve a table for three, for tomorrow night at XYZ restaurant?

明日の夜、XYZ レストランでの３人席の予約をお願いできますか？

How do we get from the Plaza Hotel to the ABC company main office?

プラザホテルから ABC 社の本社まではどのように行けますか？

What's the best way to get to the office from Central Station?

中央駅からオフィスまで、どうやって行くのが一番良い方法ですか？

How long will it take to get to JFK Airport from here?

ここから JFK 空港までどのくらいかかりますか？

---

4. 海外出張中のトラブル対応　　　Track 118

I overslept due to jet lag this morning.

今朝、時差ぼけで寝坊しました。

Can you get to the station as soon as possible?

できるだけ早く駅に行ってくださいますか？

I have a very important appointment.

私はとても大事な約束があります。

Can you make it in 10 minutes?

10 分以内に着くことができますか？

Are we almost there?

そろそろそこに着きそうでしょうか？

I'm low on cash right now.

現金の持ち合わせがありません。

Do you take credit cards?

クレジットカードは使えますか？

I left my wallet at my office.

会社にお財布を忘れました。

Can I go get my wallet at my office?

会社にお財布を取りに行ってもいいですか？

I think that the check is wrong.

お勘定が間違っているように思います。

What is this charge?

これは何の値段ですか？

5. 体調が良くない時   Track 119

I feel sick.

具合が悪いです。

Do you have any pain killers?

鎮痛剤はありますか？

Where's the nearest hospital?

一番近い病院はどこですか？

Please call a doctor.

医者を呼んでください。

Is there a doctor who speaks Japanese?

日本語を話せる医者はいますか？

I feel better now.

だいぶ良くなりました。

I have an allergy to nuts.

ナッツアレルギーがあります。

パワー単語を活用して、
リーダーのフレーズを格上げしよう

　本書では数多くのフレーズをご紹介していますが、これは知らなくても良いと思うような難しい単語は一切使っていません。ビジネスシーンでの会話は、なるべく短文で、シンプルに表現するのがおすすめです。

　一方、"**パワー単語**" と言われる、前向きに響く言葉を活用すると、プロフェッショナルな感じで、文章全体が引き締まり、リーダーに相応しい力強い表現になります。パワー単語は、実は最近のカタカナ英語として、日本人に浸透しているものが多くあります。
　下記にいくつか例をご紹介します。

face（直面する）

　難題（**challenges**）にぶつかっている時、**face** を使うと、その問題に対峙して乗り越えるといった、前向きなニュアンスになります。

feedback（フィードバック）

　本書で何度も出て来ました。**comment** や **opinion** より、相手に負担をかけないニュアンスがあると同時に、ポジティブで軽快なイメージもあります。

launch（始める・発売する）

　ロケットを発射するという時にも使われる **launch** ですが、新製品を発売したり、新しいプロジェクトを開始する時など、ビジネスで幅広く使われています。前向きで恰好いい表現です。

initiative（イニシアチブ・戦略・計画）

　来年の計画などを話す際にも、**plan** という平坦な単語ではなく、**initiatives for the next year** という表現を使えば、計画自体が一気にパワフルなものに格上げされます。

パワー単語の学び方ですが、まず周囲にプレゼンが上手な人がいたら、どのような単語を使っているかチェックしてみてください。動画などで見ることができる、海外の著名な CEO などのインタビュー動画も参考になります。

　その他、ウォールストリートなどの経済新聞でよく使われる単語をチェックしてみるとか、グローバル企業のアニュアル・レポートの CEO からのメッセージなどもおすすめです。　**どんなにビジネスが厳しい状況にあっても、必ず前向きなトーンのメッセージになるよう、パワー単語を活用**しています。

Chapter 6

グローバルリーダーの
最強フレーズ

　プレゼンには一定の "型" があり、それを意識した成り立ちにするのが、最も伝わりやすいです。また、プレゼンでの一番の課題は、予期せぬ質問を受けた時にどのように対処するかですが、それはリーダーに求められる大事なスキルの一つです。

1. プレゼンに適切な挨拶と自己紹介　　Track 120

Good morning, everyone.

皆さん、おはようございます。

Good afternoon, ladies and gentlemen.

皆さん、こんにちは。

Good evening to all.

皆さん、こんばんは。

Thank you for waiting.

お待ちいただきありがとうございます。

Thank you for coming all the way to attend our seminar.

セミナーに出席してくださり、大変ありがとうございます。

I warmly welcome you all to my presentation.

私のプレゼンテーションにようこそ。

Thank you for attending our conference this afternoon.

今日の午後に私たちのコンフェレンスに出席していただきありがとうございます。

Thank you for taking some time out of your busy schedule.

お忙しいところ、お時間をいただきましてありがとうございます。

I hope you all had a pleasant trip today.

今日ここに来るまで、良い旅であればよかったのですが。

On behalf of the organizing committee, I would like to welcome you here today.

組織委員会を代表して、今日ここで皆さんを歓迎いたします。

I would like to take the opportunity to thank you for coming to this seminar with great enthusiasm.

熱意をもってこのセミナーに参加してくださり、ありがとうございます。

I am delighted to see that so many of you could be with us today.

今日は非常に多くの方が参加してくださりうれしいです。

It's great to meet so many people from around the world all together in this conference.

世界中から非常に多くの方にこのコンフェレンスでお会いできてうれしいです。

Welcome to our 2nd Annual Sales Leadership Conference.

第2回、年次セールスリーダーシップコンフェレンスへようこそ。

It is a great pleasure to be here today.

本日ここでお話しする機会を得られて大変光栄です。

It's a great privilege for me to be invited as a keynote speaker today.

今日、基調講演者として招待されることは私にとって大きな特権です。

I would like to thank the association for inviting me to this global conference.

このグローバル会議に私を招待してくれた協会に感謝したいと思います。

I have been looking forward to this event for many weeks.

何週間もこのイベントを楽しみにしていました。

I am very pleased to have the opportunity to talk about our new services today.

本日は私たちの新しいサービスについて話す機会をいただき、大変うれしく思います。

I am glad to have this opportunity to offer a few thoughts on this latest topic.

この最新の話題について、いくつか考えを述べさせていただく機会をいただき、光栄に思います。

I appreciate the opportunity to make a presentation this afternoon.

今日午後、プレゼンテーションをする機会をいただいたことを感謝しております。

First, let me introduce myself.

まず、自己紹介させてください。

Let me start by saying just a few words about my own background.

私自身の経歴について少しお話しすることから始めます。

For those of you who don't know me already, my name is Ken Suzuki and I am in charge of the Tokyo office.

まだ私を知らない方もいらっしゃいますが、私は東京オフィスの責任者のスズキ・ケンです。

I am Taro Yamada from Yokohama branch, ABC company.

私は ABC 社の横浜支店の山田太郎です。

I am Taro Yamada, the representative from ABC company.

私は ABC 社の代表、山田太郎です。

I am in charge of business development in headquarters.

私は本社で事業開発を担当しています。

I am responsible for domestic sales.

私は国内営業の責任者です。

Hello. I'm Ken and I am the head of sales of ABC company.

こんにちは。ABC 社の営業統括のケンです。

To begin with, I would like to briefly talk about our company's history.

はじめに、私たちの会社の歴史について簡単にお話しします。

Our company consists of 10 divisions around the world.

当社は、世界中にある 10 の部門で構成されています。

My team consists of 30 people from different backgrounds.

私のチームは、様々なバックグラウンドの 30 人で構成されています。

Chapter 6

We are one of the leading companies in the digital marketing industry.

私たちは、デジタルマーケティング業界のトップ企業の１つです。

We just merged with two local companies.

当社は地元の２社と合併したところです。

We are a startup company formed in 2010 in Tokyo.

私たちは2010年に東京で設立されたスタートアップ企業です。

We have a capital alliance with one of the global trading companies, called ABC company.

当社はABC社という世界的な商社と資本提携をしています。

We have several partnerships with local companies around the world.

世界中の地元企業といくつかのパートナーシップを結んでいます。

We specialize in small business consulting.

中小企業のコンサルティングを専門としています。

We are based in New York.

私たちはニューヨークに拠点を置いています。

We have two regional headquarters in Asia and Europe to support our global business.

グローバルビジネスをサポートするために、アジアとヨーロッパに２つの地域本社があります。

We have ten factories all over the world and have about a thousand employees.

世界中に 10 の工場があり、約 1,000 人の従業員がいます。

We have a dominating market share in this segment.

このセグメントの市場シェアは圧倒的です。

We are aggressively expanding our global business.

グローバルビジネスを積極的に拡大しています。

We have three core businesses, including system development, software development, and after-services.

システム開発、ソフトウェア開発、そしてアフターサービスを含む 3 つのコアビジネスがあります。

Our parent company is an established manufacturing company in Japan.

当社の親会社は日本で定評のある製造業者です。

We have a strong presence in Southeast Asia.

当社は東南アジアで圧倒的なプレゼンスを持っています。

We went public last year.

当社は昨年公開しました。

We are planning to do an Initial Public Offering next year.

来年、新規株式公開を行う予定です。

Our parent company is listed on NASDAQ.

親会社は NASDAQ に上場しています。

In the next few minutes, I would like to talk about who we are.

次の数分で、私たち自身についてお話しします。

Then I will talk about how we can help your personal development.

そして、私たちがあなたの個人的な成長をどのように助けることができるかについて話したいと思います。

Now, I would like to introduce my colleague Ken Suzuki.

それでは、同僚のスズキ・ケンを紹介します。

He will present our sales strategy.

彼が私たちの営業戦略をお話しします。

2. プレゼンの目的を効果的に伝える Track 121

Today I would like to talk about our sales strategy for this year.

本日は、我々の今年の営業戦略について話したいと思います。

My presentation is divided into three parts.

私のプレゼンテーションは3つのパートに分かれています。

Here is my schedule today.

こちらが今日の予定です。

I am here today to talk about our new product.

今日ここで新製品についてお話しします。

The theme of my presentation is "corporate social responsibility".

私のプレゼンテーションのテーマは「企業の社会的責任」です。

My presentation today consists of five sections.

今日の私のプレゼンテーションは5つのセクションで構成されています。

I have four main points to talk about today.

今日は4つのポイントを話します。

First, I will show you the results of last year.

まず、昨年の成果をお話しします。

Then I am going to talk about the key issues.

その後、重要な課題についてお話しします。

Chapter 6

And finally, I will present the plan for this year.

そして最後に、今年の計画を発表します。

At the end of my presentation, I will touch on our new product.

プレゼンテーションの最後に、新製品について触れます。

In today's presentation, I am going to talk about our latest market trends in AI technology.

本日のプレゼンテーションでは、AI 技術における最新の市場動向についてお話しします。

My objective today is to give you the full pictures of our priorities next year.

私の今日の目的は、皆さんに来年の我々の優先事項の全体像をお伝えすることです。

The purpose of this presentation is to introduce our new services for the first time.

このプレゼンテーションの目的は、私たちの新しいサービスを初めてご紹介することです。

My presentation is particularly relevant to those of you who are interested in global leadership.

私の発表は、グローバルリーダーシップに興味を持っている皆さんに特に関連があります。

This presentation is intended for managers who lead diversified groups.

このプレゼンテーションは、多様なグループを率いるマネージャーを対象としています。

Today I am here to talk about our sales strategy next year.

今日は、来年の私たちの販売戦略について話します。

Before I start, does anyone know about the latest service, called ABC?

プレゼンを始める前に、ABC という最新のサービスを聞いたことがある方はいますか？

As you all know, today I am going to talk to you about our new products for next year.

皆さんご存知の通り、今日は来年の新製品についてお話しします。

Let me start by giving you some overview of my presentation.

プレゼンテーションの概要を紹介することから始めさせていただきます。

I would like to kick off my presentation with a brief explanation about today's topics.

今日の話題について簡単に説明して、プレゼンテーションを開始したいと思います。

Let me begin by explaining the current status.

現在の状態を説明することから始めましょう。

First, I will give you a quick overview of our last year financial results.

最初に、昨年の決算の概要を簡単に説明します。

What I am going to talk about today is how social media has impacted our lives for the last ten years.

今日お話しすることは、ソーシャルメディアが過去 10 年間に私たちの生活にどのような影響を与えたかについてです。

Chapter 6

Today I am going to report on the results of the field research we carried out for the last six months.

今日は、過去6ヶ月間に実施したフィールド調査の結果について報告します。

As I have limited time to present today, I would like to focus on three major discoveries.

本日の発表の時間は限られているので、3つの大きな発見に集中してお話しします。

Let me start by giving you some background information about my research.

私の研究について、あなたにいくつかの背景情報を与えることから始めましょう。

Today, I want to make a short presentation about the budget for the new year.

今日は、新年の予算について簡単に説明します。

Today I would like to talk about our new strategy in detail.

今日、私たちの新しい戦略を詳細にお話しします。

I would like to limit my discussion on our upcoming merger today.

今日は私たちの合併に関する議論に限ってお話ししたいと思います。

By the end of my presentation, I hope you will be familiar with our new services.

プレゼンテーションの終わりには、我々の新サービスを十分ご理解いただけると思います。

By the time I'm done today, you will be very excited about our new product.

今日の私の話が終わるまでに、私たちの新製品に大きく期待していただけると思います。

I am sure you will enjoy my seminar today.

今日のセミナーを楽しんでいただけると確信しています。

I am sure you will have a few takeaways from my presentation.

私のプレゼンで持ち帰っていただけることがいくつかあると確信しています。

My presentation will take around 30 minutes, then a Q&A session will follow.

私のプレゼンは30分くらいかかり、その後Q&Aセッションがあります。

I expect to be presenting for no more than 30 minutes.

プレゼンは30分以上かからない予定です。

I will be speaking today for about one hour.

今日は約1時間お話しします。

Now, I am going to start with some general information on the current market.

それでは、現在の市場についての一般的な情報から始めます。

Please feel free to interrupt me if you have any questions.

ご質問がありましたら、遠慮なく私にご質問ください。

I will give you a handout of the slides at the end of my talk.

私のお話の最後に、スライドの配布資料をお送りします。

Please take one on your way out.

お帰りの途中に 1 部を取ってください。

The handout has additional data for your information.

配布資料には、情報として追加データがあります。

I would like you to focus on the presentation rather than taking notes.

ノートを取るより、プレゼンに集中していただきたいと思います。

Please refer to your copies of the slides where needed.

必要に応じて、スライドのコピーを参照してください。

I have put all the important information on a handout for you.

配布資料に全て重要な情報を入れています。

After the presentation, I can email the PowerPoint presentation to anybody who requests it.

プレゼンの後、ご希望の方にはパワーポイントのプレゼン資料をＥメールでお送りします。

We will distribute a quick survey after the presentation.

プレゼンテーション後に、簡単なアンケートを配布します。

The survey will take only a few minutes to complete.

アンケートはたった数分で完了します。

It will be greatly appreciated if you could fill out the survey before you leave.

お帰り前にアンケートにご記入いただければ幸いです。

3. 相手に語りかけて関心を引く　　　Track 122

Think about why we are having this off-site meeting.

なぜこのオフサイトミーティングを開いているのか考えてください。

How many of you have ever had trouble remembering goals?

ゴールを見失いそうになった人は皆さんの中でどれくらいいますか？

Have you ever heard of "Webisode"?

「ウェビソード」という言葉を聞いたことがありますか？

Has anyone heard of the new tax benefits?

新しい税制優遇措置を聞いたことがある人はいますか？

So, what has changed?

それで、何が変わったのでしょうか？

Can anyone tell what's going on in this market?

誰もがこの市場で何が起こっているのかわかりますか？

Let's find out the reasons for this.

その理由を見つけましょう。

Could you tell what this chart is indicating?

このチャートが何を示しているかわかりますか？

According to market information, our competitors plan to cut their prices dramatically.

市場情報によると、競合他社は劇的に彼らの価格を引き下げることを予定しています。

According to statistics, we will see the population growing more in this area.

統計によると、この分野での人口増加が見られます。

Given our financial situation, we need to consolidate our business.

財務状況を考えると、ビジネスを統合する必要があります。

How would you respond to this situation?

この状況にどう対応しますか？

With all of these challenges, what do we hope to accomplish?

これら全ての課題がある中、私たちは何を達成したいのでしょうか？

Here is what we found.

こちらが、私たちが発見したことです。

Well, how about reducing the price further?

では、さらに価格を下げるのはどうですか？

Is this too aggressive?

これはアグレッシブすぎますか？

Where do you want to go from here?

ここからどうしますか？

How do you feel about this proposal?

この提案についてどう思いますか？

What's going to happen if we don't move now?

今行動を起こさなければ、どうなると思いますか？

Does anyone have a good explanation for this issue?

この問題をきちんと説明できる人はいますか？

Did you know that we received great feedback?

すばらしいフィードバックを受けていることを知っていましたか？

What did we learn from this challenge?

この試練から何を学びましたか？

What does this mean for us?

これは私たちにどのような意味がありますか？

What have we learned from past failures?

過去の失敗から私たちは何を学びましたか？

What about your idea?

あなたの考えはどうですか？

How are you going to deal with this challenge?

この課題にどのように対処しますか？

Let's work together to overcome this challenge.

この課題を克服するために協力しましょう。

1. メインパートをわかりやすく伝える　　Track 123

I am going to begin by explaining the market trend in the Tokyo metropolitan area.

東京の首都圏の市場傾向を説明することから始めます。

Now, I would like to explain the details of our services.

では、サービスの詳細を説明します。

I would like to explain the details later.

詳細は後ほどご説明いたします。

Let's begin with the result of last year.

昨年の結果から始めましょう。

Now, we are going to look at our market trend.

では、市場の動向を見ていきましょう。

First, I am going to give you some details of our great accomplishments last year.

まず、昨年我々が成し遂げたすばらしい結果の詳細をお伝えします。

We are going to look at our current market share.

最新の我々の市場シェアを見てみましょう。

Our market share has achieved a historical record for three months in a row.

当社の市場シェアは、3ヶ月連続で過去最高の記録を達成しています。

I am going to explain the change in consumer awareness.

消費者意識の変化について説明します。

Then I'll talk about where we go from here.

そして、ここからどうしていくべきかをお話しします。

Now, please take a look at the graph on page 3.

では、3 ページのグラフを見てください。

I have highlighted the key figures in blue.

重要な数字を青でハイライトしています。

Turning our attention to the next slide, now I would like to explain the features of our new product.

次のスライドをよく見ていただいて、我々の新製品の機能について説明したいと思います。

As you can see from this slide, our products have had a very strong start after the launch.

このスライドが示す通り、当社の製品は発売後、非常に力強いスタートを切っています。

I would like to highlight that the new product with a higher-margin has contributed to our profitability.

利益率の高い新製品が収益性に貢献したことを強調したいと思います。

As you can see from this chart, our product portfolio has significantly diversified after the acquisition.

このチャートからわかるように、当社の製品ポートフォリオは買収後に大幅に多様化しています。

Based on our findings, 60% of our market is made up of sales from Kanto.

私たちの調査結果によると、市場の60%は関東からの販売で構成されています。

According to our study, 50% of working people in this area spend more than $10 for lunch.

私たちの調査によると、この地域で働く人の50%が昼食に10ドル以上を使っています。

Based on our analysis, we propose to raise our service fees.

分析に基づいて、サービス料金の引き上げを提案します。

Assuming that our market research is correct, there are great demands for catering in this area.

当社の市場調査が正しいと仮定すると、この地域でのケータリングに対する需要は大きいです。

Please turn to page 7.

7ページを開いてください。

Please refer to the attached documents for the price information.

価格情報については、添付の資料をご参照ください。

Our sales were $500,000 last month.

先月の売上高は50万ドルでした。

In other words, our sales increased 10% from a month earlier.

言い換えれば、当社の売上高は前月比で10%増加です。

As this figure indicates, the average price is continuously declining.

この数字が示すように、平均価格は継続的に下落しています。

As a result of the competition with foreign companies, our market share has been steadily declining.

外国企業との競争の結果、当社の市場シェアは着実に減少しています。

When we closely look at these trends, I am sure that my point becomes clearer.

これらの傾向を詳しく見ると、私のポイントがより明確になると確信しています。

I assume that this trend will continue for the time being.

この傾向は当面続くと思います。

We should assume this problem won't go away so soon.

この問題はすぐにはなくならないと考えるべきでしょう。

Our data shows that more than 60% of men in this city prefer to buy a smaller car.

私たちのデータによると、この都市の男性の60％以上が小さな車を購入することを好んでいます。

There is a possibility of another competitive entry to the market.

市場に新たな競合他社が参入する可能性があります。

We should also remember that the global economy could slow down in the next couple of years.

また、今後数年間で世界経済が減速する可能性があることも考慮しなければいけません。

Contrary to our prediction, our sales of existing products have been strong.

予想に反して、既存製品の売上は好調です。

Now I would like to expand on my point about the new market trend.

では、新しい市場の傾向について、さらにお話ししたいと思います。

Before I move on to the next topic, I would like to answer your question.

次の話題に移る前に、ご質問にお答えします。

Let me give you some examples.

いくつか事例をご紹介します。

I am going to share a couple of case studies with you.

いくつか事例をシェアします。

Let's see our Nagoya branch case.

名古屋支店の事例を見てみましょう。

I will show you another case later.

後で別のケースを紹介します。

Therefore, we strongly recommend that you invest now.

従いまして、我々は御社がすぐに投資することを強くおすすめします。

Due to the fact that consumer preferences shift, we may change our marketing strategy.

消費者の嗜好が変化しているという事実に基づき、当社はマーケティング戦略を変更する可能性があります。

In my opinion, we should look for the other option.

私の意見では、別のオプションを探すべきです。

I would like to change direction and talk about an alternative solution.

方向を変えて、代替策についてお話ししたいと思います。

I would like to briefly cover our second strategy as an alternative.

代替案として、2番目の戦略について簡単に説明します。

I hope it's clear by now that we need to move on quickly.

これまでの話で、早急に動く必要があるとおわかりいただけたことを願います。

There are three advantages to this idea.

このアイデアには3つの利点があります。

There are three stages of implementing this program.

このプログラムの実施には3つの段階があります。

We propose two types of services.

2タイプのサービスをご提案します。

There are two kinds of services available at this moment.

現在、2種類のご利用できるサービスがあります。

This ties in with one of our strategic directions.

これは、当社の戦略的方向性の1つと関連しています。

The first one offers a free trial period, while the other option requires immediate purchase with a 10% discount.

最初のものは無料試用期間を提供しますが、他のオプションは10%割引で即時購入を必要とします。

Even if we accept the point that we have increased our market share, that still leaves the question of declining prices.

マーケットシェアを拡大したという点を受け入れても、それでも価格を下げるという問題が残ります。

Do you have any questions at this point?

この段階で何か質問がありますでしょうか？

For the next 10 minutes or so, I will focus on this problem.

次の10分間ほど、この問題に焦点を当てます。

For the rest of my presentation, I am going to explain the details of my proposal.

プレゼンテーションの残りの時間では、私の提案の詳細を説明します。

Now let's turn to the last part of my presentation, which is about the project schedule.

それでは、プレゼンテーションの最後のパートの、プロジェクトのスケジュールについてお話しします。

This concludes my first part of today's presentation.

これで今日のプレゼンテーションの最初のパートは終わりです。

Now, I hand over to Mike, our next presenter.

では、次のプレゼンターであるマイクに引き渡します。

Before I move on, does anyone have any comments?

先に進む前に、何かコメントがある方はいますか？

2. グラフやデータを使って効果的に説明する　Track 124

In this part of my presentation, I will be showing you some charts to explain more detail.

プレゼンテーションのこのパートで、チャートをお見せしながら詳細を説明したいと思います。

Let me use a graphic to explain this.

これを説明するためにグラフィックを使用します。

Now, I am going to show you some interesting data.

ここで、いくつかの興味深いデータを紹介します。

I would like to show you a short video.

短いビデオをお見せしたいと思います。

Let's look at the survey results.

では調査結果を見ていきましょう。

Please look at the graph on the screen.

スクリーンのグラフを見てください。

Let me explain this further by showing the graphs.

グラフを見せながら、これをさらに説明します。

The figure is based on government reports.

この図は政府の報告に基づいています。

The price trend of raw materials is shown in the blue line.

原材料の価格動向は青い線で示されています。

If you look at this chart, you will see the declining trend.

このチャートを見ると、減少傾向が見られます。

These figures indicate that we are losing our shares to the competitors.

これらの数字は、競合他社にシェアを失いつつあることを示しています。

This chart shows the price of raw material X for the past few years.

このチャートは、過去数年間の原材料 X の価格を示しています。

The price increased dramatically from 2012 to 2014.

価格は 2012 年から 2014 年に劇的に上昇しました。

Then the price remained stable for a couple of years.

それから価格は数年間、安定したままでした。

Since the beginning of 2017, it's been declining gradually.

2017 年の初めから、それは徐々に減少しています。

We expect the price will continue going down for the time being.

当面、価格は下がり続けると予想しています。

If you take a look at the pie chart, you will see the distribution of our product portfolio.

円グラフを見ると、当社の製品ポートフォリオの分布がわかります。

Now we are going to spend a few moments reviewing our marketing data.

では、少しマーケティングデータを見てみましょう。

This chart shows a breakdown of the materials we use in our new product.

このチャートは、新製品で使用した材料の内訳を示しています。

Let's look at the year-over-year movement.

前年比の動きを見てみましょう。

This steady increase illustrates our new strategy is working well.

この着実な増加は、新しい戦略がうまく機能していることを示しています。

This chart shows the breakdown of the revenue by region.

このチャートは、地域ごとの収益の内訳を示しています。

The source of this information comes from our R&D database.

この情報は当社の R&D のデータベースから来ています。

This line graph deals with our sales figures for the past decade.

この折れ線グラフは、過去 10 年間の売上高を示しています。

The green line represents the budget this year.

緑の線は、今年の予算を表しています。

The solid lines in black are our historical data.

黒の実線は、過去のデータです。

On the horizontal axis, you can see the years of service.

横軸には、勤続年数が表示されます。

On the vertical axis, you can see the ages.

縦軸には、年齢が表示されます。

The horizontal axis indicates years from 2008 to 2018.

横軸は、2008 年から 2018 年を示します。

You can see some major fluctuations during this period.

この期間中に大きな変動があることがわかります。

The solid black line shows actual sales.

黒の直線は、売上実績です。

The broken blue line represents projected sales.

青の破線は、売上予想を示します。

This line graph clearly shows the significant seasonal variations in sales during the course of a year.

この折れ線グラフは、年間の売上高の季節ごとの大きな変動を明確に示しています。

As you can see from the chart, there was a slight decrease in sales in August and December.

グラフからわかるように、8 月と 12 月の売上高はわずかに減少しました。

The revenues increased sharply in the spring.

収益は春に急増しました。

Our sales increased 10% this year.

今年の売上は 10% 伸びました。

Sales bottomed out in May.

売上高は 5 月に底打ちしました。

We have achieved a double-digit sales increase two years in a row.

2 年連続で 2 桁の売上増を達成しました。

Our productivity has improved 20% this year.

今年の生産性は 20％改善しました。

On the other hand, sales peaked in October.

一方、売上高は 10 月にピークに達しました。

With these bar charts, I would like to bring you up to date with our progress.

これらの棒グラフをお見せして、これまでの進捗状況をお知らせしたいと思います。

This bar chart shows the sales trend of our product A, B, C for the last three years.

この棒グラフは、過去 3 年間における当社の製品 A、B、C の販売動向を示しています。

You can see that although Product A is the highest-selling, its sales have gradually declined over the three-year period, while sales of the other two have continued to grow.

製品 A が最も売れ行きが良いですが、その売上は 3 年間で徐々に減少し、他の 2 つの売上は伸び続けているのがわかります。

Chapter 6

409

What can we learn from this trend?

この傾向から学べることは何でしょうか？

When you see this declining trend, it is obvious that we need a drastic plan.

この減少傾向を見ると、抜本的な計画が必要であることは明らかです。

When you see these results, we can say our plan has been working well.

これらの結果を見ると、計画がうまく機能していると言えます。

How should we interpret these figures?

これらの数字をどう解釈すべきでしょうか？

Perhaps Product A is suffering from stiffer competition than the other two models.

製品 A は他の 2 つのモデルよりも厳しい競争にさらされているのではないでしょうか。

This means we need to do something to revitalize Product A urgently.

これは、製品 A のてこ入れを早急にする必要があることを意味します。

As you can see, this graph shows the new trend of the market.

ご覧のように、このグラフは市場の新しい傾向を示しています。

It means that we are no longer a leader in the market.

つまり、私たちはもはや市場のリーダーではありません。

As this figure indicates, the upside of the market growth is limited.

この図が示すように、市場成長の上昇は限られています。

I must say that our revenue will continue to be stagnant unless we do something.

何もしない限り、収益は停滞し続けると言わざるを得ません。

The study of these data implies a decrease in consumer interests.

これらのデータの調査は、消費者の関心の低下を示唆しています。

This graph shows the growth of the population in Prefecture X from 1985 to 2015.

このグラフは、X 県の 1985 年から 2015 年までの人口増加を示しています。

The data is taken from the statistics of local government.

データは、地方自治体の統計に基づいています。

There are three lines in the chart.

グラフには 3 つの線があります。

The black line shows the total growth of the population.

黒い線は総人口の伸びを示しています。

While the blue line represents the population relocated from other prefectures, the green line shows the natural increase of the population.

青い線は他の都道府県から移住した人口を表し、緑色の線は（同県の）人口の自然増加を示しています。

Chapter 6

411

During these periods, the population of Prefecture X has been stable despite the gradual decline of natural increase.

これらの期間中、X県の人口は自然増加の緩やかな減少にもかかわらず、安定しています。

We can tell that the relocated people from other areas offset the decline in the natural increase in Prefecture X.

他の地域からの移住者が、X県の自然増加の減少を相殺したと言えます。

From this data, I think it's fair to say that people are spending less these days.

このデータから、人々の支出が最近減ってきていると言うことができると思います。

This evidence seems to indicate that we have been losing shares to competitors.

この証拠は、私たちが競合他社にシェアを失っていることを示していると言えます。

As this figure indicates, we are recovering our market shares.

この数字が示すように、当社は市場シェアを回復しています。

3. 相手の理解の確認をする　　　　　　　Track 125

Are you with me?

よろしいでしょうか？

Are you following me so far?

ここまで私が言ったことの理解は大丈夫？

Does that make sense?

おわかりになりますでしょうか？

Have I made everything clear so far?

ここまで、全て明確にできていますでしょうか？

Are we all on the same page?

みんなご理解いただいていますか？

I would be happy to clarify anything that's not clear.

不明な点があれば、ご説明します。

If you don't mind, I would like to repeat the main point.

よろしければ、要点をもう一度繰り返します。

Let me put it another way to help your understanding.

ご理解を助けるために、別の言い方をしてみましょう。

4. 大事なメッセージを強調する方法　　Track 126

I would like to focus on the emerging trend in the market.

市場での新たな傾向に注目したいと思います。

Let me focus on the marketing strategy.

マーケティング戦略にフォーカスさせてください。

In fact, this is the most important feature of our new product.

実際、これは当社の新製品にとっても最も重要な機能です。

The problem is that the production cost is quite high.

問題は生産コストがかなり高いことです。

The problem is that the initial investment is too high.

問題は、初期投資が高すぎることです。

The issue is that we don't have enough labor resources.

問題は、十分な労働力がないことです。

The real challenge is profitability.

本当の課題は収益性です。

This is an extremely important point.

これは非常に重要な点です。

This point is extremely important for several reasons.

このポイントはいくつかの理由で非常に重要です。

Let me elaborate on this matter further, as this is critical.

これは非常に重要なので、この問題についてさらに詳しく説明します。

What I would like to emphasize is its cost performance.

私が強調したいのは、コストパフォーマンスです。

What I'm saying is that we need to increase our price.

私が言っているのは、価格を引き上げる必要があるということです。

What I would like to propose is to introduce a new system.

私が提案したいのは、新しいシステムを導入することです。

What we would like to suggest this time is to reconsider your marketing strategy.

今回提案するのは、マーケティング戦略を再検討することです。

It's obvious that we have to find a new location.

新しい場所を見つける必要があることは明らかです。

To put it simply, we have to live with a smaller budget.

簡単に言えば、少ない予算でやっていかなければならないということです。

That's the main reason why I strongly recommend the new strategy.

これは私が新しい戦略を強く推奨する主な理由です。

Now, I come to the most important message today.

いよいよ今日最も大事なメッセージをお話しします。

I would like to highlight that we need additional funding to continue our project.

私はプロジェクトを続けるために追加資金が必要であることを強調したいと思います。

Chapter 6

The significance of this is that we will have a cost advantage.

これの重要性は、コスト面で有利になることです。

This is important because any marketing effort should help to boost demand for our products in the long run.

あらゆるマーケティング活動は、長期的には当社製品の需要を押し上げることにつながるので、これは重要なことです。

As I pointed out this at the beginning of my presentation, this is the most imminent matter.

プレゼンテーションの始めにこれを指摘したように、これが最も差し迫った問題です。

Global warming is a growing and pending problem in the world.

地球温暖化は、世界で増え続けている懸案事項です。

For this reason, I intend to focus on proposing immediate solutions.

このため、私は早急な解決策の提案に焦点を当ててお話しします。

Let me go back to what I said earlier about the cost structure once again.

もう一度、コスト構造について先ほど述べたことに戻ります。

It should be emphasized that we made great progress.

私たちが大きな進歩を遂げてきたことが強調されるべきです。

Another significant point is that we need corrective action.

もう1つの重要な点は、是正措置が必要であることです。

Let's go back to page 10 to look at the numbers once again.

10ページに戻って、もう一度、数値を見てみましょう。

What I mean to say is that we need to upgrade our products before a competitor's entry.

私が言いたいのは、競合他社が参入する前に製品をアップグレードする必要があるということです。

I would like to end by emphasizing the main issues.

主な問題を強調することによって私は終わりたいと思います。

I would like to draw your attention to this point once again.

もう一度、この点に注目ください。

So I can present our plan in detail, let's go and put it into practice.

プランの詳細をお話しできましたので、これからは実践していきましょう。

First, I am going to talk about our vision.

まず、私たちのビジョンについて話します。

First of all, I would like to thank you for inviting me today.

まず始めに、本日ご招待くださったことにお礼を申し上げます。

Firstly, I will go through our results last year.

まず、昨年の結果について説明します。

Secondly, I will present the budget this year.

次に、今年の予算を発表します。

Thirdly, I will share the strategy.

第三に、私は戦略を共有します。

Finally, I am going to summarize our discussion today.

最後に、今日の私たちの議論をまとめます。

Lastly, I will take a couple of questions from the audience.

最後に、皆さんからいくつか質問を受けます。

Next, I will show you some pictures.

次に、何枚かの写真をお見せします。

Then, I will update you with our progress.

そして、進捗状況をお知らせします。

Now, let me turn to the second point I would like to discuss today.

それでは、本日の2番目の論点に移ります。

Let me skip this slide for now.

いったん、このスライドは飛ばします。

I will come back to this slide later.

のちほど、このスライドに戻ります。

Let's move on to the next topic.

次の話題に移りましょう。

Moving on to the next topic, let's take a look at our domestic market.

次のトピックに移って、国内市場を見てみましょう。

There are two steps involved in the project. The first step is planning and the second step is execution.

このプロジェクトには2つのステップが含まれます。最初のステップは計画であり、2番目のステップは実行です。

As a result of this, we decided to go ahead.

この結果、私たちは先に進むことにしました。

In addition to opening a new branch last year, we acquired a local company there.

昨年、新しい支店を開設したことに加え、そこで現地企業の買収もしました。

Furthermore, we are planning to open an R&D facility.

さらに、研究開発施設の開設を計画しています。

＊R&D：Research and Development（研究開発）

In terms of price, we are very competitive.

価格の面では、非常に競争力があります。

In terms of quality, we have significantly improved through this innovation.

品質に関しては、この革新により大幅に改善してきました。

Because of our sales staff shortage, we were unable to cover potential clients last year.

営業人員が不足していたため、昨年は見込み客をカバーできませんでした。

Despite the fact that we did not do any advertising, we made huge sales.

宣伝をまったくしなかったのにもかかわらず、大きな売上をあげました。

Although we had a smaller advertising budget, we sold more products.

広告予算が少なかったにもかかわらず、より多くの商品を販売しました。

In spite of higher material costs, we made more profit.

材料費が高騰したにもかかわらず、利益を上げました。

This leads me to my next point, which is the new function of our new product.

この件は私の次のポイント、新製品の新機能につながります。

Compared with our competitors, our products have additional functions.

競合他社と比較して、当社の製品には追加機能があります。

Compared with the older generation, the younger generation prefers a smaller model.

古い世代と比較して、若い世代はより小さなモデルを好みます。

Some of you have probably heard this before.

前に聞いたことがある方もいらっしゃるかもしれません。

Another reason why this idea is critical is cost-effectiveness.

このアイデアが重要なもう１つの理由は、費用対効果です。

For instance, the timing of the expansion is important.

例えば、拡大のタイミングが重要です。

For example, we plan to provide 24/7 services.

例えば、私たちは年中無休のサービスを提供する予定です。

Besides, this has staying power.

その上、これは耐久性があります。

In addition, we have increased our customer service representatives.

加えて、私たちはカスタマーサービス担当者を増やしました。

By the way, have you tried our competitor's product?

ところで、競合他社の商品を試したことはありますか？

Actually, this won't be an issue for us.

実は、これは問題にならないでしょう。

So far, I have covered new initiatives.

ここまでは、新しい取り組みについて話しました。

Let's summarize briefly what we've looked at so far.

これまでに見てきたことを簡単に要約しましょう。

Turning our attention now to our competitors, they might launch new products next spring.

競合他社に目を向けると、来春には新製品を発売する可能性があります。

Overall, it was a great year.

総じて、良い年でした。

At the same time, we have to consider our production capacity.

同時に、生産能力を考慮しなければなりません。

It would also be interesting to consider the alternative.

別の手段を考えてみるのもおもしろいでしょう。

On the other hand, this is cost-effective.

一方、これは費用対効果が高いです。

In spite of this, the market is growing.

これにもかかわらず、市場は成長しています。

However, we don't have any alternatives.

しかしながら、他に選択肢はありません。

Nevertheless, this option is worth exploring.

それにもかかわらず、このオプションは検討する価値があります。

In short, this will be the most efficient process.

短く言うと、これが最も効率的なプロセスになります。

Putting it simply, we need to increase our sales force.

要するに、セールス力の増強が必要です。

In other words, they are reluctant to move forward.

言い換えると、彼らは進めることを躊躇しています。

As I said at the beginning, we will have a breakout session this afternoon.

冒頭で述べたように、今日の午後には分科会があります。

As you already know, the economy is likely to continue to expand next year.

既にご存知の通り、来年も経済は拡大を続けるでしょう。

As you can see from this slide, we have successfully grown our market share.

このスライドでおわかりいただけるように、市場シェアを伸ばしてきています。

As I mentioned before, the competition will be getting tougher.

先ほどお話しした通り、競争はより激しくなるでしょう。

As we saw earlier, this will be our advantage.

前にご覧いただいた通り、これは我々の有利なところです。

Consequently, we will propose a different approach.

その結果として、私たちは異なるアプローチを提案します。

As you're aware, this product is quite sophisticated.

お気づきの通り、この商品はかなり洗練されています。

In conclusion, I am confident to beat the competitors with our new product.

結論として、我々の新製品で競合他社に勝てると確信しています。

This concludes my presentation today.

これで今日のプレゼンテーションは終わりです。

3 質問への対応

1. プレゼンの流れに沿った質問の受け方　　Track 128

Please stop me anytime, if you have questions.

ご質問があれば、いつでも聞いてください。

If you have any questions, please don't hesitate to ask.

ご質問がある場合は、どうぞご遠慮なく聞いてください。

I will be happy to answer your questions at the end of each part.

それぞれのパートの最後で、ご質問にお答えします。

My presentation will be followed by a Q&A session.

私のプレゼンの最後に、質疑応答のセッションを予定しています。

It would be great if you could wait for questions until then.

それまでご質問はお待ちいただければ幸いです。

We will have 10 minutes for Q&A at the end of the presentation.

プレゼンテーションの最後に、10 分間の質疑応答があります。

Please stop me if there is something that needs clarification before moving on.

先に進む前に説明が必要な場合は、私を止めてください。

Otherwise, we have time for discussion at the end.

そうでなければ、最後に議論する時間があります。

May I come back to that question later?

後でその質問に戻ってもいいですか？

I'll come back to this question later in the second part of my presentation.

プレゼンテーションの第2パートでこの質問に戻ります。

Well, I plan to cover the point in detail later on.

では、その点については後で詳しく説明します。

Your question leads directly to my next point.

あなたのご質問は、ちょうど次にお話ししようとしている点につながります。

2. 質問へ移行する   Track 129

Before I take your question, I will make a quick summary of what I talked about.

あなたのご質問を受ける前に、私が話したことの簡単なサマリーをします。

Now, I would like to move on to the Q&A session.

それでは、Q&A セッションに移りたいと思います。

I would be very interested to hear your comments and questions.

皆さんのコメントや質問を伺いたいと思います。

Now let's open it up for your questions and comments from the floor.

では、会場からの質問やコメントをお聞きしたいと思います。

Are there any questions?

何かご質問はありますか？

Please go ahead.

どうぞ進めてください。

Thank you for your great question.

良い質問をありがとうございます。

We just have time for a few questions.

2〜3のご質問を受ける時間があります。

That's a very good question.

とても良い質問です。

I am glad you brought that up.

その件を質問いただき、うれしいです。

I assume you are referring to one of my earlier slides.

最初のほうのスライドのことをおっしゃっていますよね。

I assume you are talking about our warranty.

当社の保証のことをおっしゃっていますよね。

Is my understanding correct?

私の理解は正しいでしょうか？

Is that correct?

正しいですか？

Well, I see your point.

ええ、そうですね。

That's right.

その通りです。

That's an interesting observation.

それは興味深い意見です。

Your question relates to what I explained at the beginning.

あなたのご質問は最初に説明したことに関連していますね。

Let me expand that point once again.

その点をもう一度、説明させてください。

Let me restate what I said about this issue.

この問題について私が言ったことをもう一度、述べさせてください。

I would like to explain this issue in a slightly different way once again.

この問題を少し異なる方法で再度、説明したいと思います。

Would you say that again, please?

もう一度、言っていただけますか？

Sorry, I didn't quite catch that.

すみません、よく理解できませんでした。

Could you ask your question in another way?

別の表現で再度ご質問していただけますか？

I am sorry, but I don't see what you mean.

すみません、ちょっとおっしゃる意味がわかりません。

Could you just repeat your questions, please?

ご質問を繰り返していただけますか？

Let me just check that I have understood your question.

あなたのご質問を理解できているか、ちょっと確認させてください。

Does this answer your question?

これはあなたのご質問へのお答えになっていますでしょうか？

I agree with your point.

あなたの意見に同意します。

I basically agree with your argument.

基本的にあなたのおっしゃる通りだと思います。

Is that the kind of information you were looking for?

このような情報で大丈夫でしょうか？

I would like to take one more question if time permits.

時間があれば、もう1つご質問を受けたいと思います。

I see your point but I have a somewhat different perspective.

おっしゃる意味はわかりますが、私は少し異なる見方をしています。

Not necessarily.

必ずしもそうではありません。

Hopefully not.

そうでなければ良いのですが。

That's true to some extent.

ある程度、当たっています。

It depends.

場合によります。

I think we have time for one more question.

あと1つご質問を受ける時間があります。

3. 予期せぬ質問への対応　　　　　Track 130

That's a bit of a difficult question to answer.

それは答えるのが少し難しい質問ですね。

I apologize but I have no idea about that.

申し訳ありませんが、それについてはわかりません。

I am sorry that we are unable to disclose that data at this moment.

申し訳ありませんが、現時点ではそのデータを開示できません。

I must say that this is confidential.

それは極秘だと言わなければなりません。

I'm afraid that I'm not the best person to answer that.

あいにく、それに答えるには、私は適任ではありません。

Well, I think that goes beyond the scope of my expertise.

えっと、それは私の専門分野を超えるようです。

I don't have that information with me today. I would like to follow it up via e-mail, if it's ok with you.

今日はその情報を持っていません。よろしければメールでフォローさせていただきます。

That's a very good question. However, I don't have any data on that to give you an accurate answer.

とても良い質問ですが、正確にお答えするためのデータを持ち合わせていません。

Let me talk to you individually after this presentation.

このプレゼンテーションの後に、個別にお話しさせてください。

I would like to talk to you more if you have time later.

後ほどお時間があれば、もっとお話ししたいと思います。

If I understand you correctly, you are asking me if we need to consider other options. Is that right?

あなたのご質問を正しく理解しているとすると、他のオプションも考える必要があるのではということですか？合っていますか？

Unfortunately, that's not my area of expertise.

あいにく、それは私の専門分野ではありません。

I think the other presenters today may know the answer to that.

今日の他のプレゼンターがそれに答えられるのではないかと思います。

Can anyone jump in to answer that question?

どなたかその質問に答えられる人はいませんか？

Have you any questions on the three proposals that I've talked about today?

今日お話しした3つの提案について、何かご質問がありますか？

I think it would be better if I got a little more information about your situation.

あなたの状況についてもう少し情報があれば、もっと良いかと思います。

Then I will be able to provide a bit more helpful answer to you.

それから、もう少し役に立つ答えを提供することができるでしょう。

Can we meet at the reception after the presentation?

発表後のレセプションでお会いできますか？

Unfortunately, we are running out of time.

残念ながら、私たちは時間を使い果たしています。

I will be happy to answer any remaining questions at the reception after the conference.

会議後のレセプションで、残りのご質問にお答えします。

For the sake of time, I will skip some details, which you can find in the handout.

時間の都合上、配布資料に記載されている詳細の一部は省略します。

I don't have those requested figures today, but I am sure that my staff has them in the office.

おたずねになったそれらの数字を今日は持ち合わせていませんが、オフィスにいる私のスタッフが持っているはずです。

I would be happy to ask her to send them to you, if you could leave your contact information.

あなたの連絡先を残していただければ、彼女にそれらを送らせますが。

I am sorry that your point falls outside of my objectives today.

すみません、その点は今日の私の（プレゼンの）目的からはずれます。

That's not my point, unfortunately.

あいにく、それは私のポイントではありません。

Not exactly.

そうとも言えません。

Let me put together my thinking on this matter.

この問題について、考えをまとめさせてください。

Perhaps can we discuss later that particular matter privately?

その特定の事柄については、後ほど個別にお話しできますか？

I'm afraid I need to move on to the next person.

次の方のご質問に移りたいと思います。

Any other questions?

他にご質問は？

4. 本題と無関係な質問を受けた場合の対応　Track 131

Good question.

良い質問です。

I really don't have an answer.

わからないですね。

What do you think?

どう思われますか？

That may not be relevant to the topic today.

それは今日のトピックには関係ないかもしれません。

Let me cover that topic in detail at the presentation next month.

そのトピックについては、来月のプレゼンテーションで詳しく説明します。

If you don't mind, I would like to defer your question to the next session.

よろしければ、次のセッションまであなたのご質問を延期したいと思います。

I'm afraid I'm unable to answer that at the moment.

あいにく、現時点ではそれに答えられません。

Perhaps, I can get back to you later.

たぶん、後ほどお答えできるでしょう。

1. 効果的にまとめる   Track 132

Finally, I would like to close my presentation with a quick summary.

最後に、簡単にまとめて私のプレゼンテーションを終わりにしたいと思います。

I would like to conclude now with a few remarks about my presentation.

私のプレゼンテーションに関していくつかお話しして、これで終わりにしたいと思います。

I would like to sum up my presentation.

プレゼンテーションをまとめたいと思います。

Finally, I would like to highlight one key issue.

最後に、1つ大事な問題を強調したいと思います。

In summing up, I would like to recommend this project with three reasons as discussed.

まとめると、お話しした3つの理由で私はこのプロジェクトをおすすめします。

Well, we've looked at the three issues we are facing.

さて、私たちが直面している3つの問題を見てきました。

I would like to sum up my recommendation now.

では、私の提案をまとめたいと思います。

Well, this brings me to the end of my presentation.

ええと、これで私のプレゼンテーションの終わりになります。

To summarize, we must prepare for the tougher competition.

まとめると、我々はより厳しい競争に向けて準備しなければならないということです。

To recap what I've gone over so far, we must invest for additional production capacity.

これまでにお話ししたことをまとめると、我々は生産設備への追加投資が必要だということになります。

Here is a quick recap of the main points of this presentation.

今回のプレゼンテーションの主要な点のまとめです。

I think that's everything I wanted to say about our proposal.

我々の提案について言いたいことはこれで全てです。

I hope you have understood that there are several advantages and disadvantages in short.

要するに、いくつかの長所と短所があることをご理解いただけたことと思います。

I've covered all the points that I wanted to talk about today.

今日お話ししたいことは全て説明しました。

That's all I want to say about our five-year business plan.

5ヶ年のビジネス計画についてお伝えしたいことは以上です。

Finally, I would like to mention that all of us at company X are really excited to be a part of your project team.

最後に、X 社の私たち全員が御社のプロジェクトチームの一員であることに本当に光栄に思っているとお伝えしたいと思います。

We are looking forward to working closely with you.

あなた方と密接に協力することを楽しみにしています。

2. 参加者へのお礼　　　　　　　　　　　　　　Track 133

Well, that's it from me.

では、私からは以上です。

That brings me to the end of my presentation.

これで私のプレゼンテーションは終わります。

Thank you for your attention.

ご注目ありがとうございます。

Thank you for paying attention.

ご清聴、ありがとうございます。

Unless anyone has anything else to add, I think that's it for today.

他にどなたか追加することがなければ、本日は以上です。

Thank you very much for your attention.

ご静聴、大変ありがとうございます。

Thank you all for listening today.

本日はご清聴ありがとうございました。

It was a pleasure being here.

ここにお越しいただきありがとうございました。

I would like to thank you for taking time out of your busy schedule to listen to my presentation.

お忙しい中、私のプレゼンテーションを聞いてくださり、ありがとうございます。

I hope this presentation was informative for you.

このプレゼンテーションがお役に立てば幸いです。

I hope my presentation today gave you some helpful insights for your future.

本日の私のプレゼンテーションで、皆さんの将来のお考えにお役に立てば幸いです。

And last but not least, I would like to thank the organizer of this event.

そして最後になりますが、このイベントの主催者に感謝します。

＊ last but not least「最後になりましたが」「大事なことを言い忘れていましたが」

Finally, I would like to end by thanking you for your attention and interest.

最後に、皆さんに注目と関心を持っていただいたことにお礼を言って終わりにいたします。

Lastly, I would like to wish you a pleasant trip back home.

最後に、良い旅でお帰りくださいと申し上げます。

Chapter 6

Column 6

ブツブツひとりごとの自主練で
アウトプットの習慣を

フレーズを実際に使えるようになるためには、自分で具体的なシナリオを想定し、"こういった場面でこんなフレーズを言おう！" という意識をもって**アウトプット（練習）すること**が効果的です。

外国人の上司や同僚、ビジネスパートナーは、同じ会社や業界であっても、発想や背景の理解が異なります。変化球の質問や想定外の疑問点が飛んでくることも多いでしょう。

何をどう簡潔に説明すれば、こちらの主張に耳を傾けてもらえるか…。これは**日頃から考える習慣**をもっておかないと、いざという時に表現できません。フレーズ練習から一歩踏み込んで、論理的に議論を展開するにはどうすればいいか、ご自身の思考を整理してください。

具体的な学習方法を一つご紹介します。

仕事からの帰り道や帰宅後、一日を振り返って、あの場面でこう言えれば良かった…という状況を思い出してください。近い将来、こんな質問があったら、自分はこういうふうに説明してみよう…そういった想像でもいいです。そういったシナリオにもとづいてフレーズを考えてください。

反対意見を効果的に言う練習も役立ちます。

例えば「その提案には賛成できません。理由は３つ…」といったふうです。この練習のポイントは、理由は３つをとりあえず言ってみることです。３つの理由を挙げることで、主張の説得力が増すと同時に、あれもこれも言わず、大事なことに絞る過程で頭の中が整理できます。

恰好良く英語でバシッと決めている自分を想像しながら、覚えるまでフレーズを自主練してください。ひとりごとでブツブツ、実際に口に出してみてください。

ビジネスシーンでは似たような状況が起きることが多いので、この自主練の成果を実感する機会は、近い将来必ずやって来るでしょう。

〈付録〉

プロフェッショナルが書く
最強文章術

　欧米流のビジネス文書・メールでは、わかりやすく端的に、ロジカルにまとめることが重要視されます。一般的には一定の“型”（日本の大学生が学ぶ論文の書き方のようなもの）があり、その型にはめてコミュニケーションするのが相手に伝わりやすいです。

■件名の書き方

問い合わせのメール

Inquiry: Your design services.
問い合わせ：御社のデザインサービスについて。

Inquiring about your design services.
御社のデザインサービスについての問い合わせ。

Request for information on your design services.
御社のデザインサービスについての情報のリクエスト。

Question: Your invoice of November 16.
質問：御社の 11 月 16 日付の請求書について。

Re: order no. XLJ 2019; goods shipped today.
Re：注文番号 XLJ 2019；本日出荷。

作業をリクエストするメール

Requesting Project X idea submissions — Due March 31.
プロジェクト X へのアイデア提出のお願い－ 3 月 31 日締切。

Employee Survey: Please take by EOD Wednesday.
従業員意識調査：水曜までに完了してください。
＊ EOD（End of Day）「1 日の終わり」

ミーティング招集のメール

Meeting Request: marketing strategy next week.
ミーティングのお願い：来週のマーケティング戦略について。

Conference Call Request: Next year budget scheduling.
電話会議のお願い：来期予算のスケジュールについて。

フォローアップのメール

Following up from our last discussion.
先日お話ししたことのフォローアップ。

Touching base: next month sales forecast.
連絡：来月の売上予測について。

Marketing Manager Interview follow up.
マーケティングマネージャーの面接フォローアップ。

リマインダーメール

Reminder: Expense report due tomorrow.
備忘：経費報告書の締切は明日。

その他

Information: ～　　　「情報：～」
Confirmation: ～　　「確認：～」
Notification: ～　　 「通知：～」
Referred by ～　　　「～に紹介されて」
Urgent:　　　　　　「緊急：」
Important:　　　　　「重要：」

■宛先の書き方

フォーマルな場合

Dear Mr.（または Ms.）＋苗字

担当者の苗字がわからない場合

Dear Sir / Madam,　各位、
To Whom It May Concern,　ご担当者様、

複数の人へ送る場合

Dear All,　皆さんへ、
Dear Team Members,　チームメンバーの皆さんへ、
Dear Finance Department Members,　財務部の皆さんへ、
Dear Sales Representatives,　営業担当の皆さんへ、

Hello + 名前、
Hi + 名前、
To + 名前、

書き出しの表現

It was a pleasure to finally meet you last week.
先週は遂にお会いすることができ、光栄でした。

This is the first time for me to send you an e-mail.
初めてメールを送らせていただきます。

My name is Ken Suzuki from ABC company and I am in charge of Marketing.
ABC 社でマーケティングを担当している、鈴木ケンと申します。

I was referred to you by Mr. Tanaka, ABC company.
ABC 社の田中さんからご紹介いただきました。

I received your company brochure and your business card at the conference last week.
先週の会議で、会社のパンフレットと名刺をいただきました。

I was given your name by Mr. John Smith of the XYZ consulting company.
XYZ コンサルティング会社の John Smith 氏からあなたのお名前を伺いました。

We met at the Technology Exhibition held at Makuhari Messe last week.
先週の幕張メッセで開催された技術展でお会いしました。

用件を述べる

I'm contacting you to inquire about your online services.
御社のオンラインサービスについてお伺いしたく、メールしています。

I am writing to apply for the position of marketing manager posted in your website.
御社のウェブサイトに掲載されているマーケティングマネージャーのポジションに応募したくメールしています。

I am writing this letter in reference to the job posting for the sales representative in Tokyo.
東京の営業担当者の求人について、このレターを書いております。

I am writing to ask for further information about your product X.
私はあなたの製品 X の情報をさらにいただきたくメールしております。

I'm reaching out in regard to the email I sent a few weeks ago about our new service.
当社の新サービスについて数週間前にお送りしたメールについて、ご連絡しています。

I know you are busy, but I would like to ask you to have a look.
お忙しいことと思いますが、ぜひご覧ください。

Please contact me when you have any questions.
ご不明な点がございましたら、ご連絡ください。

This is just a quick recap of what we discussed this morning over the phone.
このメールは今朝、電話で話したことの簡単なまとめです。

お知らせする

I am pleased to inform you that our Project X completed on time.
私たちのプロジェクト X が予定通りに完了したことをお知らせいたします。

I wanted to update you about the status of Project X.
プロジェクト X の状況についてお知らせしたいと思います。

We're writing regarding the sales conference next year.
来年のセールス会議についてメールをお送りしています。

I am happy to inform you that our clients have accepted our request.
クライアントが私たちの要求を受け入れたことを、喜んでお知らせします。

I have spoken with our senior managers and would like to keep you updated.
シニアマネージメントと話をしたので、最新情報をお伝えします。

We are contacting you regarding your next reservation, scheduled on July 1st.
7月1日に予定されている次の予約について、ご連絡いたします。

We are writing to let you know that our new product is coming out next month.
来月、新製品が出ることをお知らせするためにメールをお送りしています。

I would like to inform you about changing our address on July 1st. 2019.
2019年7月1日に住所を変更したことをお知らせします。

In this email, I would like to inform you of a recent company policy change.
このメールでは、最近の会社の方針変更についてお知らせします。

We are pleased to inform you that we have delivered our budget target this year.
今年の予算目標を達成したことをお知らせします。

We are writing to inform you of the date change for the next meeting.
次回の会議の日程変更について、お知らせします。

I am writing to let you know that this meeting has been postponed until Friday.
この会議が金曜日まで延期されたことをお知らせします。

I'm writing regarding the problems you pointed out during our last conference call.
前回の電話会議であなたが指摘した問題について書いています。

Could you let me know if we could move the date of our meeting forward?
会議の日程を早めることができるかどうか教えていただけますか？

I'm afraid we have to move the meeting back.
残念ながら会議を遅らせる必要があります。

The purpose of this e-mail is to inquire about your availability for a conference call next week.
このEメールの目的は、来週の電話会議に参加可能か問い合わせるものです。

I'm writing to let you know about sales results for this quarter.
この四半期の販売結果についてお知らせするためにメールしています。

I have some information for you regarding our job opening.
求人情報についてお知らせがあります。

The purpose of this email is to update you on the status of Project ABC.
このメールの目的は、プロジェクト ABC の状況についての最新情報をお届けすることです。

I'm contacting you regarding the conference in NY next year.
来年のニューヨークでの会議について連絡いたします。

We would like to inform you that your application has been received.
申し込みが受理されたことをお知らせします。

The purpose of this email is to give you a quick update on our project.
このメールではプロジェクトの簡単なアップデートをさせていただきます。

With regard to your inquiry, we would like to answer in this e-mail.
あなたからのお問い合わせについて、このメールでお答えします。

I am writing in reference to your inquiry which we received last week.
先週いただいたお問い合わせの件で、メールを差し上げています。

Regarding your new product, which we have purchased the other day, we have a couple of questions.
御社から先日購入した新商品について、いくつか質問があります。

This is to confirm our telephone conversation this morning.
これは今朝、電話でお話ししたことを確認するものです。

Further to our conference call yesterday, I would like to send additional information.
昨日の電話会議の続きとして、追加情報を送ります。

We have an inquiry regarding your new product.
御社の新製品について、問い合わせがあります。

This is to let you know that I will be visiting NY next month on a business trip.
これは私が出張で来月ニューヨークを訪問することをあなたに知らせるためです。

In reply to your last e-mail, here is the information.
こちらは、先のお問い合わせメールにお答えするものです。

This is to inform you that your reservation was completed.
これはあなたの予約が完了したことを知らせるためです。

In this e-mail, we would like to confirm a few points in our contracts with you.
このメールで、御社との契約について数点確認させていただきたく思います。

謝罪する

We would like to apologize for any inconvenience caused.
ご不便をおかけして申し訳ございません。

We are extremely sorry for this matter.
この件について、大変申し訳ありません。

I'm sorry that I was unable to attend the last conference call.
先日の電話会議に出られず、申し訳ありません。

Apologies for taking a long time to get back to you.
お返事に長い時間がかかって申し訳ありません。

I'm sorry for the delay of the submission.
提出が遅れてすみません。

I'm sorry, but I will not be able to make it to the meeting next month.
申し訳ありませんが、来月の会議に参加することはできません。

We are sorry for the delay in responding to your inquiry.
お問い合わせへの返信が遅れ、申し訳ありませんでした。

I am sorry I haven't been in touch for a while.
しばらくご連絡しなくて申し訳ありません。

We would like to apologize for any inconvenience caused.
ご迷惑をおかけして、申し訳ございません。

Unfortunately, the product you ordered is currently out of stock.
申し訳ございませんが、ご注文いただいた商品は現在、欠品しております。

We regret to inform you that the material you ordered is no longer available.
あいにく、ご注文いただいた材料は、現在ご提供できません。

We are afraid we are not able to process your application at this moment.
残念ながら、現時点では申請を受け付けられません。

Please accept our apologies for the delay of the shipment.
出荷が遅れ、おわび申し上げます。

We're deeply sorry that these issues have caused some inconvenience at your operation.
これらの問題がお仕事でご不便をおかけして大変申し訳ございません。

We are very sorry that our product shipped to you on June 20th was defective.
6月20日に出荷した当社の製品に欠陥があり、大変申し訳ございません。

We understand your disappointment and understand the inconvenience this must have caused your company.
今回の件では失望され、御社でご不便をおかけしたと存じます。

We would like to offer our sincere apologies for our mistake the other day.
先日の間違いには、心より謝罪申し上げます。

Please accept my sincere apologies for this matter.
この件について、心からおわび申し上げます。

Please accept this as our formal apology for the inconvenience we caused.
今回ご不便をおかけしましたことを正式におわび申し上げます。

状況を説明する

It appears that our explanation was insufficient at the time of our contract.
契約時点では当社の説明が不十分だったようです。

It appears that there was an internal communication problem.
社内でのコミュニケーションの問題があったようです。

I would like to explain what caused the problem this time.
今回は問題の原因をご説明したいと思います。

Could you spare half hour or so for us sometime this week?
今週中に30分ほどお時間を割いていただけますか？

I would like to express my deep regrets about what happened last week.
先週起きたことについて、深く遺憾の意を表します。

I would like to apologize on behalf of our department.
私たちの部署を代表して、おわび申し上げます。

As a result of our overlook, we have created an unnecessary problem.
我々の見落としの結果、不必要な問題が発生しました。

I understand that the lack of internal communication caused this issue.
内部コミュニケーションが欠如していたため、この問題を引き起こしたと理解しています。

I understand that this issue must have been frustrating for you.
この問題が大きなフラストレーションになっていたと存じます。

We understand how difficult it must have been for you to deal with this problem.
この問題に対処することは大変難しいものであったのではないかと存じます。

Now I am fully aware of the situation.
今、状況を完全に把握しました。

We will get this fixed as soon as possible.
できるだけ早くこれを解決します。

We will contact you as soon as this issue has been fixed.
この問題が解決したらすぐに、ご連絡いたします。

We will immediately investigate how to resolve this issue.
この問題をどう解決するか、すぐに調査します。

I will be in touch with you once the situation is fixed.
状況が解決しましたらご連絡いたします。

I highly appreciate your patience.
ご理解に感謝します。

We have just tightened the internal process to improve quality control.
品質管理を改善するために内部プロセスを厳しくしました。

We've increased our efforts to ensure that the shipment will be made on time.
出荷が予定通りに行われるように、一層努力します。

We initiated actions in place to improve internal communication so that this situation won't repeat itself.
この状況が二度と繰り返されないように、社内コミュニケーションを改善するための行動を起こしました。

If there is anything else that we can do to minimize your inconvenience, please contact us at any time.
ご不便を最小限に抑えるためにできることがあれば、いつでもご連絡ください。

Again, I apologize for this problem and regret any inconvenience caused as a result.
再度、この問題とその結果ご迷惑をおかけしてしまったことを謝罪させていただきます。

リクエストまたは情報や確認を求める

Please let me know if you can attend the meeting on November 5th.
11月5日の会議に参加できるかお知らせください。

Could you set up a meeting with the sales manager?
セールスマネージャーとのミーティングを設定していただけますか？

I would like to know whether you have a seminar room in your hotel.
あなたのホテルにセミナールームがあるか知りたいです。

We would be grateful if you could send the broachers to us.
パンフレットをお送りくだされば幸いです。

Could you also send us the current price list?
最新の価格表もお送りいただけますか？

Could you please send me the documents at the address below?
下記の住所に書類をお送りいただけますか？

Could you urgently email me the results of the customer survey?
顧客調査の結果を至急、私にメールで送ってもらえますか？

I would like you to fax me the most recent price information.
最新の価格情報をファックスで送ってください。

I would be so grateful if you could send me the presentation draft early.
プレゼンのドラフトを早めに送ってもらえたら助かります。

Please have your budget proposals on my desk by the end of this month.
今月末までに予算の提案書を私の机に置いてください。

都合をたずねる、アポを取る

Is there any chance you could meet me sometime next week?
来週、どこかで会えますか？

What does your schedule look like this week to talk?
今週のご予定はいかがですか？

Are you available for a call next Friday at 3 pm?
次の金曜の午後3時にお電話でお話できますか？

Let's meet on Friday to discuss the upcoming project.
金曜日に会い、今後のプロジェクトについて議論しましょう。

I really think we can make this work.
この仕事をうまく進めることができると思います。

Could you please let me have your proposal by March 5th?
3月5日までに提案をお願いできますか？

We would like to visit your office to explain our services.
私たちのサービスを説明するために、御社のオフィスを訪問したいと思います。

We have time in the afternoon of Nov. 3rd and Nov. 6th.
11月3日と11月6日の午後に時間があります。

If neither of these dates works for you, please suggest some other times.
これらの日付のどちらも都合が良くない場合は、他の時間をいくつか提案して
ください。

We would like to arrange the meeting with you to follow up on our conversation over the phone.
電話での会話をフォローアップするために、あなたとのミーティングを設定したいと思います。

Could you just drop me a line when you are ready?
準備できたら教えてくださいますか？

Have you had a chance to work on the sales report?
販売レポートを作成する機会はありましたか？

Could you brief me on the status of the preparation?
準備の状況について、簡単に説明してもらえますか？

I would really appreciate it if you could send me the summary.
サマリーを送っていただけると本当に助かります。

I would appreciate a quick response and look forward to receiving the information.
迅速な対応に感謝し、情報をいただけることを楽しみにしています。

Would it be possible for you to send me the historical data?
過去のデータを送っていただくことは可能ですか？

Would you kindly send me your response by the end of this week?
今週末までにお返事をいただけますか？

Would you mind answering the question in my previous e-mail?
以前のメールの質問に答えていただけますか？

要望を伝える

I was wondering if you could meet us sometime next Monday.
来週の月曜日にお会いできるでしょうか。

I would be very grateful if you could take action in the next few days.
今後、数日以内に対応していただければ幸いです。

I'd really appreciate it if you could help me resolve this issue.
この問題の解決にご協力いただければ幸いです。

I am afraid that I don't exactly understand what you meant by "synergy" in your last e-mail.
前回のメールであなたが言う「相乗効果」の意味を正確に理解していません。

Could you provide more details?
もっと詳細を教えてくださいますか？

Regarding the new product, are you proposing that we should lower the price?
新製品について、価格を下げるべきだと提案していますか？

Could you clarify what you recommended in your last e-mail?
前回のメールでおすすめしていたことを明確にしていただけますか？

Would you send me any additional information about the price information?
価格情報に関する追加情報を送ってもらえますか？

I would like to follow up on our earlier conversation about our new product.
私たちの新製品に関する、以前の会話をフォローアップしたいと思います。

Have you had a chance to look over the product features in the catalog?
カタログにある製品の機能を確認する機会がありましたでしょうか？

Please let me know if you would like to try our sample.
サンプルを試されたい場合は、ご連絡ください。

We would be happy to arrange the shipment.
発送を手配させていただきます。

We would like to visit your office and give a presentation and product demonstration.
貴社のオフィスを訪問し、プレゼンテーションと製品デモを行いたいと思います。

If you are interested, please let me know a couple of times when you are available.
ご興味がある場合は、ご都合の良い時間をいくつかお教えください。

I will arrange my schedule accordingly.
こちらのスケジュールを調整いたします。

Let's discuss this matter over the phone.
この件は電話で話しましょう。

How about 8:00 am JST on February 23rd / 6:00 pm EST on February 22nd?
日本時間の 2 月 23 日の朝 8 時、米国東海岸時間の 2 月 22 日の午後 6 時ではいかがでしょうか？
＊ JST（Japan Standard Time の略）：日本の標準時
＊ EST（Eastern Standard Time の略）：米国東部の標準時

Would you be available to discuss this over the phone between 4:00 pm and 6:00 pm on February 22nd your time?
あなたの（現地）時間の 2 月 22 日の午後 4 時から午後 6 時の間で、この件について電話で話せますか？

I would like to update our progress for the ABC project.
ABC プロジェクトの進捗をアップデートしたいと思います。

Would you be available between 4:00 pm and 6:00 pm on February 22nd, Singapore time?
シンガポール時間の 2 月 22 日の午後 4 時から午後 6 時の間は空いていますか？

見積もりを依頼する、発注する

Would you please quote your most competitive rate for the maintenance services?
メンテナンスサービスのためのあなたの最も競争力のある料金をお伝えくださいますか？

Please find the attached purchase order.
添付の注文書をご確認ください。

Please process the purchase order attached to this email.
このメールに添付されている注文書を処理してください。

We are writing to notify you about the delivery delay of order no. XYZ123.
注文番号 XYZ123 の配送が遅れていることをお知らせいたします。

Could you tell me the minimum order on X-351?
X-351 の最小注文個数はどのくらいですか？

We would like to order 100 units of the X-351 model.
X-351 モデルを 100 台、注文します。

Could you confirm the availability of the X-351 model?
X-351 モデルの在庫の確認をお願いできますか？

I would like to place an order for the following.
下記の注文をお願いします。

I would like to order fifty copies of the book as follows.
下記の本 50 冊の注文をお願いします。

Would you let us know the earliest possible delivery time?
最も早い納期はいつになるでしょうか？

In case you are out of stock, how long do we need to wait?
在庫がなくなった場合、どのくらい待つ必要がありますか？

Would you tell me who I should contact to talk about the price?
価格について話すために、誰に連絡すればよいか教えてくださいますか？

We would like to follow up on our quotation letter sent to you on July 4th.
7 月 4 日にお送りした見積書はいかがでしょうか。

We have not heard from you since then.
それ以来、まだお返事をいただいておりません。

We are happy to provide more information if needed.
必要であれば、追加の情報を提供させていただきます。

We are looking forward to your response soon so that we could be ready to supply the goods you requested.
リクエストいただいた商品の供給準備ができるよう、速やかにご返事いただけることをお待ちしております。

We would like to make sure that you received the quote we sent last week.
先週お送りした見積書をお受け取りになったか確認したいと思います。

Would you let us know that you received it and if you had any questions?
お受け取りになられたか、そして何かご質問がないかお知らせいただけますか？

質問する

Could you tell me more about your new service?
新しいサービスについて、もっと詳しく教えてくださいますか？

Please find my three questions below.
以下の3つの質問をご確認ください。

First of all, I would like to know about the new features of the product.
まず、製品の新機能について知りたいです。

My second question is about the maintenance services.
2番目の質問は、保守サービスについてです。

Finally, I would also like to know the price range.
最後に、価格帯も知りたいです。

You asked us about the range of our services when we met last time.
前回お会いした時に、サービスの範囲についてたずねられました。

Please find my answers below.
以下がお答えとなります。

Thank you for your interest in our products.
当社の製品に関心をお寄せいただき、ありがとうございます。

The answers to your questions are below.
あなたのご質問に対する答えは、以下の通りです。

請求・支払いについて

Would you review to confirm the invoice with the details of the transaction?
取引の詳細と合わせて、請求書をご確認いただけますでしょうか？

Please regard this as an invoice for our professional services provided between Jan. 10 to Jan. 20.
これは 1 月 10 日から 1 月 20 日に提供した、プロフェッショナルサービスの請求書です。

Please don't hesitate to contact us if you need any clarification on the details.
詳細について何か説明が必要なようでしたら、お気軽にお問い合わせください。

Thank you for doing business with us.
当社とお取引をありがとうございます。

We highly appreciate having the opportunity to serve you.
お取引の機会を大変感謝しております。

It has come to our attention that we have not received your payment yet.
まだお支払いをいただいていないようです。

Our records show that your monthly installment is past due.
当社の記録によると、毎月の分割払いの支払い期日が過ぎています。

Your current balance of 34,000 yen was due on March 31.
34,000 円のお支払い期日は 3 月 31 日でした。
＊ current balance：現在の金額の状況。

Would you send payment at your earliest possible timing?
できる限り早期に支払いをお願いできますか？

If your payment was already made, please disregard this notice.
もし既にお支払いをいただいているようでしたら、このお知らせは破棄してください。

If you have any concerns or questions on this matter, please contact us at the following number.
この件でご懸念やご質問があるようでしたら、下記の番号にお電話ください。

Thank you in advance for your cooperation in this matter.
本件についてのご協力ありがとうございます。

We hope to continue doing business with you in the future.
今後もお取引の継続を願っております。

返信する

Thank you for contacting us to set up a meeting.
ミーティングの設定についてお問い合わせいただき、ありがとうございます。

In fact, we prefer to have a face-to-face meeting instead of e-mail.
実際、Eメールではなく、直接会いたいと思います。

I appreciate it if you can visit our office in Shinjuku.
新宿にある私たちのオフィスを訪れていただければ幸いです。

Please refer to our website for a map to our office.
オフィスへの地図については、当社のウェブサイトを参照してください。

Alternatively, we can meet somewhere near Tokyo station.
また、東京駅の近くで会うこともできます。

Please let me know if you have any preferences for the location.
場所のご希望があれば教えてください。

Unfortunately, I will be out of the office the entire next week due to the business trip.
残念なことに、私は出張のために来週いっぱい不在です。

How about sometime in the following week?
翌週はどうでしょうか？

I will let you know my cell phone number just in case.
念のため、私の携帯電話番号をお知らせします。

Please feel free to call me if you need any help.
何か必要でしたら、ご遠慮なくお電話ください。

I am looking forward to meeting you.
あなたにお会いするのを楽しみにしています。

お礼のメール

Thank you for contacting us.
ご連絡いただきありがとうございます。

Thank you for your prompt reply.
迅速なご返信をありがとうございます。

Your cooperation is greatly appreciated.
ご協力どうもありがとうございます。

Thank you for your understanding and support.
ご理解およびご協力をありがとうございます。

Thank you for your attention to this matter.
この件について関心を持っていただき、ありがとうございます。

Thank you for bringing this issue to my attention.
この問題について教えてくれてありがとうございます。

Thank you for all your assistance the other day.
先日、いろいろご協力いただきありがとうございます。

Thank you for your kind cooperation.
快くご協力いただきありがとうございます。

Thank you for your hospitality.
あなたのおもてなしをありがとうございました。

Thank you for your consideration.
ご考慮いただきありがとうございます。

I appreciate your immediate attention to this matter.
この問題にすぐにご注目いただき、ありがとうございます。

We appreciate your quick response to our inquiry about inventory information.
在庫情報に関するお問い合わせに迅速に対応していただき、ありがとうございます。

I am writing to thank you for your kind hospitality during my business trip to Tokyo.
私は東京への出張中にあなたの親切なもてなしに感謝してメールしています。

Thank you for sending the details of your services to us.
御社のサービスの詳細を送ってくださり、ありがとうございました。

I would like to express my gratitude for all your help during my last trip.
先の出張中は大変お世話になりまして、お礼を述べたいと思います。

Thank you again for everything you've done during my stay in NY.
私のニューヨーク滞在中はいろいろお世話になり、再度お礼を申し上げます。

Thank you for your great assistance during the last workshop.
先のワークショップでは、すばらしいサポートをありがとう。

Thank you for your quick response in providing me with the information I requested for the sales report.
営業報告書に必要な情報を迅速に対応してお送りくださり、ありがとうございます。

I would like to take this opportunity to express my gratitude toward you for your wonderful support for the past year.
この機会に、この1年間のすばらしい支援に対して、感謝の意を表したいと思います。

I would like to extend my sincerest gratitude towards you for your dedication to the last project.
最後のプロジェクトへのあなたの献身に心から感謝します。

On behalf of Company ABC, I want to convey our sincere gratitude to you for giving us an opportunity to serve you.
ABC会社を代表して、御社とのお取引の機会をいただきましたことに、心からの感謝を表したいと思います。

It was truly a great opportunity to do business with a rapidly growing organization like yours.
御社のように急成長している組織とのお取引は大変すばらしい機会でした。

Thank you very much for taking the initiative to lead this project.
このプロジェクトを率先して主導していただき、どうもありがとうございます。

Thank you very much for acting proactively to find a solution to the problem.
問題の解決策を見つけるために積極的に行動してくれてどうもありがとう。

I am really proud of the commitment you have put into this project.
あなたがこのプロジェクトに投入したコミットメントを本当に誇りに思います。

You have made a great contribution to the team.
あなたはチームに多大な貢献をしてくれました。

Thank you for remaining loyal to the company.
会社に忠実であり続けてくれてありがとう。

We appreciate your confidence and hard work.
あなたの信頼と努力に感謝します。

The solution you proposed for this problem was outstanding.
この問題に対して提案してくれた解決策は卓越していました。

Thank you for taking the time to tell our services to your clients.
弊社のサービスについて、クライエントの方々にお話しいただきましてありがとうございます。

We'll do our best to deserve your confidence.
信頼にお応えできるよう、最善を尽くします。

確認、連絡のメール

As agreed, we will schedule our next national sales meeting in Oct.
合意した通り、10月に次の全国販売会議を予定します。

I'm just writing to confirm the time of our meeting next week.
来週の会議の時間を確認したいと思います。

I am writing to confirm your appointment with our Sales Director next week.
来週、営業部長とのアポイントを確認させていただきます。

Your appointment will take place at 2 pm on Thursday 18 May at our headquarter in Tokyo.
アポイントは5月18日木曜日の午後2時、東京の本社です。

462

As was agreed in the manager meeting on Monday, we will hold once a month staff meeting from the next month.

月曜日のマネージャー会議で合意されたように、我々は来月から月に一度、スタッフ会議を開催します。

I am sending this letter to confirm the policies we discussed in our meeting last Friday. The policies are the following.

先週の金曜の会議で議論した方針を確認するために、このレターを送っています。ポリシーは次の通りです。

I would like to let you know that we have products that you inquired regarding the inventory.

在庫に関してお問い合わせいただいた商品があることをお知らせします。

I am afraid the item you inquired about is currently out of stock.

お問い合わせいただいた商品は、現在あいにく在庫がありません。

This will confirm that we received your order.

ご注文をお受けしたことを確認させていただきます。

This is to confirm that we have arranged the shipment based on your order instructions.

これは、ご注文の指示に基づいて出荷を手配したことを確認させていただくものです。

This confirms your request for a conference room booking.

会議室のご予約のリクエストを確認いたしました。

お祝いのメール

We would like to congratulate you on the opening of your new opening in Osaka.

大阪での新規オープンおめでとうございます。

I would like to congratulate you on your recent accomplishment.

最近の功績にお祝いを申し上げます。

I would like to congratulate you on your promotion to Senior Partner.

シニアパートナーへの昇進を祝福します。

I just heard you got the Director's job.
ディレクターになられたと伺いました。

Congratulations on the new position.
新しいポジション、おめでとうございます。

Congratulations on getting the broader responsibility.
より責任範囲の広いポジションを得られて、おめでとうございます。

I am happy to hear that your new product launch went well.
新製品の発売が順調に進んだと聞いて、うれしく思います。

フォローアップ・リマインダーメール

I would like to follow up with my previous email.
前回のメールの件、どうなっているでしょうか。

If you haven't already, please take a moment to complete the survey.
まだなようでしたら、お時間をとってアンケートをご記入ください。

This is just a friendly reminder that I am waiting for your confirmation.
確認のお返事をお待ちしていると、念のためお伝えいたします。

This is just a reminder of the starting time of our dinner tonight and no response needed.
これは今夜のディナーの開始時間を念のためお知らせするもので、返信は不要です。

This is just a friendly reminder to ask you to send your report by the end of this week.
念のためお知らせします。レポートの提出は今週末までにお願いします。

This is just to let you know that we need your report by tomorrow.
明日までに報告書が必要ですので提出をお願いします。

I would highly appreciate if you could respond to my below email.
下記のメールに返信いただけると大変助かります。

Your early response will be greatly appreciated.
早期のご返信、お願いいたします。

I would be grateful if you could reply to my inquiry that I sent on Nov. 6th.
11月6日にお送りしたお問い合わせについて、ご返信をお願いいたします。

This is a reminder to ask you to submit your expense report, which deadline was yesterday.
昨日が締切であった、経費報告書の提出を忘れずにお願いします。

I understand the busy schedule you are following.
あなたがお忙しいのは承知しています。

However, I would like to request you to submit your report on time.
しかしながら、レポートは期日通りに提出いただくようお願いします。

Please contact Ken in the accounting department if you need further instructions.
さらにインストラクションが必要な場合は、経理部のケンにお問い合わせください。

I am writing in order to remind you that our promotional period will end soon.
まもなくプロモーション期間を終了することをお知らせしたくメールしています。

Is there any chance you could send me the latest price list?
最新の価格表を送ってくれる可能性はありますか？

Can you just drop me a line to let me know if you can meet sometime tomorrow?
明日のどこかで会えるかどうかを知らせてくれますか？

Could you kindly let me know whether you can send your report by email?
レポートをメールで送信できるかどうか教えてくださいますか？

Could you do me a favor and send me your latest product catalog?
お願いがあります。最新の製品カタログを送ってくれますか？

You'd really be helping me out if you could send me the invoice at your earliest convenient time.
最も早くご都合の良い時間に請求書をお送りいただければ、本当に助かります。

It would be great to receive it by the end of this month.
今月末までに受け取っていただければ幸いです。

I would really appreciate it if you could set up a meeting next week.
来週に会議を設定できたら、本当にありがたいです。

I would be so grateful if you could spare some time with me while I will be in town.
私がこの町にいる間、お時間をいただければ幸いです。

Would it be possible for you to provide a discount?
割引いただくことは可能でしょうか？

We urgently require this order to be processed today. Would it be possible?
本日、至急この注文を処理していただく必要があります。可能でしょうか？

I would like to remind you about the conference call we have scheduled at 3:00 pm on March 22nd your time.
3月22日の午後3時（あなたの時間）に、電話会議を予定していることをご確認ください。

We will discuss next year sales target and please be prepared to provide your input.
来年の売上目標について話し合いますので、準備しておいてください。

I wanted to let you know that I've scheduled a meeting with the HR department at 3 pm, this Friday, March 3rd to discuss our recruitment plan for new graduates.
3月3日金曜日の午後3時に、新卒採用計画について話し合うために人事部とのミーティングを予定しています。

Would you please let me know if you could join this meeting?
このミーティングに参加できるか教えてくださいますか？

I would like to get together with you all to share some updates on our current project.
現在のプロジェクトの最新状況をシェアするために、皆さんと集まりたいと思います。

It's at 10 am tomorrow in the conference room A. Please let me know if you can make that time.
明日の午前 10 時に会議室 A で予定しています。その時間に参加できるかお知らせください。

I would like to know the status of my job application which I sent to you on January 19th, 2020.
2020 年 1 月 19 日にお送りした応募書類の状況を伺いたいと思います。

Could you kindly go through my job application as I am strongly interested in working with your company?
御社で働くことに大変興味を持っていますので、私の応募書類をご確認いただけますでしょうか？

I have not heard from you about the next step after the job interview last week.
先週の就職面接の後の次のステップについて、まだご連絡をいただいておりません。

Would you please let me know the status of my hiring?
採用の状況をお知らせいただけますでしょうか？

If there are any updates on the hiring process, please let me know.
採用のプロセスに進展がありましたら、ご連絡ください。

There has not been any reply after we sent our complaints on your product last month.
先月に御社の製品についての苦情を知らせてから、何もお返事をいただいていません。

Could you look into the matter urgently to find out how to resolve this issue?
この問題を解決する方法を見つけるために、緊急に問題を調べてもらえますか？

Have you given any additional consideration to our proposal, which we proposed a few months ago?
数ヶ月前にご提案した件、その後、考慮いただけたでしょうか？

クレームのメール

As of June 10th, we have not received our order yet.
6月10日時点で、まだ注文を受け取っていません。

Based on the contract, the delivery should have been made within ten working days from the order, which was June 15th.
契約書によると、納品は発注から10営業日以内の6月15日に行われるべきでした。

We would like to bring to your attention that the products (order number XYZ) was damaged during transportation.
輸送中に製品（注文番号XYZ）が破損したことをお知らせします。

The quality of shipped products did not match with our order specification.
出荷された製品の品質が注文の仕様と一致しませんでした。

Regrettably, I was not quite happy with the services I received the other day.
残念ながら、私は先日受け取ったサービスにあまり満足していません。

Unfortunately, the product you sent me was not really what I expected.
残念なことに、あなたが私に送ってくれた製品は、本当に私が期待したものではありませんでした。

Regrettably, your delivery of our order (order number XYZ) was delayed for a week from the originally promised date.
残念ながら、当社の注文（注文番号XYZ）の配達が、最初に合意した日から1週間遅れました。

We would like to let you know that we were very disappointed with this.
この件で大変失望したとお知らせしたいと思います。

I would like to draw your attention to an issue we had with your product.
私たちがあなたの製品に関して抱えていた問題に注目していただきたいと思います。

Not only has one month already passed since the original delivery date, but we also found that most of the parts were damaged.
最初の納品日からすでに1ヶ月が経過しているだけでなく、ほとんどの部品が破損していることもわかりました。

It was very disappointing as we have been your loyal customer for over three years.
私たちが 3 年以上に渡って御社の忠実な顧客であったため、非常に残念でした。

To make matters worse, we have not received any response to our request for the replacement.
さらに悪いことに、交換のリクエストに対する回答がありません。

As you are aware, the delay of your shipment brings a serious impact on our production line.
ご承知の通り、出荷の遅延は当社の生産ラインに深刻な影響をもたらします。

Please do whatever is necessary to deliver the replacement to our factory by the end of this week, July 5th.
今週の終わり、7 月 5 日までに交換品を工場に配送するために必要なことは何でもしてください。

Unless this issue is resolved promptly, we will be forced to take further action, unfortunately.
この問題が早急に解決されない限り、残念ながら、さらなる措置を講じることを余儀なくされます。

I trust this matter can be resolved very quickly so that we can get the production-line on track shortly.
この問題は非常に迅速に解決できるため、すぐに生産ラインを軌道に乗せることができると信じています。

We will return your product along with a request for a full refund.
私たちは全額払い戻しの要求と共に、製品を返します。

As a result, we could not maintain our operation as we hoped.
その結果、通常の業務を運営することができませんでした。

We consider this to be a very serious issue.
当社はこれを大変深刻な問題と受けとめています。

We expect that you take this matter seriously.
この問題を真剣に考えてください。

It would be unfortunate, but we have to consider doing business elsewhere if this problem happens again.
再度、このような問題が発生した場合は、残念ながら、他社との取引を検討しなければなりません。

During the inspection of arrival goods, we have found 10 defective parts.
到着した商品の検査中に、10 個の不良部品が見つかりました。

We request an immediate replacement or full refund.
直ちに交換するか、全額返金をお願いします。

We are waiting for your decision regarding these defective parts.
これらの不良部品をどうするかの決定をお待ちしております。

Please note that we have decided to cancel our order.
注文をキャンセルすることにしました。

In addition, we may require you to compensate us for damages caused by your shipment delay.
さらに、御社の出荷の遅れによって受けた損害に対しての賠償請求を検討しています。

Your immediate action to replace the goods will be appreciated.
すぐに商品を交換いただけると大変助かります。

We believe that it was an unintended mistake.
意図せぬ間違いであったと信じております。

We are confident that you will take a necessary step to stop recurring this kind of problem in the future.
御社は将来このような問題の再発防止に必要な策を講ずると、確信しております。

添付ファイルについて

Please find the attachment.
添付の資料をご覧ください。

Attached to this e-mail is the detail information you have requested.
リクエストいただいた詳細情報をこのメールに添付しています。

Please refer to the attached document for further details.
詳細については、添付書類をご覧ください。

Please read the attached documents in advance and bring the copy with you to the meeting.
会議の前に添付の資料を読み、当日コピーを持って来てください。

As per the attached file, we will launch our new product next month.
添付のファイルの通り、来月、弊社の新製品を発売します。

I would highly appreciate your reviewing the attached materials before the meeting.
会議の前に添付の資料をご覧いただければ幸いです。

Please replace the file I sent the other day with the attachment.
先日お送りしたファイルを、添付のもので差し替えてください。

Please download the files from the link below.
以下のリンクからファイルをダウンロードしてください。

Please expand the compressed zip file attached in this e-mail.
この E メールに添付されている圧縮 zip ファイルを解凍してください。

For your reference, please find some data attached to the e-mail.
ご参考までに、E メールに添付されているデータをご覧ください。

Please visit the website below for more details.
詳細については、以下のウェブサイトをご覧ください。

If you look at the first section of the attached document, you will find the data you requested.
添付文書の最初のセクションを見ると、リクエストしたデータが見つかります。

The parts in red of the attached report are my comments on your draft.
添付のレポートの赤い部分は、あなたの下書きに対する私のコメントです。

I've inserted some graphs in the attached PowerPoint for your review.
レビュー用に、添付のパワーポイントにいくつかのグラフを挿入しました。

Here's the prior contract that I mentioned the other day.
先日申し上げた、以前の契約はこちらです。

More information on this is available on our company website below.
これについてのさらなる情報は、以下の当社のウェブサイトをご覧ください。

The file is password protected and the password will be sent to you in a separate e-mail.
ファイルはパスワードで保護されており、パスワードは別のEメールであなたに送信されます。

If you cannot open the attached file, please let me know. I will come back to you with an alternative.
添付ファイルを開けない場合は、ご連絡ください。別の手段をお知らせします。

説得力を持つフレーズ

I am certain that we can meet your requirements.
私たちはあなたの要件を満たすことができると確信しています。

I am sure that our product will dramatically increase your productivity.
当社の製品が生産性を劇的に向上させると確信しています。

I would like to emphasis that this is a fair price considering the extra services and current exchange rate.
追加サービスと現在の為替レートを考慮すると、これが公正な価格であることを強調したいと思います。

Please let us know your decision as soon as possible before the current offer expires.
現在のオファーの有効期限が切れる前に、できるだけ早く決定をお知らせください。

Obviously, this is the best service available in the market.
明らかに、これは市場で利用可能な最高のサービスです。

用途に従い、適切なクロージング

We are pleased to offer you the full-time position of marketing manager at ABC company.
ABC社のフルタイムの、マーケティングマネージャーの役職の内定通知をさせていただきます。

Please fill out the enclosed documents and bring the identification with you on your first day.
同封の書類を記入し、身分証明書を出社初日にお持ちください。

Please confirm your acceptance of this offer by signing in the space below of this letter.
このレターの下のスペースにサインインして、このオファーの受け入れを確認してください。

After we acknowledge your acceptance, we can take the final steps in the hiring process.
承諾を確認させていただいた後、採用プロセスの最終ステップに進みます。

If you have any questions about this offer, feel free to call me.
このオファーについてご質問がある場合は、お気軽にお電話ください。

Please notify us in writing within the next two weeks regarding your decision.
あなたの決定に関して、今後2週間以内に書面で通知してください。

Should you decide to accept this offer, we can proceed with administrative matters.
このオファーを受け入れることに決めていただいた後、事務的なお話を進めます。

I hope that I may have the pleasure of working with you.
一緒に仕事ができることを楽しみにしています。

I would like to let you know that I am happy to accept the job offer from you.
御社からの内定を喜んでお受けするとお知らせいたします。

I am very excited to learn that your company offers excellent growth opportunities for all employees.
御社が全ての従業員にすばらしい成長の機会を提供していることを知って、非常に興奮しています。

I want to thank you again for how honored I am to be considered for this exciting position.
このエキサイティングな地位について、私がいかに光栄に思っているかをあらためて感謝します。

I highly appreciate you sharing these details.
これらの詳細をいただき、本当にありがとうございます。

As briefly talked the other day, I would like to discuss my compensations and working conditions.
先日、手短に述べたように、報酬と労働条件についてお話ししたいと思います。

Please let me know when we can discuss this matter.
この問題について、いつお話しできるか教えてください。

Thank you for sending your job offer today.
本日、オファーをお送りいただきありがとうございます。

I accept with pleasure the position of Finance Manager.
財務マネージャーの立場を喜んで受け入れます。

I look forward to meeting you and other members of the department's staff.
私はあなたと部門のスタッフの方々にお会いできるのを楽しみにしています。

I look forward to contributing to the team's efforts.
チームの努力に貢献できることを楽しみにしています。

I appreciate the documents you sent on the company's retirement and insurance programs.
会社の退職および保険プログラムについての書類、ありがとうございます。

I may have some questions concerning these benefits and come to see you after my orientation on the first day.
これらのベネフィットに関していくつか質問がありますので、初日のオリエンテーション後に伺います。

I hope to hear from you soon.
すぐのお返事をお待ちしております。

We look forward to receiving your reply.
お返事をお待ちしています。

Please let us know what you think about our proposal.
我々の提案についてどう思うか教えてください。

We expect to hear from you sometime soon.
近いうちにご連絡いただきたいと思います。

We would highly appreciate it if you could share your thoughts sometime soon.
近いうちにご意見をお聞かせいただければ幸いです。

Please let me know if you have any questions.
ご質問があれば、教えてください。

Please do not hesitate to contact me, if you have any questions.
ご質問があれば、遠慮なくご連絡ください。

If you have any further questions, feel free to contact us.
さらにご質問がある場合は、お気軽にお問い合わせください。

Please let us know immediately if this causes any concerns.
これが何か懸念を生じるようであれば、すぐにお知らせください。

Your early reply would be highly appreciated.
迅速にご返答いただけますと、幸いです。

I always value your input, so please let me know what you think of this matter.
いつもあなたの意見を尊重していますので、この問題についてどう思うかお知らせください。

Would you please send me your feedback by this Thursday, as I plan to finalize this report by the end of this week?
今週末までにこの報告書を完了する予定のため、今週の木曜までにフィードバックをくださいますか？

Please reply at your earliest convenience.
ご都合の良い時になるべく早く返信ください。

I would be grateful for your immediate reply regarding this matter.
本件に関し、迅速なお答えをいただけますと幸いです。

If you have further questions, please let us know at any time.
さらにご質問がある場合は、いつでもお知らせください。

If we can be of any help, please do not hesitate to contact us again.
何かお助けできることがあれば、ご遠慮なくまた知らせてください。

Please let me know when it will be convenient for you.
いつご都合が良いか、教えてください。

Please let me know how I can assist you with any other questions.
他にご質問がある場合もお手伝いできるよう、ご連絡ください。

Please contact me with any requests you might have.
どんなリクエストも私に連絡してください。

Please let me know if I can help you in any way in the future.
将来、何かお手伝いできることがあれば、いつでもご連絡ください。

We hope that we can serve you again in the near future.
近い将来、またお取引できますことを願っております。

It is always a pleasure to work with you.
あなたと一緒にお仕事ができてうれしかったです。

We really enjoyed working with you on this project.
このプロジェクトで皆さんと一緒にお仕事ができて、本当に楽しかったです。

Thank you for all of your hard work.
いろいろ頑張ってくれてありがとう。

We sincerely appreciate everything you did for us.
私たちにしてくださったこと、本当に感謝しています。

Thank you again for all your help.
あらためて本当にありがとう。

Once again, thank you for bringing this matter to my attention.
この問題を私にお知らせくださり、再度、お礼を申し上げます。

I hope this email answers all your questions.
このメールで全てのご質問にお答えできていたらと思います。

I hope that helps.
お役に立てば幸いです。

I am sorry I couldn't be more help at this time.
申し訳ありませんが、今回はこれ以上、お役に立てません。

I hope the information in this email meets your requirements for now.
このメールの情報で、現時点でご要望にかなっていたらと思います。

If I can be of any service to you in the future, please don't hesitate to contact me.
将来お手伝いできることがあれば、ご遠慮なくご連絡ください。

Best regards,
よろしくお願いいたします。

Sincerely,	心から
Best wishes,	ご多幸を祈る
All the best,	ごきげんよう
Warm regards,	敬具

おわりに

　本書を最後までお読みいただき、どうもありがとうございます。
すぐに使えそうなフレーズから、自分にはしばらく使う機会はないの
ではないかと感じたフレーズがあったかもしれません。フレーズを学
ぶと同時に、欧米流の仕事の進め方や、彼らの考え方を理解するきっ
かけにもなれば幸いです。

　ビジネスで使う英語をマスターすることは、外国人と働く上での一
つのステップにすぎません。

　私自身、長年外国人と一緒に働いてきましたが、百戦錬磨にどんな
外国人ともすぐに、仕事でわかり合えるというわけではありません。
一定期間、相手の考え方や価値観などを理解するのに時間が必要です。
考えてみれば、日本人同士であっても、新しい上司や部下とは、しば
らく一緒に働くことで、お互いを理解することができるわけですから、
当然のこととも言えます。

　相手が外国人の場合、文化的背景や育った環境が大きく違いますし、
同じ業界や会社であっても、物事の捉え方が違うことが多いので、わ
かり合うプロセスにより時間が必要になるでしょう。

　突っ込みどころが違ったり、想定外の問題意識を持っていたり、そ
もそも前提条件の理解が違ったりということは、最初から想定してい
るほうがストレスになりません。英語力の問題というより、理解し合
うことに時間が必要なのだと割り切って考えてみると、肩の力が少し
抜けると思います。

　その上で、相手を理解する努力を惜しまない、信頼関係を築くため
のコミュケーションは何かを考え、努力し続けるのが大事なのではな
いかと思っています。大げさな表現を使ったり、バシッと言い切るこ
とに慣れてくると、英語でコミュニケーションすることが快感になっ
てきます。

　異文化の外国人と働くことは、驚きがあるからこそ、チャレンジング。
新しい発見の連続が楽しいと思いながら、グローバルな環境で活躍す
る日本人リーダーが増えていくことを、心から応援しています。

小林真美

●著者紹介●
小林真美（こばやし　まみ）

津田塾大学学芸学部国際関係学科卒業。外資系証券会社を経てニューヨーク大学スターン・スクール・オブ・ビジネスに留学し、MBA取得。帰国後、フォード自動車の金融子会社に入社し、オーストラリアにあるアジア統括本部に財務マネージャーとして2年間勤務。その後、ジョンソン、日本アルコンで財務管理職を務め、外資系企業勤務は通算22年に及ぶ。現在はビジネスパーソンへの英語指導やオンライン教材の開発を行う。TOEIC 970点。英検1級。
著書に『出世する人の英語　アメリカ人の論理と思考習慣』（幻冬舎）、『だれとでも会話がとぎれない！1分間ペラペラ英会話』（ダイヤモンド社）がある。
ウェブページ：https://bizeigojuku.com/

本書の内容に関するお問い合わせは弊社HPからお願いいたします。

音声DL付き　リーダーのためのビジネス英会話フレーズブック

2020年　6月27日　初版発行

著　者　小　林　真　美
発行者　石　野　栄　一

〒112-0005 東京都文京区水道2-11-5
電話 (03) 5395-7650 （代　表）
(03) 5395-7654 （FAX）
郵便振替 00150-6-183481
http://www.asuka-g.co.jp

明日香出版社

■スタッフ■
編集　小林勝／久松圭祐／藤田知子／田中裕也
営業　渡辺久夫／奥本達哉／横尾一樹／関山美保子／藤本さやか
財務　早川朋子

印刷　株式会社フクイン
製本　根本製本株式会社
ISBN978-4-7569-2096-6 C0082

世界で戦う　伝わるビジネス英語

浅見ベートーベン

出張、メール、電話、プレゼン、会議など、ビジネスで英語を使わなくてはいけなくなった方へ。あらゆるビジネスシーンを想定して会話例やボキャブラリーをまとめています。MP3 CD-ROM 付き。

本体価格 2200 円＋税　A5 並製〈312 ページ〉2014/08 発行　978-4-7569-1719-5

英会話フレーズブック

多岐川恵理

英語中級者・上級者ほど、何気なく日本語で思ったことを「ああ、これって英語でなんて言うんだろう？」と悩むことが多くなるもの。そんな「言えそうで言えない」フレーズが満載です。CD 3 枚付き（日本語→英語収録）

本体価格 2500 円＋税　B6 変型〈384 ページ〉2007/08 発行　978-4-7569-1110-0

イギリス英語フレーズブック

ジュミック今井

イギリスへ旅行したり、留学・転勤などでイギリスで生活する人たちが日常の様々なシーンで使える会話表現集。色々な場で使える会話フレーズ（2900）を場面別・状況別に収録。CD 3 枚付き（日本語→英語収録）

本体価格 2700 円＋税　B6 変型〈392 ページ〉2018/01 発行　978-4-7569-1948-9